# A Category of Specific Non-Straightforward Tangential Rate Manifold Constraint in Coolant Force Interactions



Theodoros Archon

A Category of Specific Non-Straightforward Tangential Rate Manifold Constraint in Coolant Force Interactions

First Edition July 2025



Written by Theodoros Archon

# Contents

# List of Tables

# Chapter 1
# Preliminaries

## 1.1 Introduction

Nonlinear differential equations describe many physical phenomena in fluid dynamics and the investigation of the exact solutions of such nonlinear equations play an important role in understanding several engineering processes. In general, it is difficult to solve nonlinear problems analytically since there are no general techniques that work for all types of equations. Recently, computers have played a great role in nonlinear science and this has caused a revolution in understanding of nonlinear problems. The studies using numerical simulation picturise the solutions of nonlinear equations very well to gain insights into their behavior and to suggest directions for future analytic research.

For some non linear differential equations, it is possible to write down their special solutions explicitly in terms of elementary functions. One way of finding such explicit solutions is to reduce them to equations of lower dimension, preferably ordinary differential equations, which can often be solved exactly. But there still remains certain systems for which general solutions have not been found both analytically and numerically. One such equation is the well known Navier-Stokes equations that govern most of the flow phenomena. These equations are simultaneous system of partial differential equations which are highly nonlinear. Its simpler version known as Boundary layer equations present a great insight to several flow analysis. Depending upon the nature of the flow being incompressible or compressible; steady or unsteady; viscous or viscoelastic; two dimensional or three dimensional, the flow behavior has a wide range of mathematical variations and solution procedures and, today, this is a stimulating research area in applied mathematics and computational fluid dynamics.

The importance of fluid dynamics studies is that, it focuses on the construction and solution of governing equations for the different categories flow phenomena and their characteristics. Many mechanical, chemical and engineering processes depend upon the solution a certain fluid dynamics studies. The famous partial differential equation Navier-Stokes equations which is highly non linear have been known for 150 years or more but not its exact solution.

There are several analytic methods for solving non-linear problems that are based on the existence of small or large perturbation quantities. But, it was realized that certain non-linear problems do not contain such perturbation quantities at all. Then came the non-perturbation methods that are independent upon small or large parameters. For certain complex problems, both the perturbation and non-perturbation techniques fail to convert the non-linear problems into linear sub-problems completely.

To overcome the above difficulties, a more powerful technique known as homotopy analysis method came into the literature from Liao (1992) through his PhD dissertation titled "The Proposed Homotopy Analysis Technique for the Solution of Nonlinear Problems". Though the method had its teething troubles in the beginning in terms of convergence of solution, the method was well established soon and are clearly documented by Liao as evident from his two recent books (see in Liao (2003; 2012)). Ever since, many authors have applied this method for solution of non linear differential equations.

## 1.2 Outline of the Thesis

In the present work, the method of homotopy analysis is applied to solve certain non linear differential equations arising as a mathematical model for some practical engineering problems in fluid dynamics. The thesis is arranged as follows. In the present introductory chapter, some basic concepts and terminologies associated with fluid dynamics are presented in the next section. The governing equations are either the Navier Stokes equations or the boundary layer equations, depending upon the nature of the problem. Hence those equations are presented. The different non dimensional parameters used in the thesis are defined. A review of important analytical and numerical methods is also presented. Since the present study is concerned with the analytical solutions using homotopy analysis, we present the essence of HAM and how to apply HAM for solving non linear differential equations in great detail. From the second to sixth chapter, the actual research problems together with their solutions are studied and discussed.

## 1.3 Basic definitions

In this section, we recall some basic concepts in fluid dynamics and its related terminologies. It is to be mentioned here that the list is not at all exhaustive but only very few terms which occur in the thesis chapters are defined. Most of these definitions are available in wikipedia, only a few of them are given here. The basic books on fluid dynamics concepts by Batchelor (1967) and White (1979) has all the important terms and concepts and can be referred.

*Fluids* are substances that can flow and they are classified as liquids or gases. A branch of science that deals with the behavior of fluids at rest or in motion is known as *fluid mechanics*. *Fluid dynamics* is a sub field of fluid mechanics and it studies the effect of forces on fluid motion. Any real fluid moving along a solid boundary will incur a *shear stress* on that boundary. The no-slip condition dictates that the speed of the fluid at the boundary is zero, but at some height from the boundary the flow speed must be equal to that of the fluid. The region in between these two spaces is the boundary layer. The shear stress, for a Newtonian fluid, at a surface element parallel to a flat plate, at the point $y$ is given by:

$$\tau(y) = \mu \frac{\partial u}{\partial y}$$

where $\mu$, $u$ and $y$ are the dynamic viscosity of the fluid, velocity of the fluid along the boundary and the height above the boundary, respectively.

Specifically, the wall shear stress is defined as:

$$\tau_w = \mu \frac{\partial u}{\partial y}|_{y=0}.$$

A fluid whose shear stress is linearly proportional to the velocity gradient in the direction perpendicular to the plane of shear is called *Newtonian fluid*. A fluid, whose flow properties are not described by a single constant value of viscosity is called *non-Newtonian fluid.*

The prevention of separation in any flow can be achieved by supplying additional energy to the particles in the fluid which are low in energy in the boundary layers. This can be achieved by moving along higher velocity fluid out from inside the body is called *blowing* and fluid in from out side the body is called *suction*.

A fluid which is not reduced in volume by an increase in pressure is called *Incompressible fluid.* Layer of fluid move with different velocities without great exchange of fluid particles perpendicular to the flow direction is called *laminar flow*. If the flow velocity has the same magnitude and direction at every point in the fluid region the flow is said to be *uniform flow*. If at a given instant, the velocity has not the same at every point the flow is *non-uniform*.

In practice, every fluid that flows near a solid boundary will be non-uniform as the fluid at the boundary must take the speed of the boundary, usually zero. However if the size and shape of the cross-section of the stream of fluid is constant the flow is considered uniform.

A *steady* flow is one in which the fluid properties such as velocity and pressure may differ from point to point but do not change with time. If at any point in the fluid, if these properties change with time, the flow is described as *unsteady*. In practise there is always slight variations in velocity and pressure, but if the average values are constant, the flow is considered steady.

An energy transformed from one place to another due to the temperature gradient is termed as *heat*. *Heat transfer* is an essential process and there are three modes of heat transfer, viz., *conduction*, *convection* and *radiation.* Conduction is the mode of heat transfer by means of molecular agitation within a material and convection is when the energy is transformed from a surface to a fluid owing over it or vice versa as a result of a difference between temperatures of the surface and the fluid. The third mode of heat transfer known to be radiation is defined as an energy transfer due to temperature gradient by the mechanism of electromagnetic waves.

*Free convection* is natural flow of a fluid (or) air over a surface, without any external driving force. *Forced convection* is forced flow of a fluid (or) air over a surface. *Mixed convection* is a combination of both free and forced convection, which is the general case of convection, when a flow is determined simultaneously by both an outer forcing system (i.e, outer energy supply to the fluid stream lined body system) and inner volumetric(mass) forces, viz, by the non-uniform density distribution of a fluid medium in a gravity field.

## 1.4 Governing equations

The fundamental mathematical equations governing the fluid flow studies are the continuity, momentum and energy equations. These equations tell about the physics. They are the three fundamental physical principles upon which all of fluid dynamics is based: (1) mass is conserved; (2) F = ma (Newton's second law); (3) energy is conserved. Here, we discuss the two important equations used in the present study.

***The Navier-Stokes equations:*** The motion of a continuous substance can be described by kinematic and dynamic conservation laws of mass, momentum and energy along with the thermodynamical equations of state. The system of non-linear partial differential equations governing the motion of a Newtonian fluid is known by the Navier-Stokes equations described by Stokes (1851). The Navier Stokes equations are highly nonlinear partial differential equations and it is difficult to find its exact or numerical solutions except in some special cases. These equations have been widely accepted as an excellent model of the macroscopic motions of most real fluids, including air and water.

The conservation of mass states that, the amount fluid flowing into a volume element must be equal to the amount of fluid flowing out from that volume element, and it is mathematically expressed by the continuity equation

$$\frac{D\rho}{Dt} + \rho\nabla.\vec{q} = 0. \tag{1.1}$$

For an incompressible fluid, the eq. (1.1) reduces to

$$\nabla.\vec{q} = 0. \tag{1.2}$$

The momentum equation for a Newtonian fluid is

$$\rho\left[\frac{\partial\vec{q}}{\partial t} + (\vec{q}.\nabla)\vec{q}\right] = -\nabla p - \rho(T)g\hat{k} + \mu\nabla^2\vec{q}. \tag{1.3}$$

The left side of the momentum equation represents the rate of change of momentum per unit volume. The first, second and third terms on the right side represent, respectively, the pressure force due to normal stress, body force due to gravity and the viscous force arising due to shear.

The equation for conservation of energy can be written as:

$$\frac{\partial T}{\partial t}+(\vec{q}.\nabla)T=\chi\nabla^2 T. \tag{1.4}$$

The Navier-Stokes equations are considered sufficiently general to describe the Newtonian fluids appearing in hydro-and aerodynamics. Finding the solution of these equations is a complex task. It was realized that the Navier-Stokes equations contain terms that can be neglected in large parts of the flow domain. This allows the equations to be simplified. The terms that describe the viscous shear stresses offer such a possibility for such simplification.

***The boundary-layer equations:*** In 1904, a little-known physicist, Ludwig Prandtl, revolutionized fluid dynamics with his notion that, the effects of friction are experienced only very near an object moving through a fluid. It is Prandtl (1952) who first introduced the concept of a boundary layer suggesting that a thin layer in the immediate vicinity of a bounding surface where the effects of viscosity are significant.

There are different kinds of boundary layers, such as, velocity boundary layer, thermal boundary layer and concentration boundary layers. Using the scale analysis and certain logical assumptions, the well-known governing Navier-Stokes equations of viscous fluid flow can be greatly simplified to the boundary layer equations within the boundary layer.

The boundary layer equations of motion for steady two-dimensional incompressible flow are

$$\frac{\partial u}{\partial x}+\frac{\partial v}{\partial y} = 0, \tag{1.5}$$

$$u\frac{\partial u}{\partial x}+v\frac{\partial u}{\partial y} = -\frac{1}{\rho}\frac{\partial p}{\partial x}+\nu\left(\frac{\partial^2 u}{\partial x^2}+\frac{\partial^2 u}{\partial y^2}\right), \tag{1.6}$$

$$u\frac{\partial v}{\partial x}+v\frac{\partial v}{\partial y} = -\frac{1}{\rho}\frac{\partial p}{\partial y}+\nu\left(\frac{\partial^2 v}{\partial x^2}+\frac{\partial^2 v}{\partial y^2}\right), \tag{1.7}$$

where $\rho$ is the fluid density.

The boundary layer technique has now become one of the most powerful methods and researchable topic in the area of applied mathematics and engineering. The solution to the laminar boundary layer problem on a horizontal plate has been analyzed by the Prandtl's student Blasius (1908) for the first time. He solved the problem by transforming the partial differential equations into ordinary differential equation by introducing a new independent variable, called the similarity variable. The analysis of steady boundary layer flow over a moving surface with constant velocity was first presented by Sakiadis (1961). Significant differences were found from this study to the behavior of the boundary layer in a moving fluid over a steady surface. Tsou *et al.* (1967) made an experimental and theoretical treatment of the boundary layer on a continuously moving surface.

Investigation of fluid flow over continuous moving surfaces have attracted considerable attention in recent years due to its vital role in numerous engineering applications in industrial manufacturing processes such as hot rolling, wire drawing, glass-fiber, aerodynamic extrusion of plastic sheets, the cooling of an infinite metallic plate in a cooling bath, drawing of plastic films, metal and polymer extrusion and metal spinning etc. Convective heat transfer studies are very important in processes involving high temperatures such as gas turbines, nuclear power plants, thermal energy storage and so on.

Thermal properties of fluid play a vital role in heating as well as cooling applications in industrial processes or other technological applications.

## 1.5 Non-dimensional parameters

A quantity which has no physical dimension is said to be a dimensionless quantity. They are widely used in many fields in science and engineering. The ratio of two quantities with the same dimensions is always dimensionless irrespective of the units used to calculate them. While conducting experiments, to answer questions such as what are the parameters involved in the given flow and what is their relative significance etc., the dimensional analysis becomes very useful. The strategy is to vary only the non-dimensional numbers, which are a certain combinations of the parameters involved in the experiment .

In present research study, several non dimensional parameters are used. They are defined as follows.

The ***Biot number*** $(Bi)$ is a non dimensional quantity used in heat transfer calculations. It is the ratio of the heat transfer resistances inside and at the surface of a body. It is defined as

$$Bi = \frac{hL_c}{k_b},$$

where, $h$, $L_c$ and $k_b$ are the convective heat transfer coefficient, characteristic length and thermal conductivity of the body, respectively.

This ratio determines whether or not the temperatures inside a body will vary significantly in space, while the body heats or cools over time, from a thermal gradient applied to its surface. Uses of $Bi$ are $Bi >> 0.1$, the heat conduction inside the body is much faster than the heat convection away from its surface, and temperature gradients are negligible inside of it. When $Bi >> 1$, the thermally simple, due to uniform temperature fields inside the body and whereas, $Bi << 1$, more difficult problems due to non-uniformity of temperature fields within the object.

The ratio of convective to conductive heat transfer across the boundary (surface) within a fluid is called ***Nusselt number***. It is denoted as $(Nu)$ and defined as

$$Nu = \frac{hL}{k},$$

where, $h$, $L$ and $k$ are the convective heat transfer coefficient of the flow, characteristic length and the thermal conductivity of the fluid, respectively. Here, convection includes both advection and diffusion. But conductive has the same conditions as the heat convection include with a stagnant (or motionless) fluid.

It may be noticed that, different between Biot Number and Nusselt number is that the thermal conductivity is of the solid body in Biot Number and the fluid is in Nusselt number.

Another non dimensional quantity is ***Prandtl number***, expressed as $Pr$, represents the ratio of momentum diffusivity to thermal diffusivity. It is given by

$$Pr = \frac{\nu}{\alpha}$$

where, $\nu$ and $\alpha$ are the kinematic viscosity and thermal diffusivity, respectively. When $Pr \ll 1$ the thermal diffusivity dominates and when $Pr \gg 1$ the momentum diffusivity dominates. Typical values for Prandtl numbers are: around 0.7-0.8 for air and many other gases, and around 7 for water (At 20 degrees Celsius).

The ratio of momentum diffusivity and mass diffusivity is called ***Schmidt number***. It is denoted as $(Sc)$ and defined as

$$Sc = \frac{\nu}{D} = \frac{\mu}{\rho D},$$

where, $\nu$, $D$, $\mu$ and $\rho$ are the kinematic viscosity, mass diffusivity, dynamic viscosity and density of the fluid, respectively. It used to characterize fluid flows in which there are simultaneous momentum and mass diffusion convection processes. It physically relates the relative thickness of the hydrodynamic layer and mass transfer boundary layer.

The ratio of inertial forces to viscous forces is called ***Reynolds number***. It is denoted as $(Re)$ and defined as

$$Re = \frac{UL}{\nu},$$

where $U$, $L$ and $\nu$ are the mean velocity of the object relative to the fluid, characteristic linear dimension and the kinematic viscosity, respectively. Fluid flow is mostly chaotic, and very small changes in the surface roughness and the geometry, can result in very different flows. Hence, $Re$ is a very important guide and is widely used to characterize different flow regimes within a similar fluid, such as laminar or turbulent flow.

The ***Grashof number***, $(Gr)$ is a dimensionless number in fluid dynamics and heat transfer which approximates the ratio of the buoyancy to viscous force acting on a fluid. It frequently arises in the study of situations involving natural convection. For example, for vertical flat plates it is defines as

$$Gr = \frac{g\beta\,(T_s - T_\infty)\,L^3}{\nu^2}$$

in which, $g$, $\beta$, $T_s$ and $T_\infty$ are the gravitational constant, volumetric thermal expansion coefficient, surface temperature and bulk temperature, respectively. The viscous force is negligible compared to the buoyancy and inertial forces, when $Gr >> 1$.

## 1.6 Analytical and Numerical methods

There are many analytic methods for solving non-linear problems popularly known as perturbation methods. They are based on the existence of some small or large perturbation quantities in the given non-linear system. A lot of important properties and interesting phenomena of non-linear problems have been revealed using these methods. For example, the astonishing success of perturbation method is the discovery of the ninth planet in the solar system, found in the vast sky at a predicted point. But, it was realized later that certain non-linear problems do not contain small perturbation quantities at all.

There are certain analytic techniques in which the dependence of perturbation parameters can be avoided by introducing a so called artificial small parameter. They are Lyapunov's artificial small parameter method by Lyapunov (1892), Adomain's decomposition method by Adomian (1976) and $\delta$- expansion method by Karmishin *et al.* (1990). These methods are valid for strongly non-linear problems and can be applied to those non-linear problem which does not contain any small or large physical parameters.

***Perturbation method:*** The general procedure of the perturbation method is illustrated by Cole (1968) and the recent developments are given in Nayfeh (1981; 1985; 2000). The essence is to identify a small parameter such that when this parameter is set to zero, the problem becomes solvable. Thematically, the approach decomposes a tough problem into an infinite number of relatively easy ones. This method is used to find an approximate solution to a problem which can not be solved exactly, by starting from the exact solution of a related problem. This method leads to an expression for the desired solution in terms of a formal power series in some small parameter, that quantifies the deviation from the exactly solvable problem. The leading term in this power series is the solution of the exactly solvable problem, while further terms describe the deviation in the solution, due to the deviation from the initial problem. This method is applicable, if the problem at hand can be formulated by adding a small term to the mathematical description of the exactly solvable problem.

***Lyapunov's artificial small parameter method:*** In 1982, Lyapunov introduced an artificial parameter $\varepsilon$ in the given equation and then calculated power series expansion over $\varepsilon$ for the solutions. In many cases Lyapunov proved that series converges for $\varepsilon = 1$. The above approach is called Lyapunov's artificial small parameter method.

***Adomian decomposition method (ADM):*** This method is a powerful analytic method for strongly non-liner problems. It is valid for ordinary and partial differential equations, no matter whether they contain small or large parameters. Moreover, approximate solutions given by ADM often contain polynomials. The power series obtained using ADM generally have small convergence region. This is mainly due to the fact that power series is often not an efficient set of base functions to approximate a non-linear problem. ADM does not provide us with freedom to use different base functions. Like the artificial small parameter method, ADM also does not provide us with a convenient ways to adjust the convergence region and rate of approximation solutions.

***The $\delta-$expansion Method:*** This method is a kind of new perturbation method depending upon an artificial small parameter $\delta$. Note that both Lyapunov's artificial small parameter method and $\delta-$ expansion method introduce an artificial parameter, although it appears in a different place and is denoted by different symbol in a given non-linear equation. Karmishin *et al.* (1990) proposed a new perturbation technique based on the artificial parameter $\delta$. In essence, the $\delta$- expansion method is equivalent to the Lyapunov's artificial small parameter method. It is to be noted that, both the $\delta-$ expansion method and the artificial small parameter method does not provide fundamental rules to determine the place where the artificial parameter $\varepsilon$ or $\delta$ should appear. Like perturbation techniques, both the $\delta-$expansion method and the artificial small parameter method themselves do not provide us with a convenient way to adjust convergence region and rate of approximation series.

In all these above perturbation and non-perturbation techniques, there are some limitations. There is very limited choice to use different base functions to approximate non linear problems in these methods. They do not provide with a convenient way to adjust and control convergence region and rate of approximation series.

The history of numerical techniques for boundary-layer equations goes back to the sixteenth century. A major input to finding numerical methods was the invention of the calculus by Newton and Leibnitz, as this led to accurate mathematical models for physical reality. These mathematical models cannot usually be solved explicitly, and numerical methods to obtain approximate solutions are needed. Newton created a number of numerical methods for solving a variety of problems, and his name is attached till today to generalizations of his original ideas. Of special note is his work on root finding and polynomial interpolation. Following Newton, many of the giants of mathematics of the 18th and 19th centuries made major contributions to the numerical solution of mathematical problems.

The numerical techniques for boundary-layer flows is popular only in the nineteenth century. The review of the boundary layer flows and some of its numerical techniques are presented by Schlichting (1979) and White (1979). The numerical schemes for the boundary-layer equations have been well developed and tested as compared to methods for viscous flows. Several research papers on numerical techniques for solving boundary layer equations are available. In the present thesis, only two numerical techniques such as the Keller-Box Method (KBM) and the Runge-Kutta-Fehlberg Method (RKFM). have been used to compute the solutions. Hence these two methods are given here very briefly.

***Runge-Kutta-Fehlberg Method (RKFM):*** The RKFM uses the analysis with a Runge-Kutta method of order four and a Runge-Kutta method of order five. One way to guarantee accuracy in the solution of the problem twice using step sizes $h$ and and compare answers at the mesh points corresponding to the larger step size. This method was initially introduced by Fehlberg (1969). At each step, two different approximations for the solution are made and compared. If the two answers are in close agreement, the approximation is accepted. If the two answers do not agree to a specified accuracy, the step size is reduced. If the answers agree to more significant digits than required, the step size is increased. The formulae and the further details of this method can be obtained from Fehlberg (1969).

***Keller-Box Method (KBM):*** To solve both nonlinear ordinary and partial differential equations, Keller-Box Method (KBM) is effectively used. This method was proposed by Keller *et al.* (1971) and subsequently this idea was further elaborated by Cebeci *et al.* (1984) which presents the detailed description of the method. Here we mention the basic steps involved in applying this numerical scheme, specifically for the non-dimensional governing equations. Thus, KBM has the following four key steps. (i) Reduce higher order differential equation to first order differential equation by introducing new independent variables. (ii) Convert the first order differential equations to a system of difference equation using central differences. (iii) Linearize the resulting algebraic equations by Newton's quasi-linearization technique and represent the same in the vector matrix form and the (iv) use the block tri-diagonal elimination technique to solve the linear system. We have used this scheme to obtain numerical solutions to few problems presented in this thesis.

Since, the present study focuses on the approximate analytical solution using homotopy analysis, this method is explained in detail in the next section.

## 1.7 Homotopy Analysis Method (HAM)

Liao, (1992) employed the basic ideas of Homotopy in topology and proposed a general analytic method for solving non-linear problems namely Homotopy Analysis method (HAM). This method has been successfully applied to solve many types of non-linear ordinary differential equations (ODEs)/ Partial differential equations (PDEs) with strong non-linearity. For a detailed description on HAM (see, Liao (1997; 1998; 2002*a*; 2002*b*: 2003*a*-2003*c*; 2004; 2005; 2006; 2009; 2010; 2012) and Nadjafi *et al.* (2012), Mallory *et al.* (2013) and Araghi *et al.* (2013)).

Some analytic and semi-analytic techniques based on the homotopy analysis method (HAM) are briefly described, including the so-called homotopy perturbation method by He (1998), the Optimal Homotopy analysis method by Yabushita (2007), Optimal Homotopy asymptotic method by Marinca (2008), Predictor homotopy analysis method by Abbasbandy (2009) and the spectral homotopy analysis method by Motsa (2010), the generalized boundary element method, and the generalized scaled boundary finite element method.

### 1.7.1 Significance of using HAM

The HAM distinguishes itself from various other analytical methods in four important aspects. First, it is a series expansion method that is not directly dependent on small or large physical parameters. Thus, it is applicable for strongly nonlinear problems, going beyond some of the inherent limitations of the standard perturbation methods. Second, it is an unified method for the Lyapunov artificial small parameter method, the $\delta$-expansion method, the Adomian decomposition method and the homotopy perturbation method. The greater generality of the method often allows for strong convergence of the solution over larger spacial and parameter domains. Third, it gives excellent flexibility in the expression of the solution and provides a great freedom to choose the basis functions of the desired solution and the corresponding auxiliary linear operator of the homotopy. Finally, unlike the other analytic approximation techniques, the HAM provides a simple way to ensure the convergence of the solution series.

Here, we present how to apply HAM technique to solve a general non linear differential equation.

Consider a nonlinear differential equation of the form:

$$N[F(\eta)] = 0, \tag{1.8}$$

where $N$ is the non linear operator and $F(\eta)$ is the solution of the differential equation.

Choose an auxiliary linear operator with the property

$$L[U(\eta)] = 0 \text{ when } U(\eta) = 0. \tag{1.9}$$

The choice of initial guess $F_0(\eta)$ of the exact solution $F(\eta)$ is to satisfy the boundary conditions. Construct the family of Homotopy

$$H(X(\eta;\gamma);c_X,\gamma) \equiv (1-\gamma)L[X(\eta;\gamma) - F_0(\eta)] - \gamma c_X H(\eta) N[X(\eta;\gamma)], \tag{1.10}$$

$$\begin{aligned}
\text{where} \quad X(\eta;\gamma) &= \text{Unknown functions of } \eta \text{ and } \gamma \\
c_X &= \text{Convergence control parameter} \\
H(\eta) &= \text{Non-zero auxiliary function} \\
\gamma \in [0,1] &= \text{Embedding parameter} \\
F_0(\eta) &= \text{Initial guess.}
\end{aligned}$$

### 1.7.2 Zeroth-order deformation problem

To obtain the HAM solution for the governing equation. (1.8), let $\gamma \in [0,1]$ be an embedding parameter and $c_X$ is the basic optimal convergence control parameter. Then the zeroth order deformation equation become,

$$(1-\gamma)L[X(\eta;\gamma) - F_0(\eta)] = \gamma c_X H(\eta) N[X(\eta;\gamma)]. \tag{1.11}$$

From eq. (1.11), at $\gamma = 0$ and $\gamma = 1$, we have

$$X(\eta;0) = F_0(\eta) \text{ and } X(\eta;1) = F(\eta). \tag{1.12}$$

Expanding $X(\eta;\gamma)$ in Taylor's series with respect to $\gamma$, we obtain

$$\begin{aligned}
X(\eta;\gamma) &= X(\eta;\gamma) + \sum_{\ell=1}^{+\infty} \frac{1}{\ell!} \frac{\partial^\ell X(\eta;\gamma)}{\partial \gamma^\ell}\bigg|_{\gamma=0} \gamma^\ell \\
&= F_0(\eta) + \sum_{\ell=1}^{+\infty} F_\ell(\eta)\gamma^\ell.
\end{aligned}$$

This is called Homotopy-Series Solution convergent at $\gamma = 1$.

### 1.7.3 Higher-order deformation problem

For obtaining the $\ell^{th}$-order deformation equations, differentiate eq. (1.11) $\ell$-times with respect to $\gamma$, and divide by $\ell!$. Setting $\gamma = 0$, we get

$$L[X_\ell(\eta) - \Omega_\ell X_{\ell-1}(\eta)] = c_X H(\eta)\Re_\ell(\vec{X}_{\ell-1}), \quad \ell \geq 1, \tag{1.13}$$

where $\Re_\ell(\vec{X}_{\ell-1}) = \frac{1}{(\ell-1)!}\frac{\partial^{(\ell-1)}}{\partial\gamma^{(\ell-1)}}N[X(\eta;\gamma)]\Big|_{\gamma=0}$ and $\Omega_\ell$ is defined as

$$\Omega_\ell = \begin{cases} 0, & \ell \leq 1 \\ 1, & \ell \geq 2. \end{cases} \tag{1.14}$$

The right side of eq. (1.13) will depend only on the terms $X_n(\eta)$ with $n < \ell$. As a result, the terms $X_\ell(\eta)$ can be obtained in order to increasing $\ell$ by solving the linear deformation equation in succession. The solution to the $\ell^{th}$-order deformation equations can be written as

$$X_\ell(\eta) = X_{hom}(\eta) + X_{par}(\eta), \tag{1.15}$$

where $X_{hom}(\eta)$ satisfies the homogeneous equation $L[X_{hom}(\eta)] = 0$ and $X_{par}(\eta)$ is a particular solution of eq. (1.13). We can express $X_{par}(t)$ as

$$X_{par}(\eta) = \Omega_\ell X_{\ell-1}(\eta) + L^{-1}[c_X H(\eta)\Re_\ell(\vec{X}_{\ell-1})]. \tag{1.16}$$

We solve the eq. (1.16) one after the other in the order $\ell = 1, 2, 3, \ldots\ldots$ by means of the symbolic computation software Mathematica.

### 1.7.4 Control of residual error

In order to choose the optimal values of the convergence control parameter $c_X$, we compute the average squared residual errors suggested by Liao (2012),

$$E_X \simeq \frac{1}{\ell}\sum_{j=0}^{i}\left(N\left[\sum_{i=0}^{\ell} X_i(j\Delta x)\right]\right)^2, \tag{1.17}$$

where $X = f,\, g,\, G,\, s$ and etc. $\Delta x = \frac{10}{\ell}$ and $\ell = 30$.

At the $\ell^{th}$-order, the optimal values of $c_X$ are computed by the minimum of the squared residual $E_X$ of the governing equations, corresponding to,

$$\frac{dE_X}{dc_X} = 0. \tag{1.18}$$

The HAM-based **Mathematica package BVPh 2.0*** has been utilized to compute the averaged residual errors of eq. (1.8). Hence, we use eq. (1.17) to find the convergence control parameters which are used for the entire solution analysis.

## 1.8 Present work and Key Contributions

In this thesis, a set of five fluid dynamics problems having important engineering applications which have no analytical forms of solutions are studied. The governing equations of the problems after suitable mathematical simplifications resulted in a coupled system of non linear ordinary or partial differential equations. The resulting equations are solved using homotopy analysis and the computer algebra software Mathematica to obtain approximate analytical solutions.

For all the study problems, the objective of the study, mathematical formulation and governing equations, parameter under study, HAM solution procedure are explained. The results obtained, the discussion of the results and the conclusions drawn are all presented in a clear manner for all the problems. In all the chapters, special cases of the results from the present analysis have been compared with the results available in the literature and found to be in very good agreement. The error estimation at higher order is obtained for all the cases. An optimal convergence control parameter valid in the whole region is computed for all the problems investigated. We have successfully derived a low-to high-order solution series from 5 to 30 by solving higher order deformation equations to obtain approximate analytical solutions. Numerical computations have been performed wherever possible to compare with the present analytical results.

Given below are the research problems studied during the course of the research and are listed chapter wise.

- Chapter 2 deals with the study of mixed convection flow due to a vertical plate in a two-dimensional viscous flow.
  - To obtain the solution of viscous, steady two-dimensional boundary layer, mixed convection flow of a laminar, incompressible hydromagnetic flow due a vertical plate in the presence of a heat source and chemical reaction. The resulting equations are a coupled system of three non linear ordinary

*Refer. http://numericaltank.sjtu.edu.cn/BVPh.htm

differential equations governing the flow. This work has appeared in the following publication.

  - Mixed convection flow due to a vertical plate in the presence of heat source and chemical reaction. ***Ain Shams Engineering Journal***, (2015).

- Chapter 3 deals with the study of Heat transfer near the stagnation point of an unsteady three-dimensional viscous flow.

  - To obtain the solution of viscous, unsteady, three-dimensional, incompressible flow of an electrically conducting fluid in the neighborhood of a stagnation region. The governing Navier-Stokes equations are simplified using similarity transformations to a simultaneous system of five non linear ordinary differential equations. The numerical solutions are obtained using RKFM with a shooting technique. This work has appeared in the following publication.
  - Heat Transfer near the stagnation point of an unsteady three-dimensional flow. ***Arabian Journal of Mathematics***, (2015).

- Chapter 4 deals with the heat and mass transfer in a two-dimensional viscoelastic fluid flow due to a stretching surface.

  - To obtain the solution of steady, two-dimensional flow of non-Newtonian incompressible viscoelastic fluid due to a continuous stretching surface. The resulting equations are a coupled system of three non linear ordinary differential equations governing the flow. This work has appeared in the following publication.
  - The Study of heat and mass transfer in a Viscoelastic fluid due to a continuous stretching surface using Homotopy analysis method. ***Journal of Applied Analysis and Computation***, (2014).

- Chapter 5 deals with the flow and heat transfer in a three-dimensional viscoelastic fluid due to a stretching surface.

  - To obtain the solution of steady, three-dimensional boundary layer flow of a non-Newtonian incompressible viscoelastic fluid due to a stretching sheet with an applied magnetic field. The resulting equations are a simultaneous system of four non linear ordinary differential equations governing the flow. This work has appeared in the following publication.

  - Flow and heat transfer in a viscoelastic fluid due to a stretching surface-An analytical solution using HAM. ***International Journal of Engineering Sciences & Research Technology***, (2013).

- Chapter 6 deals with the unsteady, non similar flow in the stagnation region of a vertical plate due to impulsive motion.

  - To obtain the solution of unsteady, two-dimensional boundary layer mixed convection flow and heat transfer near the stagnation region in the presence of buoyancy forces over a heated vertical plate. The resulting equations are a coupled system of two non linear partial differential equations governing the flow. The numerical results of the flow are computed using the KBM. This work has been communicated for publication.

  - Unsteady non similar flow in the stagnation region of a vertical plate due to impulsive motion. ***Journal of Applied Analysis and Computation***, (2015).

# Chapter 2

# Mixed convection flow due to a vertical plate in a two-dimensional viscous fluid

## 2.1 Abstract

In this Chapter, the hydromagnetic heat and mass transfer by mixed convection flow due to a vertical flat plate is considered for analysis. The governing equations are solved both analytically and numerically. The analytical solutions are obtained using the HAM while the numerical solutions are computed using KBM. Convergence of the HAM solutions for the governing non-dimensional equations are derived. A detailed error analysis is done to compute the average squared residual errors for flow, temperature and concentration. The optimal values of the convergence control parameter are computed for velocity and temperature. This study includes the effects of various parameters such as magnetic parameter, Grashof number, chemical reaction parameter, heat source parameter and Biot number on skin friction, heat and mass transfer rates as well on velocity, temperature and concentration profiles. The results are presented in the form of tables and figures and discussed in detail. The special cases of present results are compared with the existing ones available in the literature and are found to be in good agreement.

## 2.2 Introduction

The study of boundary layer flow with heat and mass transfer over a vertical plate, in the presence of magnetic field and chemical reaction has important applications in various chemical and engineering processes such as petroleum and chemical industry, thermal insulation, cooling of nuclear reactors described by Rout *et al.* (2013). The convective heat transfer studies are very useful in understanding processes involving high temperature and concentration, for example, gas turbines and thermal energy storage. Other promising applications are in the field of metallurgy such as MHD stirring of molten metal and magnetic-levitation casting.

Makinde (2010*a*; 2010*b*) studied the heat and mass transfer in the presence of magnetic field due to a moving vertical plate with a convective surface boundary condition effects numerically using higher order Runge Kutta Scheme. The flow due to a semi-infinite vertical plate with convective surface boundary condition and internal heat generation in the presence of viscous dissipation, thermal radiation and chemical reaction was studied numerically by Ibrahim *et al.* (2010; 2013). Aziz (2009) has investigated the different variations of laminar thermal boundary layer and thermal slip flow due to a flat plate in a uniform stream of fluid with a convective surface and constant heat flux boundary conditions. Most of these studies pertain to numerical methods using Runge-Kutta scheme.

Recently, Ishak *et al.* (2011) have studied the effect of radiation on the thermal boundary layer flow due to a moving plate. Olanrewaju *et al.* (2013) presented the effects of thermal diffusion, magnetic field and viscous dissipation on unsteady mixed convection flow past a porous plate with chemical reaction. Thermal radiation with buoyancy force on the MHD fluid flow on the permeable vertical stretching sheet has been considered by Rashidi *et al.* (2014).

The analytical and numerical solutions in a steady two-dimensional flow of viscous fluid with chemical reaction and heat generation were considered by Shateyi *et al.* (2010). Shehzad *et al.* (2013*c*) included the Casson fluid flow with chemical reaction and suction effects for heat and mass transfer on MHD flow.

The hydromagnetic boundary layer flow with heat and mass transfer due to a vertical plate in the presence of chemical reaction, magnetic field and a convective heat exchange at the surface was examined numerically by Gangadhar *et al.* (2012) and Gangadhar (2013). Both the works deal with the numerical solution using Runge-Kutta fourth order with shooting technique. In Gangadhar *et al.* (2012), the author has not considered the source parameter (Sr) and the concentration difference parameter (Nc), whereas in Gangadhar (2013), he has included the source parameter but not considered the concentration difference parameter.

The focus of this chapter is to obtain an approximate analytical solution for the hydromagnetic flow due to a vertical plate in the presence of a heat source and chemical reaction which has not been taken up for analysis in the literature. The flow is subjected to a convective surface boundary condition in the presence of local and modified thermal Grashof numbers and the study includes the combined effects of source parameter and the concentration difference parameter. The non linear equations governing the flow were solved analytically using HAM, whereas the numerical solutions are obtained using KBM. Gangadhar *et al.* (2012) and Gangadhar (2013), have studied the numerical approach using Runge Kutta fourth order with shooting technique whereas the present analysis is an approximate analytical solution procedure. The governing equations and the boundary conditions imposed on the concentration are different from that of Gangadhar *et al.* (2012) and Gangadhar (2013). The present study takes into account both heat source parameter and Concentration difference parameter to study the effect of magnetic and internal heat generation on the fluid. However, the problem of solving the governing nonlinear equations with suitable boundary conditions using approximate analytical solution has not been studied so far.

## 2.3 Problem formulation and governing equations

This section deals with the mixed convection flow of a laminar, incompressible hydromagnetic flow due to a vertical plate in the presence of a heat source and chemical reaction. The fluid is subjected to a uniform magnetic field of strength $B_0$. The magnetic Reynolds number of the flow is assumed to be small enough so that the induced distortion due to applied magnetic field can be neglected. On the assumption of a small magnetic Reynolds number, heat energy dissipated through viscous dissipation and the heat released due to Ohmic heating are negligible compared to the energy due to heat source since the surface is heated by convection. Hence the combined effects of viscous dissipation and Ohmic heating due to magnetics are neglected in the energy equation.

Under these assumptions, the governing equations for the steady two-dimensional boundary layer flow due to a vertical plate are given by Makinde (2010*a*),

$$u_x + v_y = 0 \tag{2.1}$$

$$uu_x + vu_y = \nu u_{yy} - \frac{\sigma {B_0}^2}{\rho}\left(u - U_\infty\right) + g_1\beta_1\left(T - T_\infty\right) + g_1\beta_2\left(C - C_\infty\right) \tag{2.2}$$

$$uT_x + vT_y = \alpha T_{yy} + \frac{Q_0}{\rho C_p}\left(T - T_\infty\right) \tag{2.3}$$

$$uC_x + vC_y = DC_{yy} - Kr_1 C. \tag{2.4}$$

The boundary conditions are

$$u = v = 0, -kT_y = h_c\left(T_f - T\right), C_w = Ax^\beta + C_\infty \text{ at } y = 0,$$
$$u \to U_\infty,\ T \to T_\infty \text{ and } C \to C_\infty \text{ as } y \to \infty. \tag{2.5}$$

The coordinate system for the two-dimensional flow is given in Figure. 2.1. The $x$-axis is considered along the direction of the plate and the $y$-axis is normal to it. A uniform magnetic field of strength $B_0$ is applied in the downward $y$-axis. The left surface of the plate is being heated by convection from a hot fluid and $T_f$ represents the left side of the surface plate of temperature that gives a heat transfer coefficient $h_c$.

Here $u$ and $v$ denote the fluid velocity along the $x$-and $y$-directions, respectively, $T$ is the temperature, $C$ is the concentration, $k$ is the thermal conductivity, $\rho$ is the fluid density, $\nu$ is the kinematic viscosity, $\alpha$, $D$ are the thermal and mass diffusivity respectively, $\beta_1$ and $\beta_2$ are the thermal and solutal expansion coefficients, $\beta$ is the power index of the concentration, $\sigma$ is the fluid electrical conductivity, $Q_0$ is the heat source, $Kr_1$ is the chemical reaction rate on the species concentration and $g_1$ is the gravitational acceleration, $A$ is the constant and $C_w$ is the species concentration at the plate, $C_p$ is the specific heat at a constant pressure and $U_\infty$, $T_\infty$ and $C_\infty$ are the free stream velocity, temperature and concentration respectively.

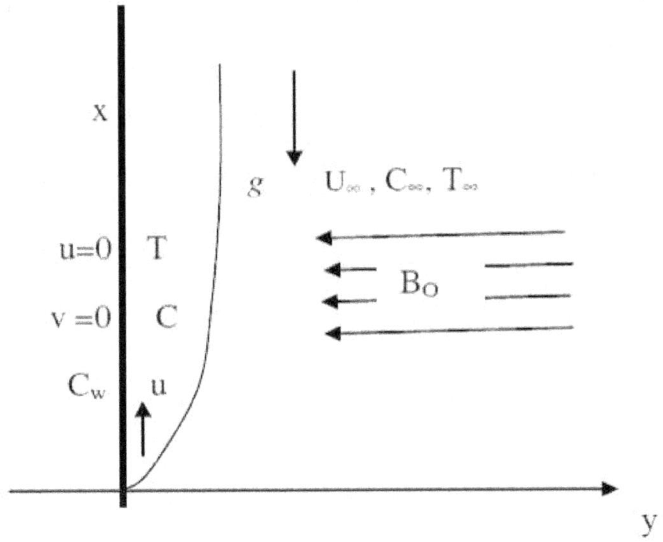


Figure 2.1: Sketch of two-dimensional coordinate system of flow.

The stream function $\psi$, satisfies the eq. (2.1) automatically with

$$u = \frac{\partial \psi}{\partial y}; v = -\frac{\partial \psi}{\partial x}. \tag{2.6}$$

It may be remarked that the partial differential equations. (2.1)-(2.6) is obtained by defining an independent variable $\eta$ and the stream function $\psi$ as follows

$$\eta = y\left(\frac{U_\infty}{\nu x}\right)^{1/2}; \quad \psi = (\nu x U_\infty)^{1/2} f(\eta). \tag{2.7}$$

The dimensionless temperature and concentration are denoted as

$$T - T_\infty = (T_f - T_\infty) g(\eta); \quad C - C_\infty = (C_w - C_\infty) G(\eta). \tag{2.8}$$

Substituting (2.6)-(2.8) into (2.1)-(2.5), we get the following coupled nonlinear ODEs;

$$f'''(\eta) + \frac{1}{2} f(\eta) f''(\eta) + M(1 - f'(\eta)) + Gr\, g(\eta) + Gc\, G(\eta) = 0 \tag{2.9}$$

$$g''(\eta) + \frac{1}{2} Pr f(\eta) g'(\eta) + Pr Sr g(\eta) = 0 \tag{2.10}$$

$$G''(\eta) + \frac{1}{2} Sc f(\eta) G'(\eta) - Sc Kr (G(\eta) + Nc) = 0, \tag{2.11}$$

eq. (2.5) can be rewritten as

$$\begin{aligned} f(0) &= f'(0)=0,\ f'(\infty)=1 \\ g'(0) &= Bi\,(g(0)-1)\,,\ g(\infty)=0 \\ G(0) &= 1,\ G(\infty)=0, \end{aligned} \tag{2.12}$$

where $\eta$ is the similarity variable, $f$ is the dimensionless stream function, $f'$ is the dimensionless velocity, $g$ is the dimensionless temperature, $G$ is the dimensionless concentration, and prime denotes derivative with respect to $\eta$.

The coefficients appearing the the non dimensional equations are given by

$$M=\frac{\sigma {B_0}^2 x}{\rho U_\infty},\quad Gr=\frac{g_1\beta_1\left(T_f-T_\infty\right)x}{U_\infty^2},\quad Gc=\frac{g_2\beta_2\left(C_w-C_\infty\right)x}{U_\infty^2},$$

$$Bi=\frac{h_c}{k}\left(\frac{\nu x}{U_\infty}\right)^{\frac{1}{2}},\quad Sr=\frac{Q_0 x}{U_\infty\rho C_p},\quad Pr=\frac{\nu}{\alpha},$$

$$Sc=\frac{\nu}{D}\quad Kr=\frac{Kr_1 x}{U_\infty},\quad Nc=\frac{C_\infty}{C_w-C_\infty}.$$

Here $M$ is the local magnetic field parameter, $Gr$ is the local thermal Grashof number, $Gc$ is the modified Grashof number, $Bi$ is the local convection heat transfer parameter, $Pr$ is the Prandtl number, $Sc$ is the Schmidt number, $Sr$ is the local heat source parameter, $Kr$ is the local chemical reaction parameter and $Nc$ is the concentration difference parameter.

It is noted that the local parameters such as $Gr$, $Gc$, $Bi$ and $M$ in (2.9)-(2.12) are functions of $x$, these local parameters must be constant and have a similarity solution, and assume the relations as follows

$$h_c=\frac{a}{x^{\frac{1}{2}}},\ \sigma=\frac{b}{x},\ \beta_1=\frac{d}{x},\ \beta_2=\frac{e}{x},\ Q_0=\frac{a_1}{x}\ \text{and}\ Kr_1=\frac{b_1}{x}, \tag{2.13}$$

where $a$, $b$, $d$, $e$, $a_1$ and $b_1$ are constants.

From (2.9)-(2.12) with $Sr=Kr=0$ (without Source and Chemical reaction parameters) reduces to Makinde (2010*a*) and Gangadhar *et al.* (2013). Also, (2.10)-(2.12) are the same as that of Rout *et al.* (2013). In this problem the physical quantities such as the local skin friction coefficient in terms of the shear stress $\tau=f''(0)$ and the local Nusselt number in terms of the heat transfer $Nu=-g'(0)$, local Sherwood number in terms of the mass transfer $Sh=-G'(0)$ are computed for different combinations of the parametric values under study.

## 2.4 Homotopy series solution

The governing non dimensional equations are solved using HAM to obtain an approximate analytical solutions. Since the method is explained in detail in the introductory Chapter, the procedure is directly applied to the equations (2.9)-(2.11).

The main components of the HAM procedure are selecting suitable initial profiles satisfying the boundary conditions of the problem and choosing an appropriate linear operator so that its solutions are simpler to evaluate analytically. The nonlinear operator is directly written from the governing equation of the problem. In HAM analysis, a system of deformation equations are derived which have to be solved. To initiate the HAM analysis, a set of base functions are required. They are taken as

$$\{\left(\eta^k e^{-n\eta}\right),\, k \geq 0,\, n \geq 0\},$$

$$f_l(\eta) = \sum_{n=0}^{\infty}\sum_{k=0}^{\infty}[A_{l,n}^k \eta^k e^{-n\eta}], \tag{2.14}$$

$$g_l(\eta) = \frac{Bi}{1+Bi}\sum_{n=0}^{\infty}\sum_{k=0}^{\infty}[B_{l,n}^k \eta^k e^{-n\eta}], \tag{2.15}$$

$$G_l(\eta) = \sum_{n=0}^{\infty}\sum_{k=0}^{\infty}[C_{l,n}^k \eta^k e^{-n\eta}]. \tag{2.16}$$

In which $A_{l,n}^k$, $B_{l,n}^k$ and $C_{l,n}^k$ are the coefficients.

The initial guesses for the flow variables are

$$f_0(\eta) = \eta - \eta e^{-\eta},\;\; g_0(\eta) = \frac{Bie^{-\eta}}{1+Bi},\;\; G_0(\eta) = e^{-\eta}. \tag{2.17}$$

The auxiliary linear operators are suitably chosen from the governing equations as

$$L_f = \frac{d^3 f}{d\eta^3} - \frac{df}{d\eta},\;\; L_g = \frac{d^2 g}{d\eta^2} - g,\; L_G = \frac{d^2 G}{d\eta^2} - G, \tag{2.18}$$

so as to obtain a simpler form of solution as

$$\begin{aligned} L_f\left[C_1 + C_2 e^{\eta} + C_3 e^{-\eta}\right] &= 0, L_g\left[C_4 e^{\eta} + C_5 e^{-\eta}\right] = 0, \\ L_G\left[C_6 e^{\eta} + C_7 e^{-\eta}\right] &= 0, \end{aligned} \tag{2.19}$$

where $C_i$'s are arbitrary constants and can be evaluated from (2.12).

### 2.4.1 Zeroth-order deformation problem

To obtain the HAM solution for the governing eqs. (2.9)-(2.11), let $\gamma \in [0,1]$ be an embedding parameter and $c_f$, $c_g$ and $c_G$ are the basic optimal convergence control parameters. Then the zeroth order deformation equation and the non-linear operators can be written as

$$(1-\gamma)L_X[X(\eta,\gamma)-X_0(\eta)] = \gamma c_X \mathscr{N}_X[X(\eta,\gamma)] \tag{2.20}$$

where, $X = f,\ g$ and $G$ and $X_0 = f_0, g_0$ and $G_0$.

The non linear operator of each of these flow variables can be explicitly written from the governing equations as

$$\begin{aligned}\mathscr{N}_f[f(\eta,\gamma)] &= \frac{\partial^3 f(\eta,\gamma)}{\partial\eta^3} + \frac{1}{2}f(\eta,\gamma)\frac{\partial^2 f(\eta,\gamma)}{\partial\eta^2} + M\left(1-\frac{\partial f(\eta,\gamma)}{\partial\eta}\right)\\ &+ Grg(\eta,\gamma) + GcG(\eta,\gamma)\end{aligned} \tag{2.21}$$

$$\begin{aligned}\mathscr{N}_g[g(\eta,\gamma),f(\eta,\gamma)] &= \frac{\partial^2 g(\eta,\gamma)}{\partial\eta^2} + \frac{1}{2}Pr\left(f(\eta,\gamma)\frac{\partial g(\eta,\gamma)}{\partial\eta}\right)\\ &+ PrSrg(\eta,\gamma),\end{aligned} \tag{2.22}$$

$$\begin{aligned}\mathscr{N}_G[G(\eta,\gamma),f(\eta,\gamma)] &= \frac{\partial^2 G(\eta,\gamma)}{\partial\eta^2} + \frac{1}{2}Sc\left(f(\eta,\gamma)\frac{\partial G(\eta,\gamma)}{\partial\eta}\right)\\ &- ScKr(G(\eta,\gamma)+Nc),\end{aligned} \tag{2.23}$$

with appropriate boundary conditions rewritten from (2.12) as,

$$f(\eta;\gamma)|_{\eta=0} = 0,\ \left.\frac{\partial f(\eta;\gamma)}{\partial\eta}\right|_{\eta=0} = 0,\ \left.\frac{\partial f(\eta;\gamma)}{\partial\eta}\right|_{\eta=\infty} = 1 \tag{2.24}$$

$$\left.\frac{\partial g(\eta;\gamma)}{\partial\eta}\right|_{\eta=0} = Bi[g(\eta;\gamma)|_{\eta=0}-1],\ g(\eta;\gamma)|_{\eta=\infty} = 0, \tag{2.25}$$

$$G(\eta;\gamma)|_{\eta=0} = 1,\ G(\eta;\gamma)|_{\eta=\infty} = 0. \tag{2.26}$$

### 2.4.2 Higher-order deformation problem

For obtaining the $\ell^{th}$-order deformation equations, differentiate eq. (2.20) $\ell$-times with respect to $\gamma$, and divide by $\ell!$. Setting $\gamma = 0$, we get

$$L_X[X_\ell(\eta) - \Omega_\ell X_{\ell-1}(\eta)] = c_X \mathscr{R}_X^\ell(\eta). \tag{2.27}$$

The boundary conditions can be redefined as

$$
\begin{aligned}
f_\ell(0) &= 0,\ f'_\ell(0)=0,\ f'_\ell(\infty)=1,\\
g'_\ell(0) &= Bi[g_\ell(0)-1],\ g_\ell(\infty)=0\\
G_\ell(0) &= 1, G_\ell(\infty)=0. \qquad (2.28)
\end{aligned}
$$

In (2.27), the term $\mathscr{R}_X^\ell(\eta)$ denotes $\mathscr{R}_f^\ell(\eta)$, $\mathscr{R}_g^\ell(\eta)$ and $\mathscr{R}_G^\ell(\eta)$. These are the remainder terms from the linear operators which are given by

$$
\begin{aligned}
\mathscr{R}_f^\ell(\eta) &= f'''_{\ell-1}(\eta)+\frac{1}{2}\sum_{j=0}^{\ell-1}[f_{\ell-1-j}f''_j]+M(1-f'_{\ell-1}(\eta))\\
&+ Gr(g_{\ell-1}(\eta))+Gc(G_{\ell-1}(\eta)) \qquad (2.29)
\end{aligned}
$$

$$
\mathscr{R}_g^\ell(\eta)=g''_{\ell-1}(\eta)+\frac{1}{2}Pr\sum_{j=0}^{\ell-1}[f_{\ell-1-j}g'_j]+PrSrg_{\ell-1}(\eta), \qquad (2.30)
$$

$$
\mathscr{R}_G^\ell(\eta)=G''_{\ell-1}(\eta)+\frac{1}{2}Sc\sum_{j=0}^{\ell-1}[f_{\ell-1-j}G'_j]-ScKr(G_{\ell-1}(\eta)+Nc). \qquad (2.31)
$$

Here the function $\Omega_\ell$ denotes the characteristic function defined as

$$
\Omega_\ell=\begin{cases} 0 & \text{if } \ell\leq 1\\ 1 & \text{if } \ell>1. \end{cases} \qquad (2.32)
$$

Expanding $X(\eta;\gamma)$ with respect to $\gamma$ using Taylor's series, we get

$$
X(\eta;\gamma)=X_0(\eta)+\sum_{\ell=1}^{\infty}X_\ell(\eta)\gamma^\ell, \text{where } X_\ell(\eta)=\frac{1}{\ell!}\frac{\partial^\ell X(\eta;\gamma)}{\partial\gamma^\ell}\bigg|_{\gamma=0}. \qquad (2.33)
$$

When the auxiliary parameter value is selected as $\gamma=0$ and $\gamma=1$ in (2.20), it is realized that

$$
X(\eta;0)=X_0(\eta) \text{ and } X(\eta;1)=X(\eta). \qquad (2.34)
$$

Thus as $\gamma$ increases from 0 to 1, $X(\eta;\gamma)$ varies from the initial guess $X_0(\eta)$ to the solution $X(\eta)$ of the governing equations. The auxiliary parameters are suitably chosen so that the series solutions converge for $\gamma=1$ and the particular solution is given by

$$
X(\eta)=X_0(\eta)+\sum_{\ell=1}^{\infty}X_\ell(\eta). \qquad (2.35)
$$

Therefore, we get the general approximate analytical solutions $f_\ell, g_\ell, G_\ell$ in terms of special solutions $f_\ell^*, g_\ell^*, G_\ell^*$ as,

$$\begin{aligned} f_\ell(\eta) &= f_\ell^*(\eta) + C_1 + C_2 e^{\eta} + C_3 e^{-\eta} && (2.36)\\ g_\ell(\eta) &= g_\ell^*(\eta) + C_4 e^{\eta} + C_5 e^{-\eta} && (2.37)\\ G_\ell(\eta) &= G_\ell^*(\eta) + C_6 e^{\eta} + C_7 e^{-\eta}. && (2.38) \end{aligned}$$

By solving (2.36)-(2.38) one after the other in the order $\ell = 1,2,3,...$ by means of the symbolic computation software Mathematica, it is shown that the solution for the profiles can be expressed as an infinite series of any desired order. The approximate analytical solutions computed for $f$, $g$ and $G$ for $\ell = 1,2,3,...$ are given in **Appendix-A**.

### 2.4.3 Convergence of the Homotopy series

In this section, it is proved that the base functions (i.e, eqs. (2.14)-(2.16)) converge to the solutions of the (2.9)-(2.11).

That is, it is shown that

$$\lim_{N\to\infty} f_N(\eta) = 0, \quad \lim_{N\to\infty} g_N(\eta) = 0, \quad \lim_{N\to\infty} G_N(\eta) = 0. \tag{2.39}$$

From (2.27) and (2.32),

$$\begin{aligned} \lim_{N\to\infty}\left[\sum_{\ell=1}^{N} c_X \Re_X^\ell(\eta)\right] &= \lim_{N\to\infty}\sum_{\ell=1}^{N} L_X[X_\ell(\eta) - \Omega_\ell X_{\ell-1}(\eta)]\\ &= \lim_{N\to\infty} L_X\left[\sum_{\ell=1}^{N} X_\ell(\eta) - \sum_{\ell=1}^{N}\Omega_\ell X_{\ell-1}(\eta)\right]\\ &= \lim_{N\to\infty} L_X f_N(\eta)\\ &= L_X \lim_{N\to\infty} f_N(\eta)\\ \lim_{N\to\infty}\left[\sum_{\ell=1}^{N} c_X \Re_X^\ell(\eta)\right] &= 0 \;\; ; \eta \in [0,\infty), && (2.40) \end{aligned}$$

where $f_N = \sum_{\ell=1}^{N}(X_\ell(\eta) - \Omega_\ell X_{\ell-1}(\eta))$ and $X = f$, $g$ and $G$. Further (2.40) gives that infinite sequences $S_1, S_2, S_3, S_4, S_5, S_6......$, where $S_N = \left[\sum_{\ell=1}^{N}\Re_X^\ell(\eta)\right]$ converges to zero.

From (2.29),

$$\sum_{\ell=1}^{N} \Re_f^{\ell}(\eta) = \sum_{\ell=1}^{N} [f'''_{\ell-1}(\eta) + M(1 - f'_{\ell-1}(\eta)) + Gr(g_{\ell-1}(\eta)) + Gc(G_{\ell-1}(\eta))] + \sum_{\ell=1}^{N} \left\{ \frac{1}{2} \sum_{j=0}^{\ell-1} [f_{\ell-1-j} f''_j] \right\} \tag{2.41}$$

$$\begin{aligned}
\lim_{N\to\infty} \left[ \sum_{\ell=1}^{N} \Re_f^{\ell}(\eta) \right] &= \sum_{\ell=1}^{\infty} \{ f'''_{\ell-1}(\eta) + M(1 - f'_{\ell-1}(\eta)) + Gr(g_{\ell-1}(\eta)) \} \\
&+ \sum_{\ell=1}^{N} \left\{ Gc(G_{\ell-1}(\eta)) + \frac{1}{2} \sum_{j=0}^{\ell-1} [f_{\ell-1-j} f''_j] \right\} \\
&= \frac{d^3}{d\eta^3} \left( \sum_{\ell=1}^{\infty} f_{\ell-1}(\eta) \right) + \frac{1}{2} \sum_{\ell=1}^{\infty} \sum_{j=0}^{\ell-1} [f_{\ell-1-j} f''_j] \\
&+ Gr \left( \sum_{\ell=1}^{\infty} g_{\ell-1}(\eta) \right) + Gc \left( \sum_{\ell=1}^{\infty} G_{\ell-1}(\eta) \right) \\
&+ M \left( 1 - \frac{d}{d\eta} \left( \sum_{\ell=1}^{\infty} f_{\ell-1}(\eta) \right) \right) \\
&= \frac{d^3}{d\eta^3} \left( \sum_{j=0}^{\infty} f_j(\eta) \right) + \frac{1}{2} \sum_{j=0}^{\infty} \sum_{m=j+1}^{\infty} [f_{m-1-j} f''_j] \\
&+ Gr \left( \sum_{j=0}^{\infty} g_j(\eta) \right) + Gc \left( \sum_{j=0}^{\infty} G_j(\eta) \right) \\
&+ M \left( 1 - \frac{d}{d\eta} \left( \sum_{j=0}^{\infty} f_j(\eta) \right) \right) \\
&= \frac{d^3}{d\eta^3} \left( \sum_{j=0}^{\infty} f_j(\eta) \right) + M \left( 1 - \frac{d}{d\eta} \left( \sum_{j=0}^{\infty} f_j(\eta) \right) \right) \\
&+ Gr \left( \sum_{j=0}^{\infty} g_j(\eta) \right) + Gc \left( \sum_{j=0}^{\infty} G_j(\eta) \right) \\
&+ \frac{1}{2} \left( \sum_{j=0}^{\infty} f_j(\eta) \right) \left( \frac{d^2}{d\eta^2} \left( \sum_{j=0}^{\infty} f_j(\eta) \right) \right).
\end{aligned} \tag{2.42}$$

From (2.42) and (2.39),

$$\begin{aligned}
0 &= \frac{d^3}{d\eta^3} \left( \sum_{j=0}^{\infty} f_j(\eta) \right) + M \left( 1 - \frac{d}{d\eta} \left( \sum_{j=0}^{\infty} f_j(\eta) \right) \right) \\
&+ Gr \left( \sum_{j=0}^{\infty} g_j(\eta) \right) + Gc \left( \sum_{j=0}^{\infty} G_j(\eta) \right) \\
&- \frac{1}{2} \left( \sum_{j=0}^{\infty} f_j(\eta) \right) \left( \frac{d^2}{d\eta^2} \left( \sum_{j=0}^{\infty} f_j(\eta) \right) \right),
\end{aligned} \tag{2.43}$$

and from (2.30),

$$\begin{aligned}\sum_{\ell=1}^{N}\Re_g^{\ell}(\eta) &= \sum_{\ell=1}^{N}[g''_{\ell-1}(\eta)+PrSr(g_{\ell-1}(\eta))\\ &+ \frac{Pr}{2}\sum_{j=0}^{\ell-1}\{f_{\ell-1-j}(\eta)g'_{\ell-1}(\eta)\}] \end{aligned} \tag{2.44}$$

$$\begin{aligned}\lim_{N\to\infty}\left[\sum_{\ell=1}^{N}\Re_g^{\ell}(\eta)\right] &= \sum_{\ell=1}^{\infty}[g''_{\ell-1}(\eta)+PrSr(g_{\ell-1}(\eta))\\ &- \frac{1}{2}Pr\sum_{j=0}^{\ell-1}\{f_{\ell-1-j}(\eta)g'_{\ell-1}(\eta)\}]\\ &= \frac{d^2}{d\eta^2}\left(\sum_{\ell=1}^{\infty}g_{\ell-1}(\eta)\right)+PrSr\left(\sum_{\ell=1}^{\infty}g_{\ell-1}(\eta)\right)\\ &+ \frac{1}{2}Pr\sum_{\ell=1}^{\infty}\sum_{j=0}^{\ell-1}[f_{\ell-1-j}(\eta)g'_j(\eta)]\end{aligned}$$

$$\begin{aligned}\lim_{N\to\infty}\left[\sum_{\ell=1}^{N}\Re_g^{\ell}(\eta)\right] &= \frac{d^2}{d\eta^2}\left(\sum_{\ell=1}^{\infty}g_{\ell-1}(\eta)\right)+PrSr\left(\sum_{\ell=1}^{\infty}g_{\ell-1}(\eta)\right)\\ &+ \frac{1}{2}Pr\sum_{j=0}^{\infty}\sum_{m=j+1}^{\infty}[f_{m-1-j}(\eta)g'_j(\eta)]\\ &= \frac{d^2}{d\eta^2}\left(\sum_{j=0}^{\infty}g_j(\eta)\right)+PrSr\left(\sum_{j=0}^{\infty}g_j(\eta)\right)\\ &+ \frac{1}{2}Pr\sum_{j=0}^{\infty}\sum_{m=j+1}^{\infty}[f_{m-1-j}(\eta)g'_j(\eta)]\end{aligned}$$

$$\begin{aligned}\lim_{N\to\infty}\left[\sum_{\ell=1}^{N}\Re_g^{\ell}(\eta)\right] &= \frac{d^2}{d\eta^2}\left(\sum_{j=0}^{\infty}g_j(\eta)\right)+PrSr\left(\sum_{j=0}^{\infty}g_j(\eta)\right)\\ &+ \frac{1}{2}Pr\left(\sum_{j=0}^{\infty}f_j(\eta)\right)\left(\frac{d}{d\eta}\left[\sum_{j=0}^{\infty}g_j(\eta)\right]\right).\end{aligned} \tag{2.45}$$

From (2.45) and (2.39),

$$\begin{aligned}\frac{d^2}{d\eta^2}\left(\sum_{j=0}^{\infty}g_j(\eta)\right) &+ \frac{1}{2}Pr\left(\sum_{j=0}^{\infty}f_j(\eta)\right)\left(\frac{d}{d\eta}\left[\sum_{j=0}^{\infty}g_j(\eta)\right]\right)\\ &+ PrSr\left(\sum_{j=0}^{\infty}g_j(\eta)\right)=0,\end{aligned} \tag{2.46}$$

and from (2.31),

$$\begin{aligned}\sum_{\ell=1}^{N}\Re_G^{\ell}(\eta) &= \sum_{\ell=1}^{N}[G''_{\ell-1}(\eta)-ScKr(G_{\ell-1}(\eta)+Nc)\\ &+ \frac{1}{2}Sc\sum_{j=0}^{\ell-1}\{f_{\ell-1-j}(\eta)G'_{\ell-1}(\eta)\}],\end{aligned} \tag{2.47}$$

$$\begin{aligned}
\lim_{N\to\infty}\left[\sum_{\ell=1}^{N}\Re_G^{\ell}(\eta)\right] &= \sum_{\ell=1}^{\infty}\{G''_{\ell-1}(\eta)-ScKr(G_{\ell-1}(\eta)+Nc)\}\\
&+ \sum_{\ell=1}^{\infty}\left\{\frac{1}{2}Sc\sum_{j=0}^{\ell-1}[f_{\ell-1-j}(\eta)G'_{\ell-1}(\eta)]\right\}\\
&= \frac{d^2}{d\eta^2}\left(\sum_{\ell=1}^{\infty}G_{\ell-1}(\eta)\right)\\
&- ScKr\left(\sum_{\ell=1}^{\infty}(G_{\ell-1}(\eta)+Nc)\right)\\
&+ \frac{1}{2}Sc\sum_{\ell=1}^{\infty}\sum_{j=0}^{\ell-1}[f_{\ell-1-j}(\eta)G'_j(\eta)],
\end{aligned}$$

$$\begin{aligned}
\lim_{N\to\infty}\left[\sum_{\ell=1}^{N}\Re_G^{\ell}(\eta)\right] &= \frac{d^2}{d\eta^2}\left(\sum_{\ell=1}^{\infty}G_{\ell-1}(\eta)\right)-\{\sum_{\ell=1}^{\infty}(G_{\ell-1}(\eta)\\
&+ Nc\}ScKr+\frac{1}{2}Sc\sum_{j=0}^{\infty}\sum_{m=j+1}^{\infty}[f_{m-1-j}(\eta)G'_j(\eta)]\\
&= \frac{d^2}{d\eta^2}\left(\sum_{j=0}^{\infty}G_j(\eta)\right)-\{\sum_{j=0}^{\infty}(G_j(\eta)\\
&+ Nc\}ScKr+\frac{1}{2}Sc\sum_{j=0}^{\infty}\sum_{m=j+1}^{\infty}[f_{m-1-j}(\eta)G'_j(\eta)]\\
&= \frac{d^2}{d\eta^2}\left(\sum_{j=0}^{\infty}G_j(\eta)\right)-ScKr\left(\sum_{j=0}^{\infty}(G_j(\eta)+Nc)\right)\\
&+ \frac{1}{2}Sc\left(\sum_{j=0}^{\infty}f_j(\eta)\right)\left(\frac{d}{d\eta}\left[\sum_{j=0}^{\infty}G_j(\eta)\right]\right). \qquad (2.48)
\end{aligned}$$

From (2.48) and (2.39),

$$\begin{aligned}
\frac{d^2}{d\eta^2}\left(\sum_{j=0}^{\infty}G_j(\eta)\right) &+ \frac{1}{2}Sc\left(\sum_{j=0}^{\infty}f_j(\eta)\right)\left(\frac{d}{d\eta}\left[\sum_{j=0}^{\infty}G_j(\eta)\right]\right)\\
&- ScKr\left(\sum_{j=0}^{\infty}G_j(\eta)+Nc\right)=0. \qquad (2.49)
\end{aligned}$$

From (2.28),

$$\begin{aligned}
&\sum_{j=0}^{\infty}f_j(0)=0,\quad \sum_{j=0}^{\infty}f'_j(0)=0,\quad \sum_{j=0}^{\infty}f'_j(\infty)=0,\quad \sum_{j=0}^{\infty}g_j(\infty)=0,\\
&\sum_{j=0}^{\infty}\left(g'_j(0)-Bi[g_j(0)-1]\right)=0,\quad \sum_{j=0}^{\infty}G_j(0)=0,\quad \sum_{j=0}^{\infty}G_j(\infty)=0. \qquad (2.50)
\end{aligned}$$

Therefore, (2.43)-(2.46) and (2.49) with (2.50) show that the (2.14)-(2.16) converge.

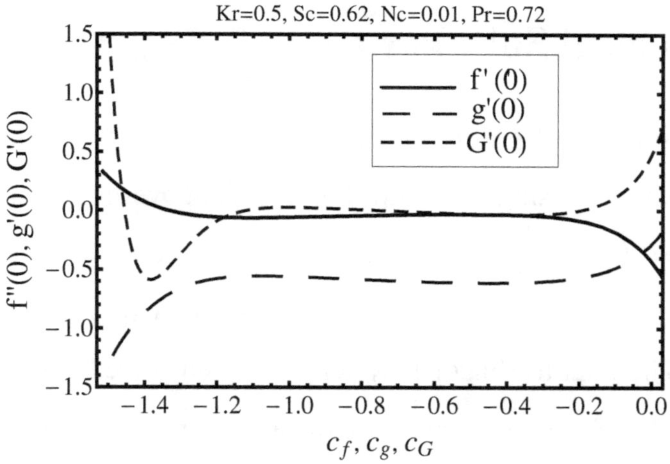


Figure 2.2: $c_X$ curve at $M = Bi = Gc = Gr = 0.1$ and $Sr = 1.0$.

It is customary in HAM analysis to plot $c_X$-curves to identify the interval of optimal convergence control parameters (i.e. $c_f$, $c_g$ and $c_G$) within which any values can be chosen to obtain convergent solutions. From Figure. 2.2, it is shown that choosing $c_f$ in the interval $[-1.3, -0.3]$ does not affect the values of shear stress rates and it is $[-1.1, -0.3]$ for both heat and mass transfer rates. The $c_f$, $c_g$ and $c_G$ curves have been drawn for $20^{th}$ order of HAM solution. The computation of average squared residual errors helps to obtain the optimal value of these $c_f$, $c_g$ and $c_G$ within that interval.

### 2.4.4 The error estimation at high orders

Use eq. (1.17) to compute the average squared residual errors of (2.9)-(2.11). At the $\ell^{th}$-order, the optimal values of $c_X$ are computed by the minimum of the squared residual $E_X$ of the governing equations, corresponding to (1.18).

The average squared residual errors at different orders of approximation for $f(\eta)$, $g(\eta)$ and $G(\eta)$ are shown in Figure.2.2. The average squared residual errors decreases much more quickly with convergence control parameters $c_f = -1.20945$,, $c_g = -1.10744$ and $c_G = -1.04288$. Obtaining these optimal values of $c_f$, $c_g$ and $c_G$ and using these values in all the further calculation of flow variables greatly influence and accelerate the convergence of series solution.

In all of the figures, we use $Pr = 0.72$, $Kr = 0.5$, $Sc = 0.62$, $Nc = 0.01$, $M = Bi = Gc = Gr = 0.1$ and $Sr = 1.0$ unless it is mentioned otherwise.

## 2.5 Numerical Solution

The numerical solution of governing eqs. (2.9)-(2.11) subject to the boundary conditions (2.12) is obtained using the KBM. For this, the governing non-dimensional equations are reduced to a first order system and the system obtained are approximated using central differences. The resultant difference equations are linearized by Newton's method. The final tri-diagonal systems are then solved using Thomas algorithm by Thomas (1949). Since the focus is on the approximate analytical solutions, the detailed mathematical derivations for numerical solutions are not presented here for sake of brevity. The numerical results and approximate analytical results agree very well in all the calculations, which are shown in the tables.

## 2.6 Results Analysis

The approximate analytical solutions are obtained in the form of general series for the flow variables $f$, $g$ and $G$. The computational software **Mathematica** is used for all algebraic and numerical calculations. The expressions for $f$, $g$ and $G$ are evaluated up to tenth order to keep the results up to seven decimal places accuracy.

Here the effect of various physical parameters such as magnetic field parameter $M$, local convective heat transfer parameter $Bi$, Prandtl number $Pr$, Schmidt number $Sc$ and local thermal Grashof number $Gr$, modified Grashof number $Gc$ and Concentration difference parameter $Nc$, local heat source parameter $Sr$ and chemical reaction parameter $Kr$ are analysed. The influence of these parameters on velocity, temperature and concentration profiles as well as on skin friction, heat and mass transfer rates discussed. Computations have been carried out for several combinations of parameters $Bi$, $M$, $Pr$, $Sr$, $Sc$, $Gr$, $Gc$, $Nc$ and $Kr$ and all results are presented here in the form of Tables 2.1-2.4 and Figures. 2.3-2.50.

Table 2.1 illustrates the convergence of skin friction $-f''(0)$, heat transfers $-g'(0)$ and $-G'(0)$ after performing up to $35^{th}$-order approximation of functions $f$, $g$ and $G$ computed from deformation equations. As seen, the computation is terminated as soon as three consecutive values agree in their seventh decimal places. Table 2.2 shows the comparison of skin friction results with that of Gangadhar (2013) and found them to be in very good agreement. Numerical calculations obtained from KBM method are carried out for various values of the dimensionless parameters of the problem.

It is seen from Table 2.3 that the heat transfer rate for *Bi*, *Gr*, *Gc*, *M*, *Pr* and *Sc* are compared in the absence of chemical reaction $(Kr)$ and source parameters $(Sr)$ with that of Rout *et al.* (2013). It is found that the values of the heat transfer rates increase with an increase in *Bi*, *Gr*, *Gc*, *M*, *Pr* and decreases in *Sc*. Similarly mass transfer rates increase in *Bi*, *Gr*, *Gc*, *M*, *Sc* and decrease in *Pr* from Table 2.4.

The Figures. 2.3-2.29 show the effects of these parameters on flow profiles and the 2.30- 2.50 show the variation of shear stress, heat and mass transfer rates.

The influence of all the parameters such as *Bi* and *M*, *Pr*, *Sr*, *Sc*, *Gr*, *Gc*, *Nc* and *Kr* on velocity profiles in the boundary layer are plotted in Figures. 2.3, 2.6, 2.9, 2.12, 2.15, 2.18, 2.21, 2.24 and 2.27. It is seen from these figures that, the velocity starts from a zero value at the plate surface and increase to the free stream value far away from the plate surface satisfying the far field its boundary conditions for all physical parameter values.

It is observed from Figure. 2.3 that, the magnetic parameter $(M)$ increases as increasing the velocity profile because the *M* presents a damping effect on the velocity field by creating a drag force that opposes the fluid motion, causing the velocity to decrease. However, in this case an increasing in *M* only slightly slows down the motion of the fluid away from the vertical plate toward the free stream velocity, while the fluid velocity near the vertical plate surface increases. Similar trend of slight increase in the fluid velocity near the vertical plate is observed with an increase in convective heat transfer parameter $(Bi)$ shown in Figure. 2.6.

The effect of *Gr* on the velocity $(f')$ profile is plotted in Figure. 2.9. It is seen that the *Gr* increase as velocity increases due to an upward accelerant of the fluid in the vicinity of the vertical plate is increasing intensity of Grashof number $(Gr)$. Further downstream of the fluid motion decelerates to the free stream velocity. The effect of *Gc* on the velocity $(f')$ profile is plotted in 2.12. There is an overshoot in the velocity profiles for higher values of *Gc*. This is due to the fact that the $x$-momentum equation is a coupled equation contains both the heat and concentration components.

Figure. 2.15 and 2.24 show a slight decrease in the fluid velocity with an increase in Schmidt number and chemical reaction parameter respectively. It can be seen that the increase in the source parameter and Prandtl number leads to a fall in the velocity as shown in 2.18 and 2.21. The effect of concentration parameter $(Nc)$ on velocity profile shown in 2.27. It is observed that the velocity increase as increasing the $Nc$.

The fluid temperature is maximum at the vertical plate surface and decrease exponentially to the free stream zero value away from the plate satisfying the boundary conditions. The effect of $M$, $Bi$, $Gr$, $Gc$, $Sc$, $Sr$, $Pr$, $Kr$ and $Nc$ on the temperature profile are plotted in Figures. 2.4, 2.7, 2.10, 2.13, 2.16, 2.19, 2.22, 2.25 and 2.28. From these figures, it observed that the thermal boundary layer thickness increase with an increase in the intensity of parameters such as $Bi$, $Sc$, $Sr$, $Pr$, $Kr$ and $Nc$. The effect of local heat source parameter $Sr$ on the temperature profile is plotted in 2.19. It is observed that the steepness of the profile increase as $Sr$ increases. Moreover, the fluid temperature is decrease with an increase in the Schmidt number $(Sc)$ and chemical reaction parameter $(Kr)$ leading to decrease in thermal boundary layer thickness. It observed that the thermal boundary layer decreases as increasing the $M$, $Gr$ and $Gc$ due to chemical reaction parameter.

Generally, the species concentration is higher at the plate surface and decreases to zero far away from the plate satisfying the boundary condition. The effect of $M$, $Bi$, $Gr$, $Gc$, $Sc$, $Sr$, $Pr$, $Kr$ and $Nc$ on the concentration profile are plotted in Figures. 2.5, 2.8, 2.11, 2.14, 2.17, 2.20, 2.23, 2.26 and 2.29, respectively. From these figures, it observed that the species concentration boundary layer thickness decreases with an increase the values of all the parameters.

The effect of all physical parameters such as $M$, $Bi$, $Gr$, $Gc$, $Sc$, $Sr$, $Pr$, $Kr$ and $Nc$ on the skin friction coefficient $f''(0)$, heat transfer rate $g'(0)$ and mass transfer rate $G'(0)$ versus $M$ are shown in Figures. 2.30-2.50. It is observed that, for any fixed parameter the shear stress rates, heat and mass transfer rates increase with increasing the concentration difference parameter $(Nc)$, Grashof number $(Gr)$, local heat transfer source parameter $(Sr)$ and Convective heat transfer parameter $(Bi)$. The effect of the $Gc$ the shear stress rates $f''(0)$ decreases, heat and mass transfer rates increase with increasing the magnetic field parameter $M$ shown in 2.36-2.38. The effect of the Schmidt number $(Sc)$ on shear stress rates, heat and mass transfer rates are plotted in 2.39-2.41. It observed that the shear stress rates and heat transfer rates are decreases, and mass transfer rates are increase with increasing the magnetic field parameter.

The effect of the Prandtl number on shear stress rates, heat and mass transfer rates are plotted in 2.45- 2.47. It observed that the shear stress rates and Mass transfer rates decrease, and heat transfer rates increase with increasing the magnetic field parameter.

The effect of the heat source parameter(Sr) on heat and mass transfer rates are plotted in Figures. 2.51-2.54. It observed that the heat and mass transfer rates increase with increasing the chemical reaction parameter $Kr$ and Prandtl number $(Pr)$. The influence of the chemical reaction parameter $Kr$ on heat and mass transfer rates are plotted in 2.55 and 2.56. It observed that the heat and mass transfer rates increase with increasing the convective heat transfer parameter $(Bi)$.

## 2.7 Summary

This study presents the analysis of the heat and mass transfer of hydrodynamic flow due to a vertical plate in the presence of chemical reaction, heat source and magnetic parameter along with the convective surface boundary condition. An approximate analytical solution using HAM is obtained for the flow velocity, temperature and concentration boundary layer equations. The coefficients of the solution series contains all the other parameters such as *Bi*, *M*, *Pr*, *Sr*, *Sc*, *Gr*, *Gc*, *Nc* and *Kr* on study variables such as velocity, temperature and concentration profiles as well as shear stress, heat and mass transfer rates. The computer algebra software Mathematica is used to perform these semi-analytical calculations. The numerical solutions are obtained from the governing equations using KBM. The present study is useful in identifying a suitable parameter that can be increased or decreased to alter the heat and mass transfer rates of the vertical plate thereby enhancing the final product to a desired characteristic.

The following conclusions are drawn from the present study.

- The velocity and temperature profiles increase for the increase in Grashof number values whereas the trend is quite opposite for the concentration profiles.

- The temperature profiles increase for the increase in the values of chemical reaction, concentration difference and Prandtl number, source parameters and local convective heat transfer parameter whereas it decrease for the increase in the values of thermal Grashof number on temperature.

- The shear stress rates increase, heat and mass transfer rates decrease for the increase in the values of magnetic field parameter for any fixed value of local heat source parameter.

- The local skin friction, and heat and mass transfer rates increase for the increase in source/ magnetic parameter.

Table 2.1: Convergence of HAM solution for different orders of approximation for $-f''(0)$, $-g'(0)$ and $-G'(0)$ when ($M = Gc = Gr = Bi = 0.1$ and $Sc = 0.62$, $Sr = 1.0$, $Kr = 0.5$ and $Pr = 0.72$.)

| $\ell$ | $-f''(0)$ | $-g'(0)$ | $-G'(0)$ |
|---|---|---|---|
| 1 | 0.7231065 | 0.5159944 | 0.4150661 |
| 5 | 0.7618803 | 0.5539803 | 0.4399820 |
| 10 | 0.8714585 | 0.5823581 | 0.4510038 |
| 15 | 0.8901475 | 0.5822144 | 0.4506601 |
| 20 | 0.9147587 | 0.5822144 | 0.4506601 |
| 25 | 0.9147587 | 0.5822144 | 0.4506601 |
| 30 | 0.9147587 | 0.5822144 | 0.4506601 |
| 35 | 0.9147587 | 0.5822144 | 0.4506601 |

Table 2.2: Comparison with Gangadhar (2013) results for the values of $f''(0)$ for various values of physical parameters.

| Bi | Gr | Gc | M | Sc | Sr | Kr | $f''(0)$ Gangadhar (2013) | Present KBM | Present HAM |
|---|---|---|---|---|---|---|---|---|---|
| **0.1** | 0.1 | 0.1 | 0.1 | 0.24 | 1.0 | 0.5 | 0.597803 | 0.5977991 | 0.5977982 |
| **1.0** | 0.1 | 0.1 | 0.1 | 0.24 | 1.0 | 0.5 | 0.651686 | 0.6516859 | 0.6516841 |
| 0.1 | **0.5** | 0.1 | 0.1 | 0.24 | 1.0 | 0.5 | 0.688034 | 0.6880329 | 0.6880327 |
| 0.1 | **1.0** | 0.1 | 0.1 | 0.24 | 1.0 | 0.5 | 0.793144 | 0.7931433 | 0.7931432 |
| 0.1 | 0.1 | **0.5** | 0.1 | 0.24 | 1.0 | 0.5 | 1.017760 | 1.0177721 | 1.0177721 |
| 0.1 | 0.1 | **1.0** | 0.1 | 0.24 | 1.0 | 0.5 | 1.500850 | 1.5008444 | 1.5008400 |
| 0.1 | 0.1 | 0.1 | **0.4** | 0.24 | 1.0 | 0.5 | 0.814486 | 0.8144179 | 0.8144179 |
| 0.1 | 0.1 | 0.1 | **0.6** | 0.24 | 1.0 | 0.5 | 0.931116 | 0.9311098 | 0.9311098 |
| 0.1 | 0.1 | 0.1 | 0.1 | **0.62** | 1.0 | 0.5 | 0.584136 | 0.5841009 | 0.5841009 |
| 0.1 | 0.1 | 0.1 | 0.1 | **0.78** | 1.0 | 0.5 | 0.579769 | 0.5797902 | 0.5797902 |
| 0.1 | 0.1 | 0.1 | 0.1 | 0.24 | **2.0** | 0.5 | −− | 0.5987366 | 0.5987366 |
| 0.1 | 0.1 | 0.1 | 0.1 | 0.62 | **3.0** | 0.5 | −− | 0.6100231 | 0.6100231 |
| 0.1 | 0.1 | 0.1 | 0.1 | 0.24 | 1.0 | **1.0** | −− | 0.5842769 | 0.5842769 |
| 0.1 | 0.1 | 0.1 | 0.1 | 0.62 | 1.0 | **1.5** | −− | 0.5774861 | 0.5774861 |

Table 2.3: Comparison with Rout *et al.* (2013) results for $-g'(0)$ with $Kr = Sr = 0.0$ for the different values of physical parameters.

| Bi | Gr | Gc | M | Pr | Sc | $-g'(0)$ Rout *et al.* (2013) | Present KBM | Present HAM |
|---|---|---|---|---|---|---|---|---|
| **0.1** | 0.1 | 0.1 | 0.1 | 0.72 | 0.62 | 0.078635 | 0.07863449 | 0.07863449 |
| **1.0** | 0.1 | 0.1 | 0.1 | 0.72 | 0.62 | 0.273153 | 0.27315107 | 0.27315107 |
| 0.1 | **0.5** | 0.1 | 0.1 | 0.72 | 0.62 | 0.079173 | 0.07917111 | 0.07917111 |
| 0.1 | **1.0** | 0.1 | 0.1 | 0.72 | 0.62 | 0.079691 | 0.07968042 | 0.07968042 |
| 0.1 | 0.1 | **0.5** | 0.1 | 0.72 | 0.62 | 0.080711 | 0.08066944 | 0.08066943 |
| 0.1 | 0.1 | **1.0** | 0.1 | 0.72 | 0.62 | 0.082040 | 0.08203891 | 0.08203891 |
| 0.1 | 0.1 | 0.1 | **1.0** | 0.72 | 0.62 | $---$ | 0.05249166 | 0.05249166 |
| 0.1 | 0.1 | 0.1 | **5.0** | 0.72 | 0.62 | 0.066156 | 0.06615556 | 0.06615561 |
| 0.1 | 0.1 | 0.1 | 0.1 | **1.0** | 0.62 | 0.081935 | 0.08193111 | 0.08193110 |
| 0.1 | 0.1 | 0.1 | 0.1 | **7.10** | 0.62 | 0.093348 | 0.09334842 | 0.09334841 |
| 0.1 | 0.1 | 0.1 | 0.1 | 0.24 | **0.78** | 0.078484 | 0.07847998 | 0.07847998 |
| 0.1 | 0.1 | 0.1 | 0.1 | 0.62 | **2.63** | 0.077915 | 0.07791442 | 0.07791442 |

Table 2.4: Comparison with Rout *et al.* (2013) results for $-G'(0)$ with $Kr = Sr = 0.0$ for the different values of physical parameters.

| Bi | Gr | Gc | M | Pr | Sc | $-G'(0)$ Rout *et al.* (2013) | Present KBM | Present HAM |
|---|---|---|---|---|---|---|---|---|
| **0.1** | 0.1 | 0.1 | 0.1 | 0.72 | 0.62 | 0.3337425 | 0.33374233 | 0.33374233 |
| **1.0** | 0.1 | 0.1 | 0.1 | 0.72 | 0.62 | 0.3410294 | 0.34102918 | 0.34102911 |
| 0.1 | **0.5** | 0.1 | 0.1 | 0.72 | 0.62 | 0.2082640 | 0.20825967 | 0.20825967 |
| 0.1 | **1.0** | 0.1 | 0.1 | 0.72 | 0.62 | 0.2928890 | 0.29288761 | 0.29288761 |
| 0.1 | 0.1 | **0.5** | 0.1 | 0.72 | 0.62 | 0.3813954 | 0.38138012 | 0.38138012 |
| 0.1 | 0.1 | **1.0** | 0.1 | 0.72 | 0.62 | 0.4176699 | 0.41766897 | 0.41766891 |
| 0.1 | 0.1 | 0.1 | **1.0** | 0.72 | 0.62 | $---$ | 0.09546261 | 0.09546261 |
| 0.1 | 0.1 | 0.1 | **5.0** | 0.72 | 0.62 | 0.1806634 | 0.18066333 | 0.18066310 |
| 0.1 | 0.1 | 0.1 | 0.1 | **1.0** | 0.62 | 0.3325180 | 0.33251459 | 0.33251457 |
| 0.1 | 0.1 | 0.1 | 0.1 | **7.10** | 0.62 | 0.3305618 | 0.33056004 | 0.33056004 |
| 0.1 | 0.1 | 0.1 | 0.1 | 0.24 | **0.78** | 0.3844559 | 0.38445444 | 0.38445444 |
| 0.1 | 0.1 | 0.1 | 0.1 | 0.62 | **2.63** | 0.7981454 | 0.79810011 | 0.79810011 |

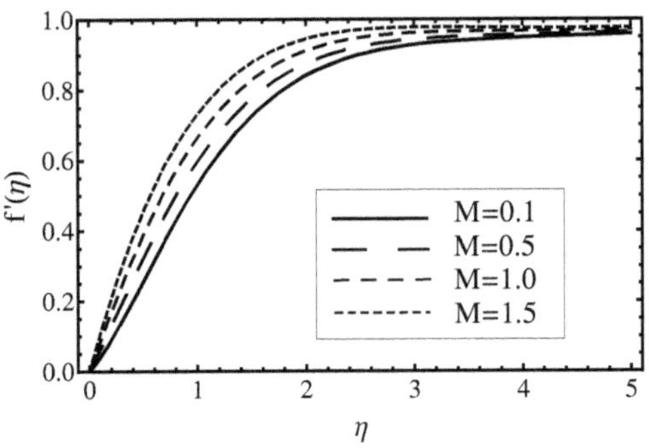


Figure 2.3: Effect of magnetic parameter on velocity profiles.

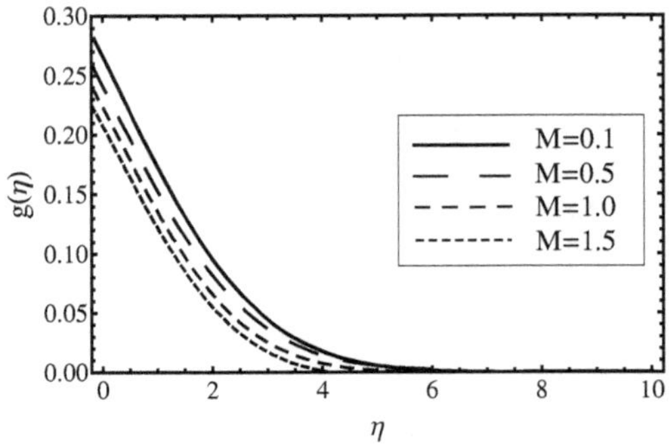


Figure 2.4: Effect of magnetic parameter on temperature profiles.

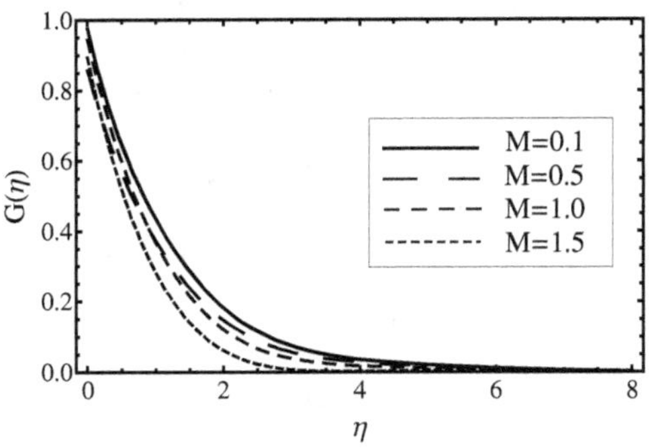


Figure 2.5: Effect of magnetic parameter on concentration profiles.

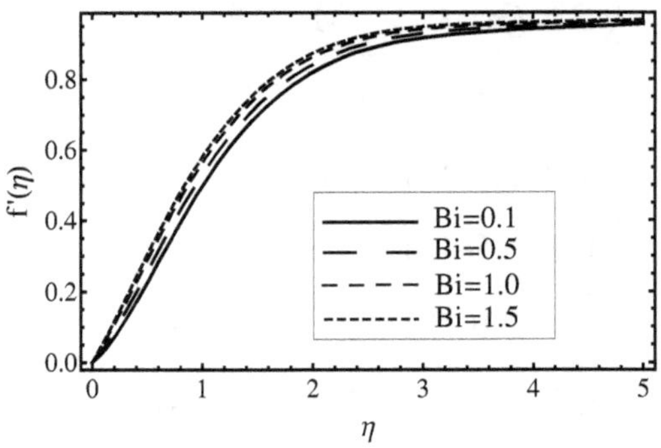


Figure 2.6: Effect of the convective heat transfer parameters on velocity profiles.

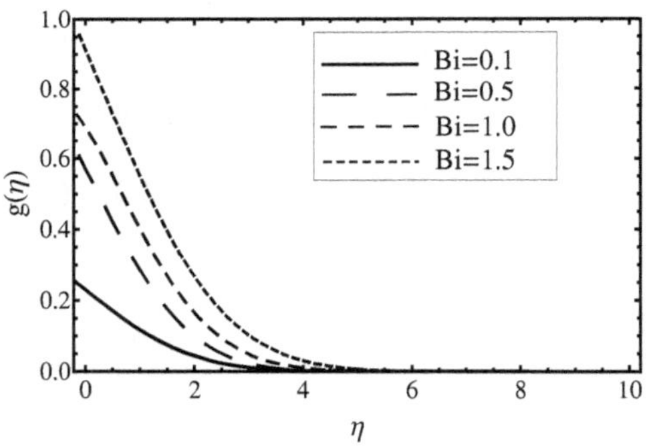


Figure 2.7: Effect of the convective heat transfer parameters on temperature profiles.

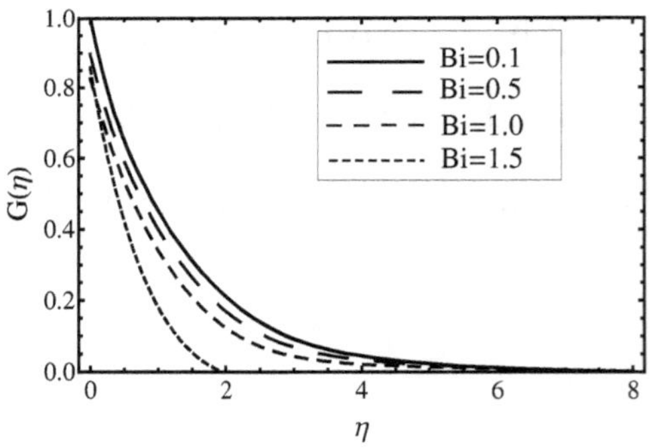


Figure 2.8: Effect of the convective heat transfer parameters on concentration profiles.

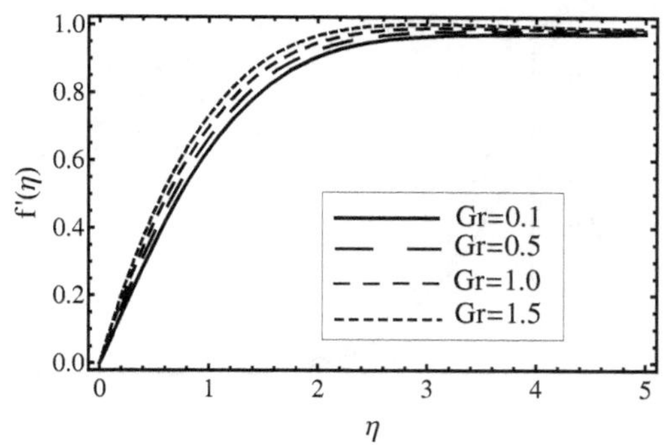


Figure 2.9: Effect of Grashof number on velocity profiles.

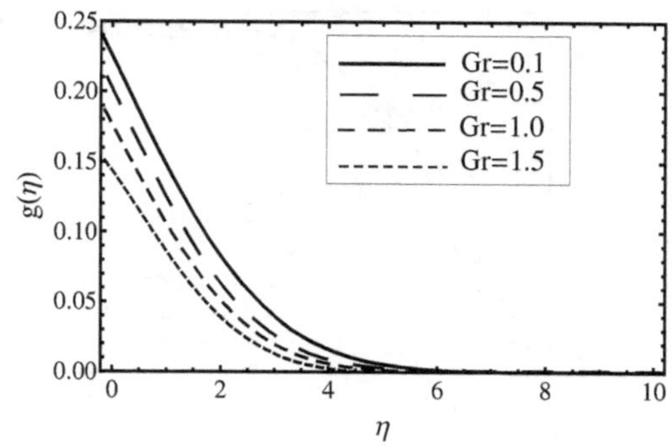


Figure 2.10: Effect of Grashof number on temperature profiles.

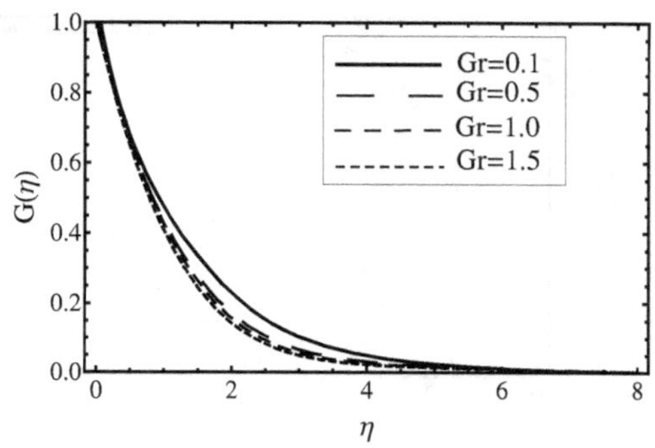


Figure 2.11: Effect of Grashof number on concentration profiles.

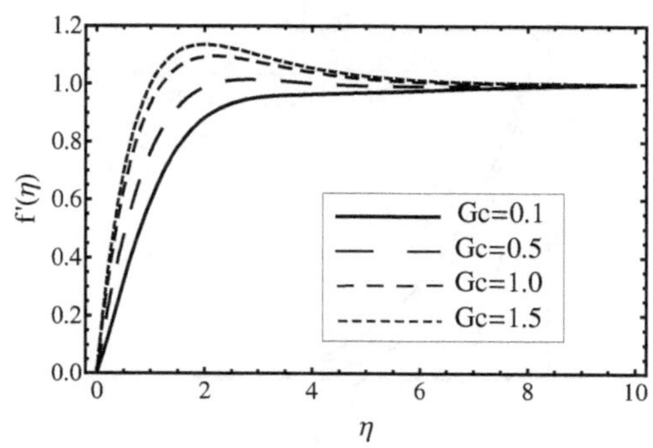


Figure 2.12: Effect of the modified Grashof number on velocity profiles.

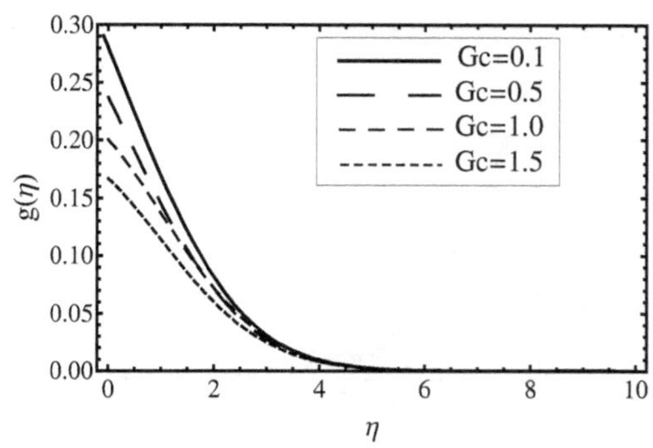


Figure 2.13: Effect of the modified Grashof number on temperature profiles.

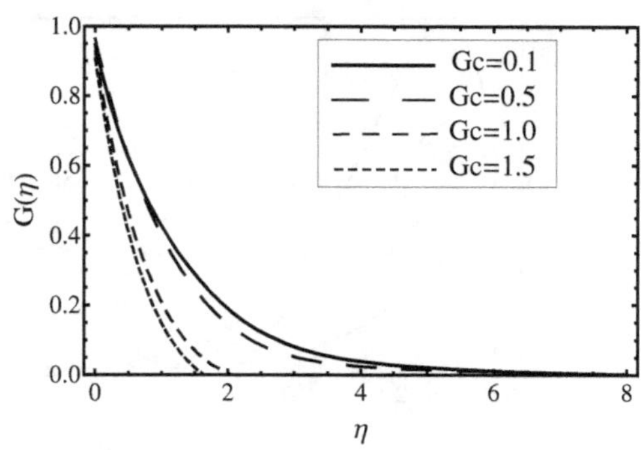


Figure 2.14: Effect of the modified Gc on concentration profiles.

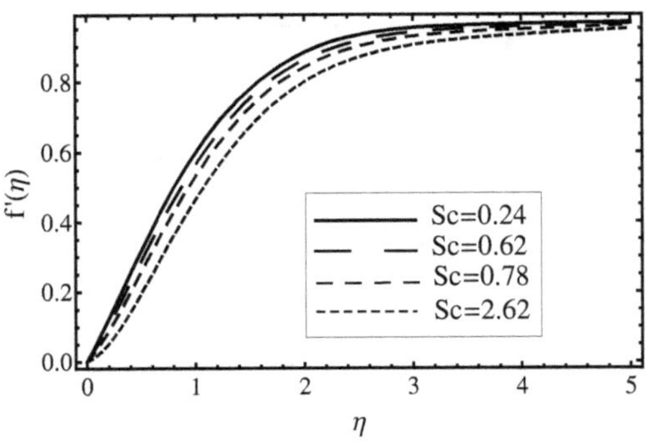


Figure 2.15: Effect of Schmidt number on velocity profiles.

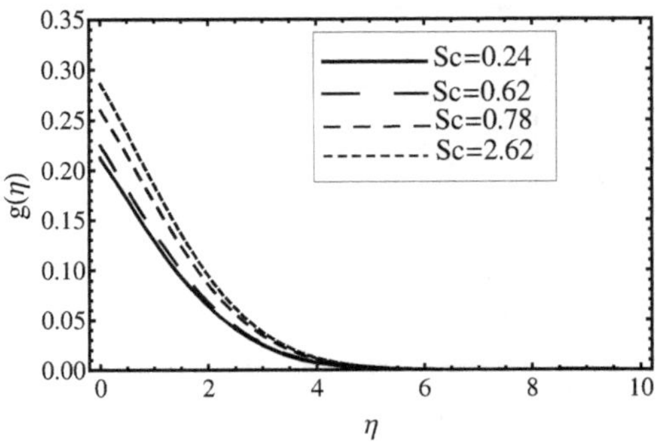


Figure 2.16: Effect of Schmidt number on temperature profiles.

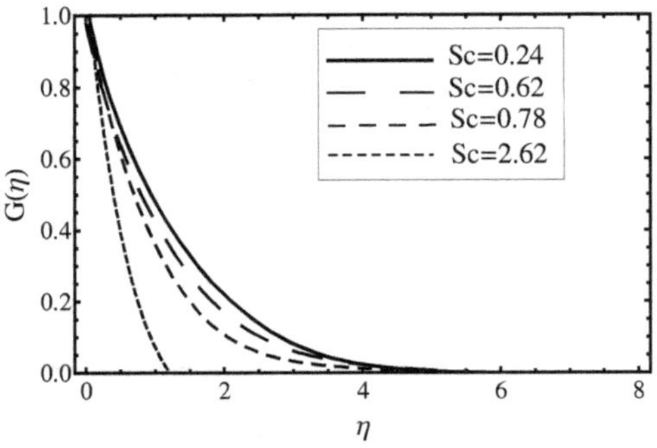


Figure 2.17: Effect of Schmidt number on concentration profiles.

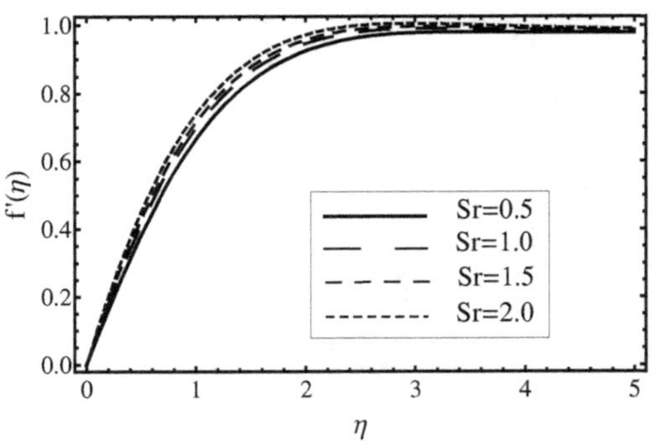


Figure 2.18: Effect of the local heat Source parameter on velocity profiles.

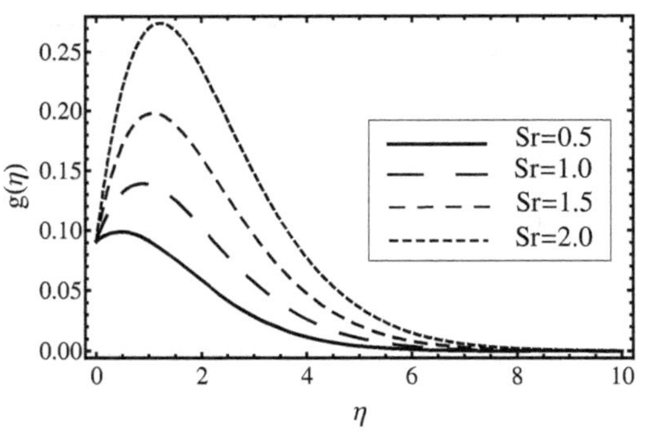


Figure 2.19: Effect of the local heat Source parameter on temperature profiles.

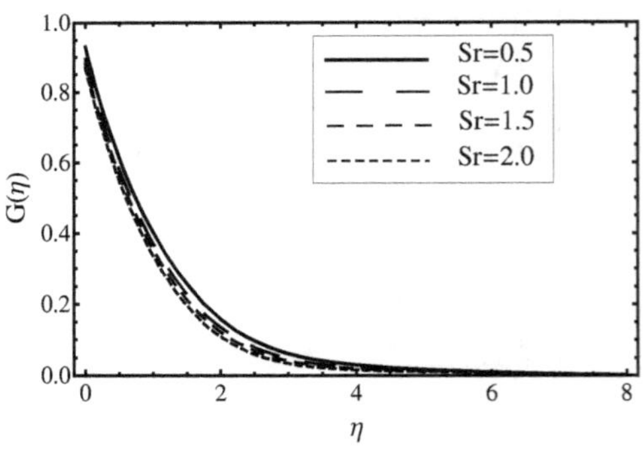


Figure 2.20: Effect of the heat Source parameter on concentration profiles.

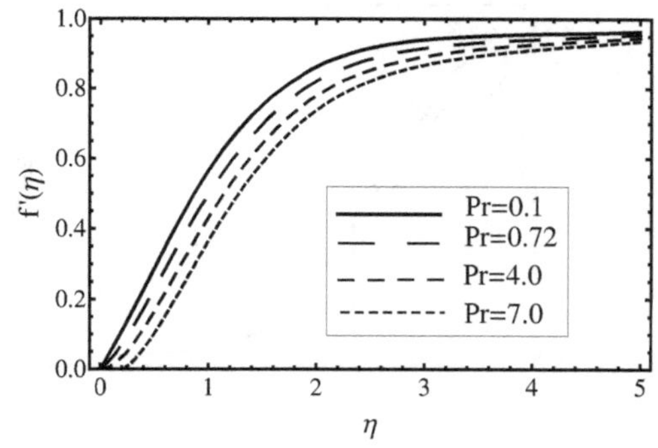


Figure 2.21: Effect of Prandtl number on velocity profiles.

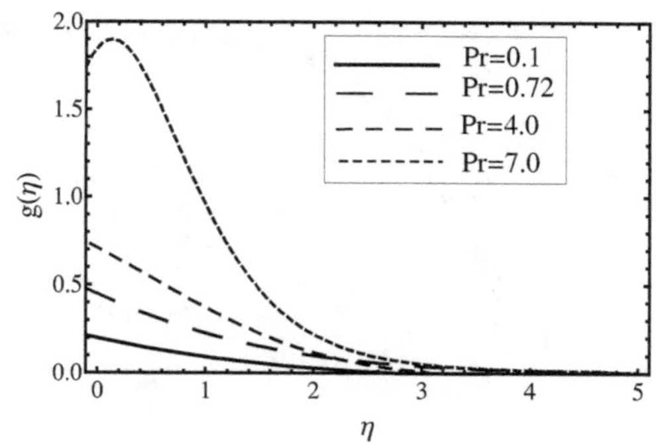


Figure 2.22: Effect of Prandtl number on temperature profiles.

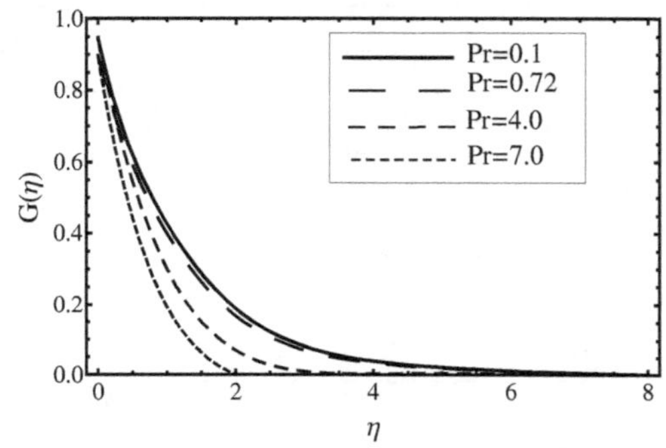


Figure 2.23: Effect of Prandtl number on concentration profiles.

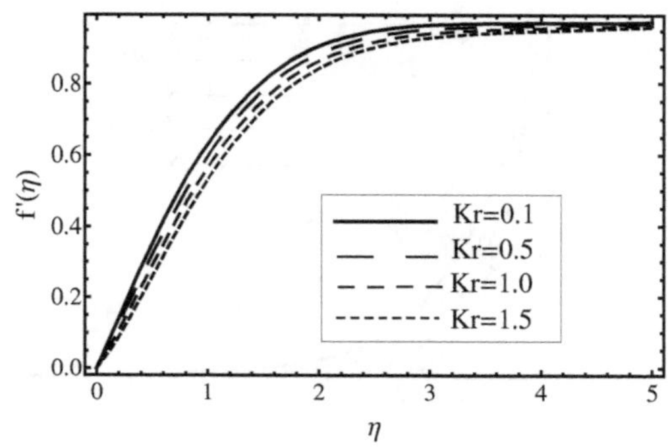


Figure 2.24: Effect of the chemical reaction parameter on velocity profiles.

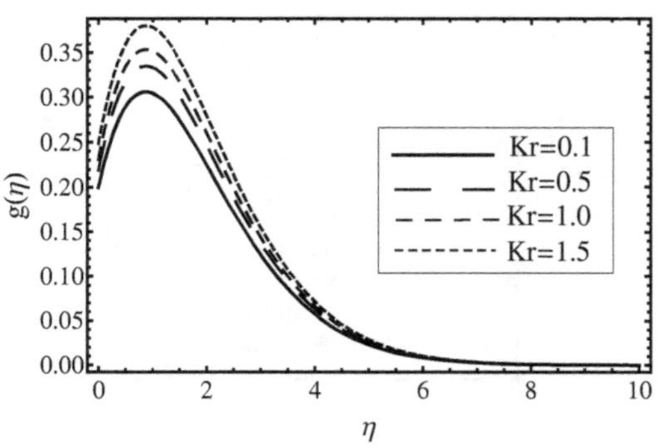


Figure 2.25: Effect of the chemical reaction parameter on temperature profiles.

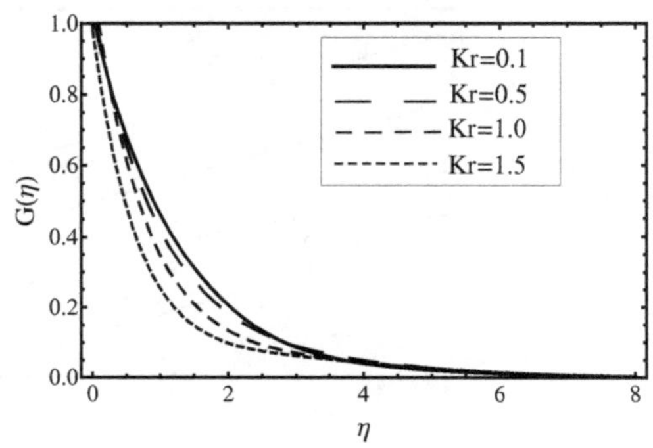


Figure 2.26: Effect of the chemical reaction parameter on concentration profiles.

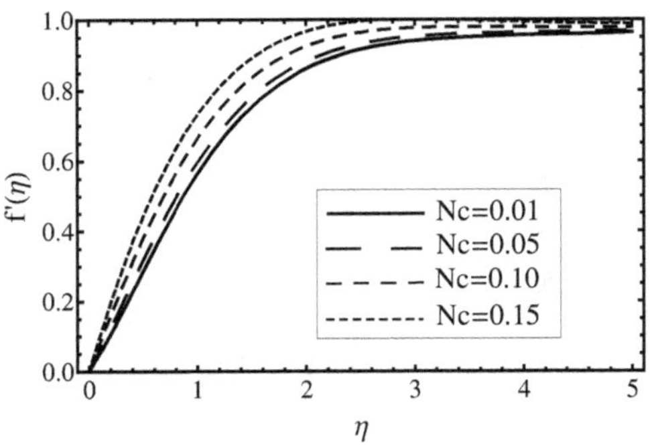


Figure 2.27: Effect of the concentration difference parameter on velocity profiles.

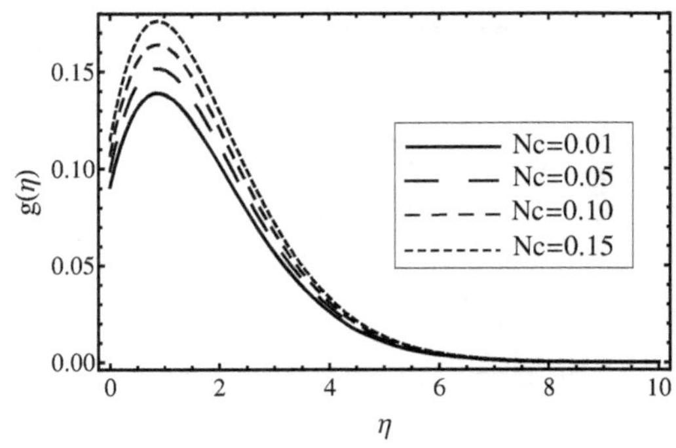


Figure 2.28: Effect of the concentration difference parameter on $g(\eta)$.

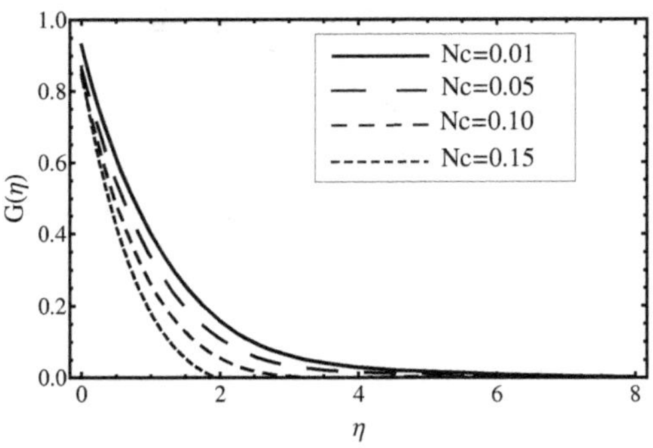


Figure 2.29: Effect of the concentration difference parameter on $G(\eta)$.

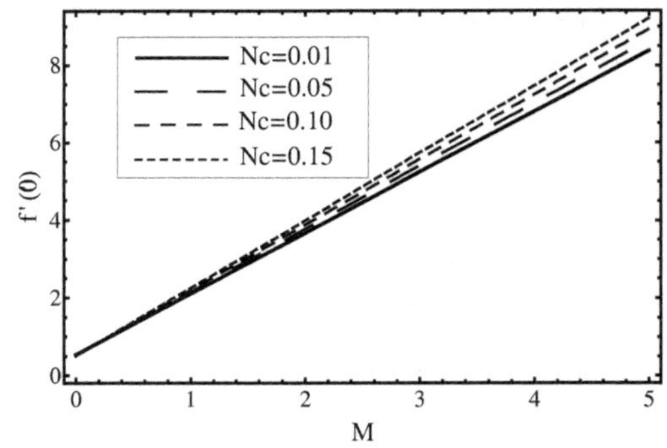


Figure 2.30: Effect of the concentration difference parameter on shear stress rate.

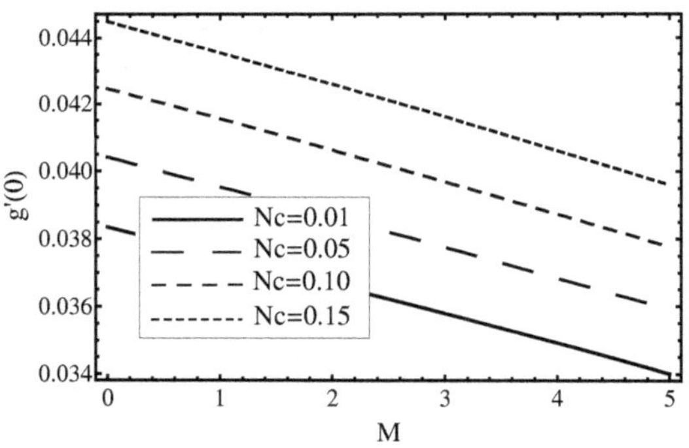


Figure 2.31: Effect of the concentration difference parameter on heat transfer rate.

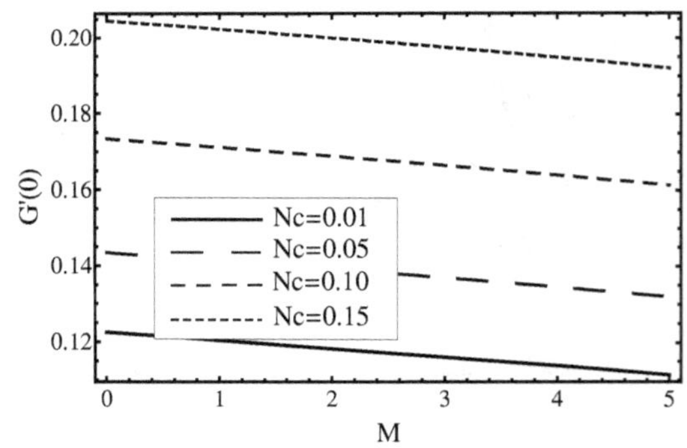


Figure 2.32: Effect of the Nc parameter on mass transfer rate.

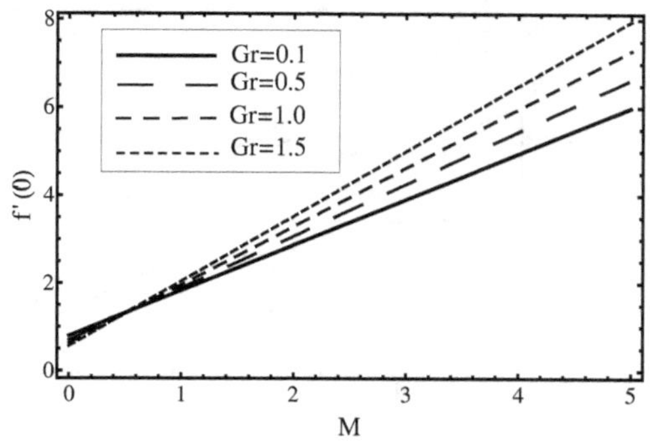


Figure 2.33: Effect of the Grashof number on shear stress rate.

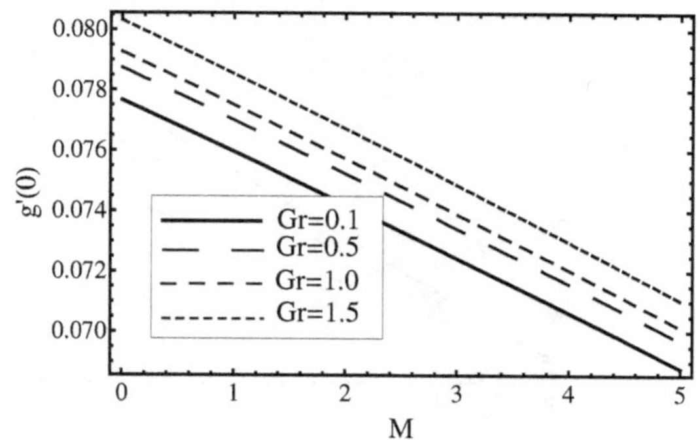


Figure 2.34: Effect of the Grashof number on heat transfer rate.

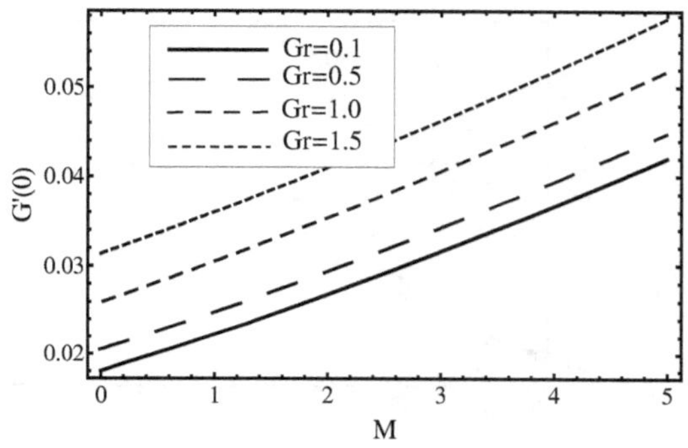


Figure 2.35: Effect of the Grashof number on mass transfer rate.

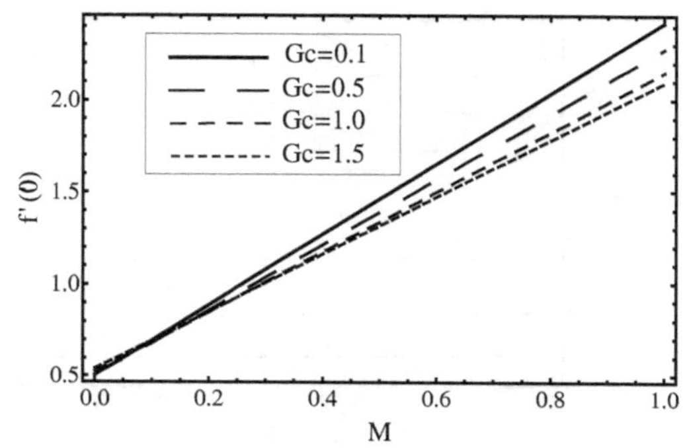


Figure 2.36: Effect of the modified Grashof number on shear stress rate.

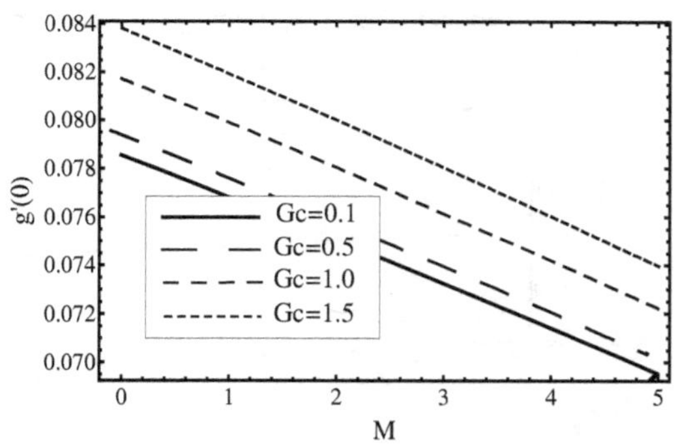


Figure 2.37: Effect of the modified Grashof number on heat transfer rate.

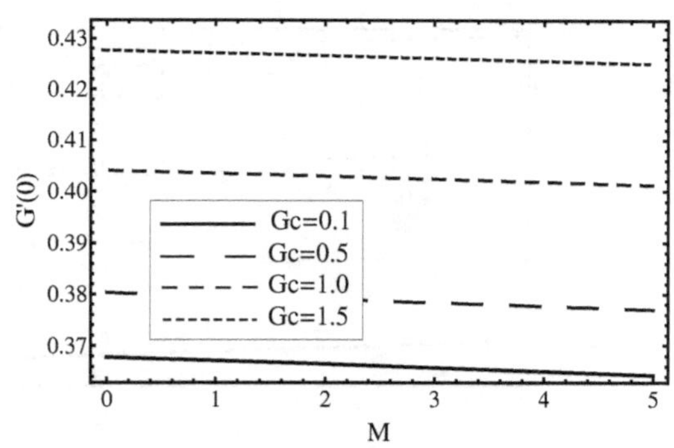


Figure 2.38: Effect of the modified Grashof number on mass transfer rate.

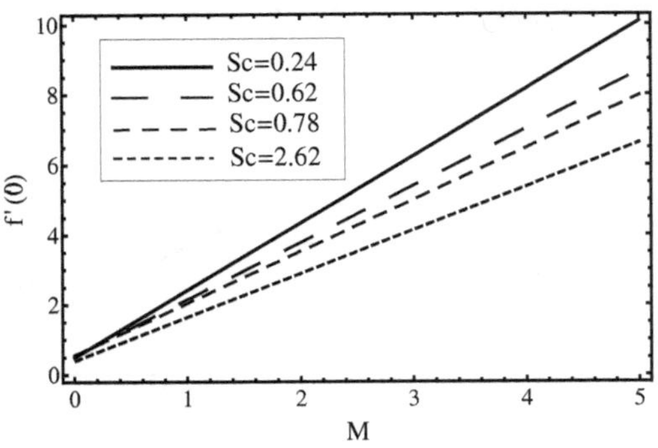


Figure 2.39: Effect of the Schmidt number on shear stress rate.

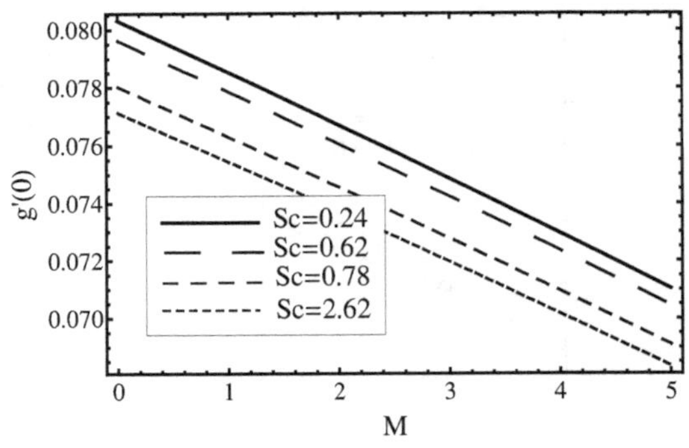


Figure 2.40: Effect of the Schmidt number on heat transfer rate.

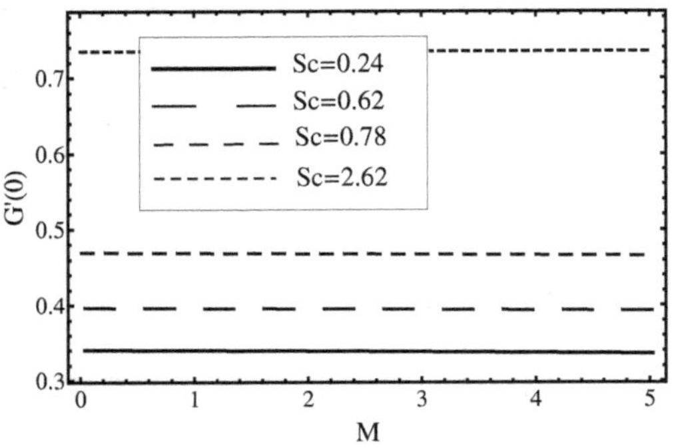


Figure 2.41: Effect of the Schmidt number on mass transfer rate.

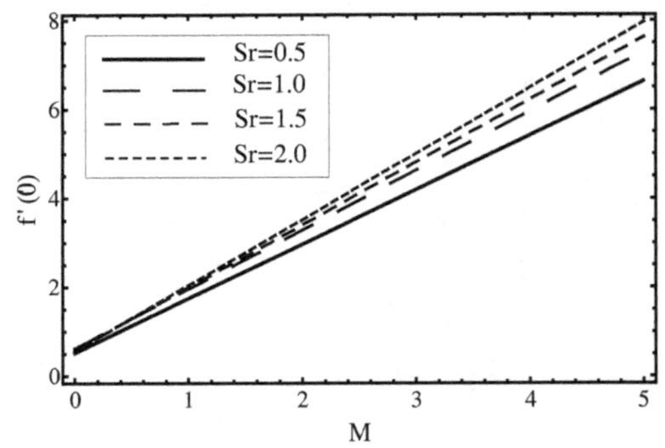


Figure 2.42: Effect of the heat source parameter on Shear stress rate.

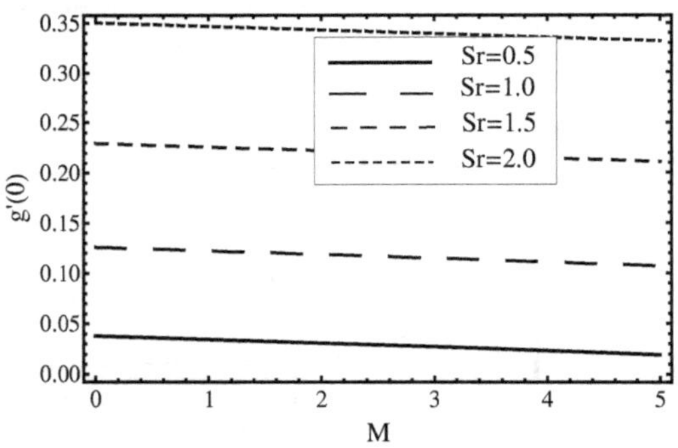


Figure 2.43: Effect of the heat source parameter on heat transfer rate.

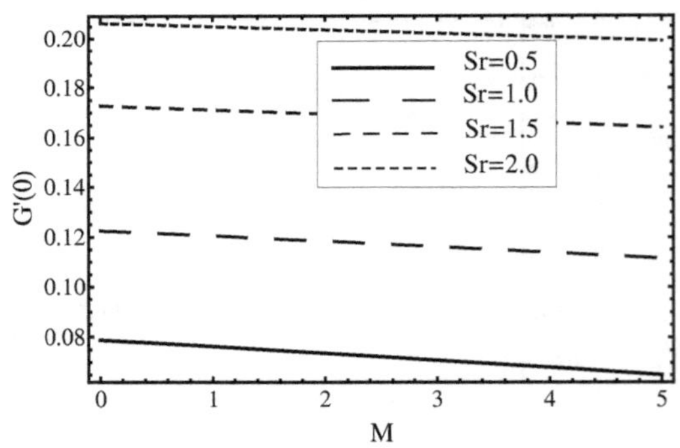


Figure 2.44: Effect of the heat source parameter on mass transfer rate.

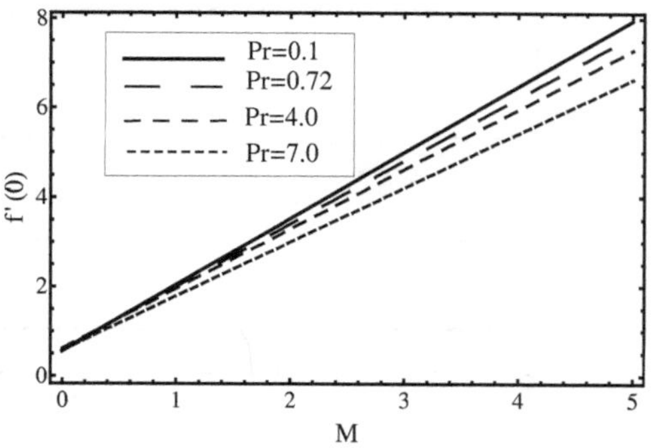


Figure 2.45: Effect of the Prandtl number on shear stress rate.

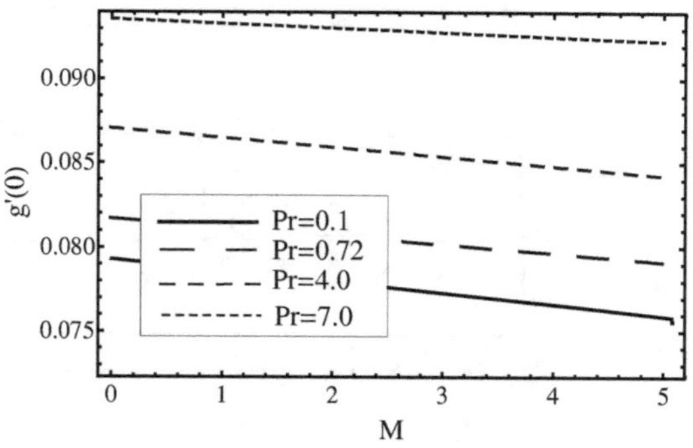


Figure 2.46: Effect of the Prandtl number on heat transfer rate.

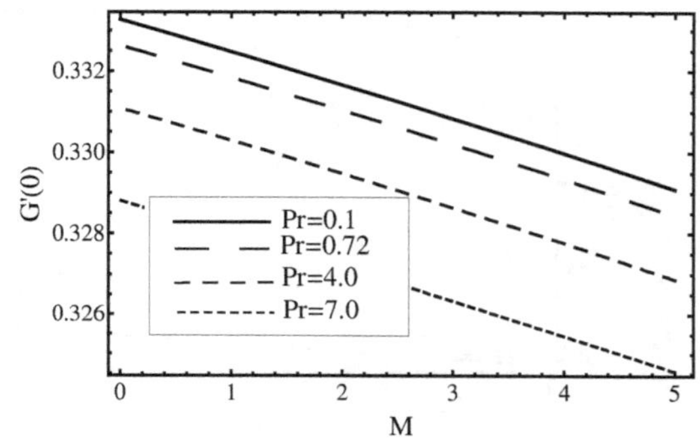


Figure 2.47: Effect of the Prandtl number on mass transfer rate.

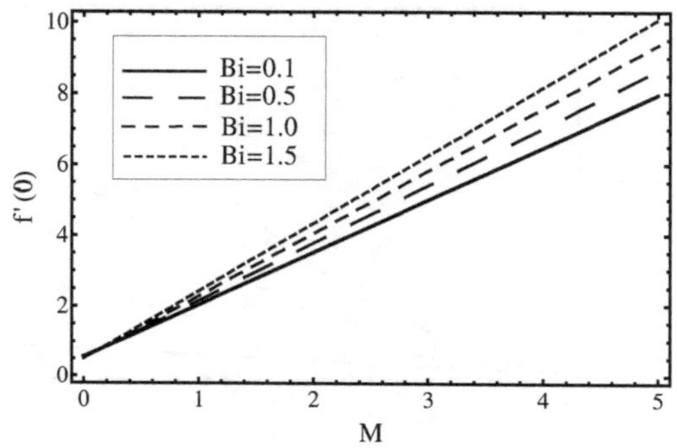


Figure 2.48: Effect of the convective heat transfer parameter on shear stress rate.

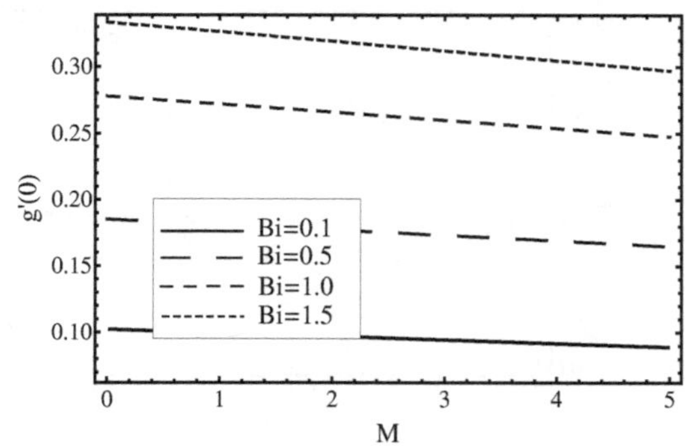


Figure 2.49: Effect of the convective heat transfer parameter on heat transfer rate.

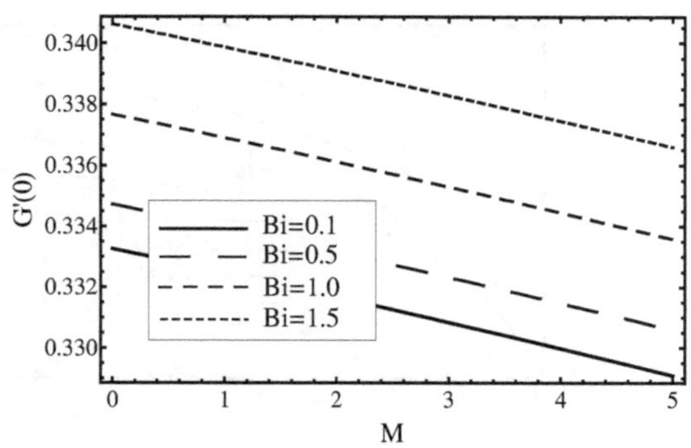


Figure 2.50: Effect of the convective heat transfer parameter on mass transfer rate.

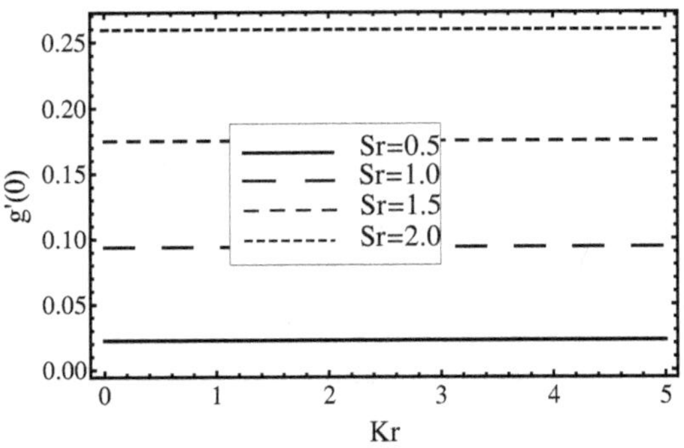


Figure 2.51: Effect of the heat source parameter on heat transfer rate.

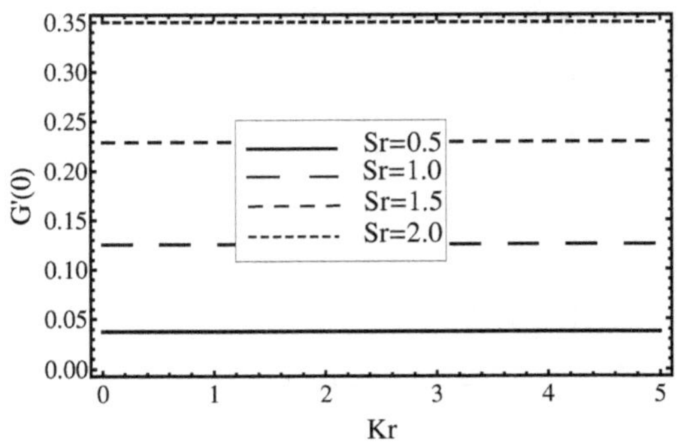


Figure 2.52: Effect of the heat source parameter on mass transfer rate.

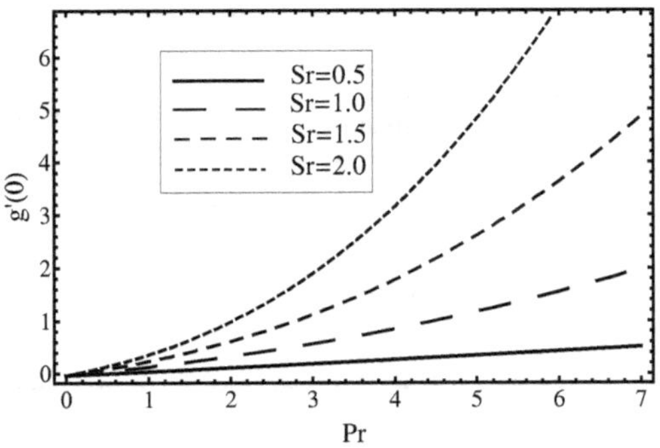


Figure 2.53: Effect of the heat source parameter on heat transfer rate.

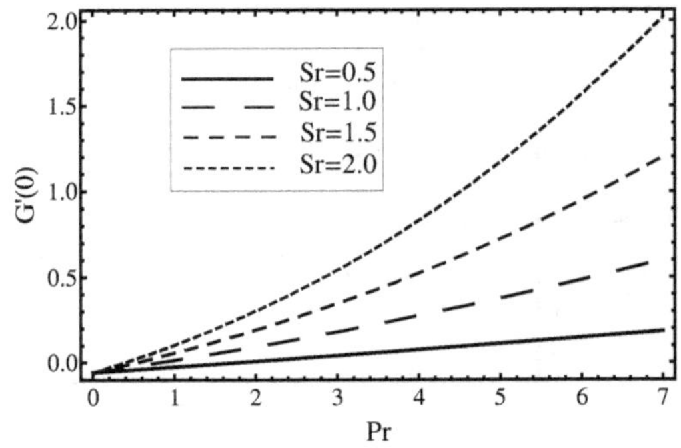


Figure 2.54: Effect of the heat source parameter on mass transfer rate.

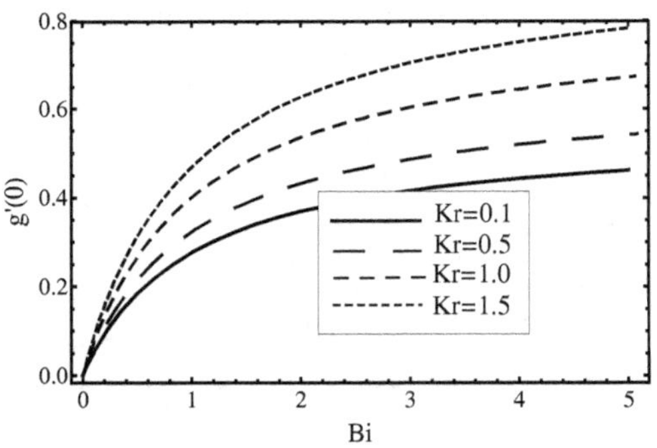


Figure 2.55: Effect of the chemical reaction parameter on heat transfer rate.

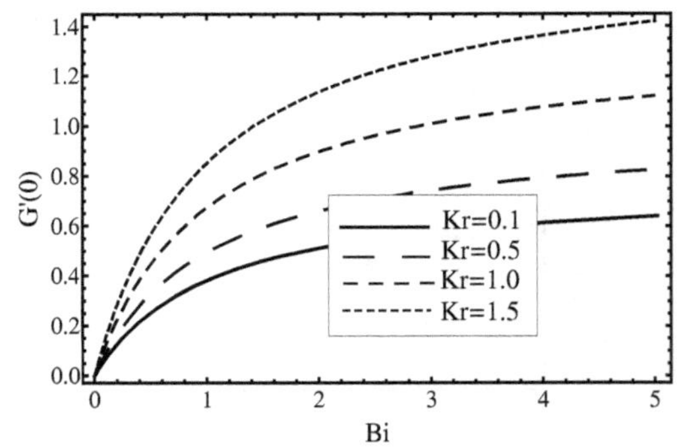


Figure 2.56: Effect of the chemical reaction parameter on mass transfer rate.

# Chapter 3

# Heat transfer near the stagnation point of an unsteady three-dimensional viscous flow

## 3.1 Abstract

In this chapter, the unsteady laminar three-dimensional flow of an incompressible viscous fluid in the neighbourhood of a stagnation point is studied. The magnetic field is applied normal to the surface and the effects of viscous dissipation and Ohmic heating are taken into account. The unsteadiness in the flow is caused by the external free stream varying arbitrarily with time. The governing equations are solved both analytically and numerically. An approximate analytical solution has been obtained for flow and heat transfer in the form of series solution using HAM while the numerical solutions are computed using the RKFM with a shooting technique. The influence of various parameters such as the viscous dissipation, unsteadiness, ratio of the velocity gradient and magnetic field effects on flow and heat transfer parameters are studied. A detailed error analysis is done to compute the average squared residual errors for velocity and temperature. The optimal values of the convergence control parameters are computed for the flow which is used for obtaining all the other results presented.

## 3.2 Introduction

The study of laminar boundary layers to variations in the external free stream with time has many practical applications in flow over helicopters; missile aerodynamics; turbomachines and in flutter phenomena involving wings. The unsteadiness increases the complexities of the problem because the dimension of the problem is increased. During recent years, the subject of unsteady boundary layer studies near stagnation region has received considerable attention.

The laminar, incompressible three-dimensional boundary-layer flow in the neighbourhood of the nodal point region ( i.e, $0 \leq c \leq 1$) was first studied by Howarth (1951). The corresponding flow near the saddle point region (i.e, $-1 \leq c < 0$) was considered by Davey (1961), where he has observed the appreciable changes in the similarity solution of boundary layer equations compared to the solution near the nodal point region. The heat transfer in the three-dimensional stagnation flow at nodal point region has been analyzed by Cheng *et al.* (1971) and a self similar solution has been obtained.

The unsteady incompressible flow of a viscous fluid near the stagnation region of a three-dimensional body was investigated by Kumari *et al.* (1978). The unsteady heat flux at a general three-dimensional body when the velocity is varying as a linear function of time was considered by Teipel (1979). A stagnation point solution near nodal and saddle point regions of an incompressible micro polar fluid was studied by Guram *et al.* (1991).

The unsteady stagnation point flow of a stretching surface in a three-dimensional flow was presented by Rajeswari *et al.* (1993). The effect of the magnetic field on the stagnation point flow and heat transfer of a viscous fluid was studied by Kumari *et al.* (1999). Various aspects of this problem were studied by the authors (Kumari *et al.* (2002); Seshadri *et al.* (2002) and Chamkha *et al.* (2011)). The unsteady laminar MHD flow of a viscous fluid with variation of Ohmic heating and viscous dissipation were studied by Osalusi *et al.* (2007), as well as Olanrewaju *et al.* (2011) and Chauhan *et al.* (2012).

The importance of studying the unsteady boundary layer flow near stagnation region is that the heat transfer is maximum near the stagnation point. When the free stream velocity varies arbitrarily with time, unsteadiness is caused in the flow field. Hence the unsteadiness influences the flow and heat transfer to a great extent. Most of the studies cited above present the numerical solutions of flow and heat transfer near the stagnation point.

The focus of this chapter is to obtain an approximate analytical solution for the flow velocity and the temperature in the form of a power series solution. Since the approximate analytical solution for the three-dimensional stagnation point boundary layer flow has not been studied, we obtain the same using HAM.

Generally, HAM solutions are always represented as a power series form in which the coefficients contains the study parameters. In this analysis the various study parameters considered are magnetic field strength ($M$), unsteadiness in the flow ($\lambda$), Prandtl number ($Pr$), the ratio of the velocity gradient ($c$) and the viscous dissipation parameters ($\alpha$) and ($\beta$). Also, computed the numerical solutions for present governing equations using the RKFM with shooting technique.

## 3.3 Problem formulation and governing equations

This section deals with the unsteady incompressible viscous flow of an electrically conducting fluid in the neighbourhood of a stagnation point of a three-dimensional surface. Let us consider the orthogonal set of coordinates $(x,y,z)$ with the origin "$O$" at the forward stagnation region, with $x$ and $y$ coordinates along the body surface and $z$ is the coordinate perpendicular to the body surface at origin as shown in Figure. 3.1. The unsteadiness in the flow field is imparted by the free stream varying arbitrarily with time. Uniform magnetic field of strength $B$ is applied normal to the surface in the positive $z$-direction. Since the magnetic Reynolds number is considered to be small, the induced magnetic field can be neglected. The effects of viscous dissipation and Ohmic heating are taken into account. The Navier-Stokes equations governing the three-dimensional flow and heat transfer are given by

$$u_x + v_y + w_z = 0 \tag{3.1}$$

$$u_t + uu_x + vu_y + wu_z = -\left(p_x - \nu\rho\nabla^2 u + \sigma B^2 u\right)/\rho \tag{3.2}$$

$$v_t + uv_x + vv_y + wv_z = -\left(p_y - \nu\rho\nabla^2 v + \sigma B^2 v\right)/\rho \tag{3.3}$$

$$w_t + uw_x + vw_y + ww_z = -\left(p_z - \nu\rho\nabla^2 w\right)/\rho \tag{3.4}$$

$$\rho C_\rho \left(T_t + uT_x + vT_y + wT_z\right) = \kappa\nabla^2 T + \mu\left(u_z^2 + v_z^2\right) + \sigma B^2\left(u^2 + v^2\right). \tag{3.5}$$

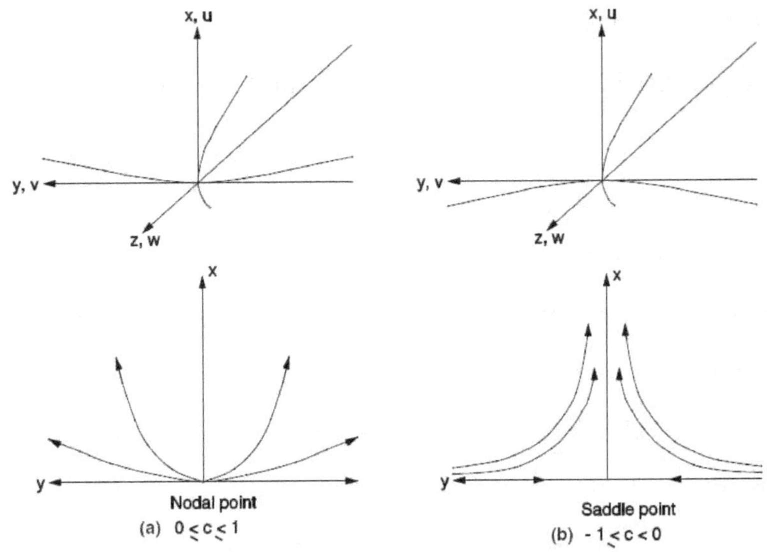


Figure 3.1: Sketch of three-dimensional coordinate system of flow.

The initial conditions when $t = 0$ are

$$u = u_i;\; v = v_i;\; w = w_i;\; p = p_i;\; T = T_i. \tag{3.6}$$

The boundary conditions are

$$\begin{aligned}
u &= v = w = 0,\; p = p_0,\; T = T_w \text{ at } z = 0,\; x \geq 0 \text{ and } y \geq 0 \\
u &\to U,\; v \to V,\; w \to W,\; T \to T_\infty \text{ at } z \to \infty,\; x \geq 0 \text{ and } y \geq 0 \\
u &= U,\; v = V,\; w = W,\; T = T_\infty \text{ at } x = 0,\; y \geq 0 \text{ and } z \geq 0 \\
u &= U,\; v = V,\; w = W,\; T = T_\infty \text{ at } y = 0,\; x \geq 0 \text{ and } z \geq 0.
\end{aligned} \tag{3.7}$$

Here $T$ is the temperature, $\kappa$ is the thermal conductivity, $p$ is the static pressure, $\rho$ is the density, $\nu$ is the kinematic viscosity, $C_\rho$ is the specific heat at a constant pressure, $p_0$ is the stagnation pressure, $B$ is the magnetic field, $U$, $V$ and $W$ are the components of velocity in the potential flow, the subscripts $t$, $x$, $y$ and $z$ denote the derivatives with respect to $t$, $x$, $y$ and $z$ respectively.

The velocity components in $x$-and $y$-directions in the potential flow vary directly as a linear function of distance and inversely as a linear function time.

$$U = (ax)/(1 - \lambda t),\;\; V = (by)/(1 - \lambda t),\;\; \text{where } \lambda t < 1. \tag{3.8}$$

The velocity components in $z$-direction is obtained from eq. (3.1), so that the continuity equation is satisfied exactly.

$$W = -az(1+c)/(1-\lambda t).$$

The magnetic field $B$ for the unsteady flow and the wall temperature $T_w$ varies as

$$B = B_0/\sqrt{(1-\lambda t)}, \quad \text{and} \quad (T_w - T_\infty) = (T_{w0} - T_\infty)/(1-\lambda t)^2, \tag{3.9}$$

where $T_{w_0}$ is the value of $T_w$ when $t = 0$. The expression of pressure $p$ can be obtained from Bernoulli equation as

$$\begin{aligned} p_0 - p &= (\rho a^2)/2(1-\lambda t)^2[(1+\lambda+M)x^2 + c(c+\lambda+M)y^2 \\ &+ (1+c)(1+c-\lambda)z^2]. \end{aligned} \tag{3.10}$$

Since the governing equations are a system of partial differential eqs. (3.1)-(3.5) with four independent variables $(x,\ y,\ z,\ t)$, we apply a suitable similarity transformation by which the partial differential equations can be converted into a system of nonlinear ordinary differential equations. The similarity transformations are,

$$\begin{aligned} \eta &= (a/\nu)^{1/2}(1-\lambda t)^{-1/2}z, \quad u = xa(1-\lambda t)^{-1}f'(\eta), \\ v &= yb(1-\lambda t)^{-1}g'(\eta) \\ w &= -(a\nu)^{1/2}(1-\lambda t)^{-1/2}[f(\eta)+cg(\eta)] \end{aligned}$$

$$\begin{aligned} T - T_\infty &= (T_w - T_\infty)[s(\eta) + (x/L)^2\Phi(\eta) + (y/L)^2\theta(\eta)], \\ &= (T_w - T_\infty)s(\eta) \end{aligned}$$

$$\begin{aligned} p_0 - p &= (\rho a^2)/2(1-\lambda t)^2[(1+\lambda+M)x^2 + c(c+\lambda+M)y^2 \\ &+ (2\nu/a)(1-\lambda t)P(\eta)], \end{aligned} \tag{3.11}$$

where $M = \sigma B_0^2/\rho a$. Here $s$, $\Phi$ and $\theta$ used in temperature represent the dimensionless temperatures without viscous dissipation, with viscous dissipation and with Ohmic heating, respectively.

Substituting eq. (3.11) into (3.1)-(3.5), we find that (3.1) is identically satisfied and (3.2)-(3.5) reduce to a system of coupled non-linear ordinary differential equations given by

$$f''' + (f + cg)\, f'' + 1 - (f')^2 + M\,(1 - f') + \lambda\,(1 - f' - \eta f''/2) = 0 \quad (3.12)$$

$$g''' + (f + cg)\, g'' + c\left(1 - (g')^2\right) + M\,(1 - g') + \lambda\,(1 - g' - \eta g''/2) = 0 \quad (3.13)$$

$$Pr^{-1} s'' + (f + cg)\, s' - 2^{-1}\eta s' - 2\lambda s = 0 \quad (3.14)$$

$$Pr^{-1}\Phi'' + (f + cg)\,\Phi' - 2f'\Phi - 2\lambda\Phi - 2^{-1}\eta\lambda\Phi' + \alpha\left[(f'')^2 + M\,(f')^2\right] = 0 \quad (3.15)$$

$$Pr^{-1}\theta'' + (f + cg)\,\theta' - 2cg'\theta - 2\lambda\theta - 2^{-1}\eta\lambda\theta' + \beta\left[(g'')^2 + M\,(g')^2\right] = 0 \quad (3.16)$$

$$\text{and } P + 2^{-1}(f + cg)^2 - (\lambda/2)\,\eta\,(f + cg). \quad (3.17)$$

Equation. (3.17) has been written after integration satisfying the condition on pressure. The boundary conditions

$$\begin{aligned} f(0) &= 0,\ f'(0) = 0,\ f'(\infty) = 1;\ g(0) = 0,\ \ g'(0) = 0,\ g'(\infty) = 1 \\ s(0) &= 1,\ s(\infty) = 0;\ \Phi(0) = 0,\ \Phi(\infty) = 0;\ \theta(0) = 0,\ \ \theta(\infty) = 0. \end{aligned} \quad (3.18)$$

Where $f'$ and $g'$ are the dimensionless velocity components in $x$-and $y$-directions, respectively, $\lambda$ is the unsteadiness parameter, $\eta$ is the similarity variable, $M$ is the magnetic parameter, $Pr$ is the Prandtl number, $a$ and $b$ are the velocity gradient along $x$-and $y$-directions in the potential flow, $c = b/a$ is ratio of the velocity gradient, $\alpha$ and $\beta$ are the viscous dissipation parameters, $L = (\nu/a)^{1/2}$ is the characteristic length and prime denotes derivative with respect to $\eta$.

Equations. (3.12)-(3.16) with $\lambda = 0$ (steady-state case) and without Ohmic heating (i.e, magnetic parameter $M = 0$) reduces to Howarth (1951) for the flow in the nodal point region ($0 \le c \le 1$) and to those of Davey (1961) in the saddle point region ($-1 \le c < 0$). Further may be noted that (3.12)-(3.16) without the last term in (3.14) for $M = 0$ are same to those of Teipel (1979).

The heat transfer coefficient in terms of Nusselt number and local Skin friction coefficients in $x$ and $y$ directions are expressed as

$$\begin{aligned} C_{fx} &= 2\mu(\partial u/\partial z)_{z=0}/\rho U^2 = 2(Re)^{-1/2} f''(0) \\ C_{fy} &= 2\mu(\partial v/\partial z)_{z=0}/\rho U^2 = 2(V/U)(Re)^{-1/2} g''(0) \\ Nu_x &= -x(\partial T/\partial z)_{z=0}/(T_w - T_\infty) \\ &= -(Re_x)^{1/2}\left[s'(0) + (x/L)^2\Phi'(0) + (y/L)^2\theta'(0)\right] \\ &= -(Re_x)^{1/2} s'(0),\ \text{ where, } Re_x = Ux/\nu. \end{aligned}$$

## 3.4 Homotopy series solution

The main features of the HAM procedure are selecting suitable initial profiles satisfying the boundary conditions of the problem and choosing an appropriate linear operator so that its solutions are simpler to evaluate analytically. The initial profiles that satisfy the initial and boundary conditions of the flow. The set of base functions, initial guesses and auxiliary linear operators as follows,

$$\{\left(\eta^k e^{-n\eta}\right), \, k \geq 0, \, n \geq 0\}.$$

Then, we can write

$$X(\eta) = A^0_{0,0} + \sum_{n=0}^{\infty}\sum_{k=0}^{\infty}[A^k_{l,n}\eta^k e^{-n\eta}], \tag{3.19}$$

where $X = f, \, g, \, s, \, \Phi$ and $\theta$; $A^k_{\ell,n}$ is the coefficient.

$$\begin{aligned} f_0(\eta) &= \eta + 1 - e^{-\eta}, \; g_0(\eta) = \eta + 1 - e^{-\eta}, \; s_0(\eta) = 1 - e^{-\eta}, \\ \text{and } \Phi_0(\eta) &= \eta e^{-\eta}, \; \theta_0(\eta) = \eta e^{-\eta}. \end{aligned} \tag{3.20}$$

$$\begin{aligned} L_f &= \frac{d^3 f}{d\eta^3} - \frac{df}{d\eta}, \; L_g = \frac{d^3 g}{d\eta^3} - \frac{dg}{d\eta}, \\ L_s &= \frac{d^2 s}{d\eta^2} - s, \; L_\Phi \frac{d^2\Phi}{d\eta^2} - \Phi, \; L_\theta = \frac{d^2\theta}{d\eta^2} - \theta. \end{aligned}$$

The Linear operators chosen for this set of equations as,

$$\begin{aligned} L_f\left[C_1 + C_2 e^{\eta} + C_3 e^{-\eta}\right] &= 0; \, L_g\left[C_4 + C_5 e^{\eta} + C_6 e^{-\eta}\right] = 0; \\ L_s\left[C_7 e^{\eta} + C_8 e^{-\eta}\right] &= 0; \, L_\Phi\left[C_9 e^{\eta} + C_{10} e^{-\eta}\right] = 0; \\ L_\theta\left[C_{11} e^{\eta} + C_{12} e^{-\eta}\right] &= 0, \end{aligned} \tag{3.21}$$

in which $C_i$'s are arbitrary constants and can be obtained from (3.18).

### 3.4.1 Zeroth-order deformation problem

To obtain the HAM solution for the eqs. (3.12)-(3.16), let $\tau \in [0,1]$ be an embedding parameter and $c_f$, $c_g$, $c_s$, $c_\Phi$ and $c_\theta$ are the basic convergence control parameters. Then the zeroth order deformation equation and the non-linear operators take the following form

$$(1-\gamma)L_X[X(\eta,\gamma) - X_0(\eta)] = \gamma c_X \mathcal{N}_X[X(\eta,\gamma)], \tag{3.22}$$

where, $X_0 = f_0,\ g_0,\ s_0,\ \Phi_0$ and $\theta_0$. The nonlinear operator is directly written from the governing equations as

$$\begin{aligned}\mathcal{N}_f[f(\eta,\gamma)] &= \frac{\partial^3 f(\eta,\gamma)}{\partial\eta^3} + (f(\eta,\gamma)+cg(\eta,\gamma))\left(\frac{\partial^2 f(\eta,\gamma)}{\partial\eta^2}\right)\\ &+ \left(1-\left(\frac{\partial f(\eta,\gamma)}{\partial\eta}\right)^2\right) + M\left(1-\left(\frac{\partial f(\eta,\gamma)}{\partial\eta}\right)\right)\\ &+ \lambda\left(1-\left(\frac{\partial f(\eta,\gamma)}{\partial\eta}\right)-\left(\frac{\eta}{2}\right)\left(\frac{\partial^2 f(\eta,\gamma)}{\partial\eta^2}\right)\right)\end{aligned} \tag{3.23}$$

$$\begin{aligned}\mathcal{N}_g[g(\eta,\gamma),f(\eta,\gamma)] &= \frac{\partial^3 g(\eta,\gamma)}{\partial\eta^3} + (f(\eta,\gamma)+cg(\eta,\gamma))\left(\frac{\partial^2 g(\eta,\gamma)}{\partial\eta^2}\right)\\ &+ c\left(1-\left(\frac{\partial g(\eta,\gamma)}{\partial\eta}\right)^2\right) + M\left(1-\left(\frac{\partial g(\eta,\gamma)}{\partial\eta}\right)\right)\\ &+ \lambda\left(1-\left(\frac{\partial g(\eta,\gamma)}{\partial\eta}\right)-\left(\frac{\eta}{2}\right)\left(\frac{\partial^2 g(\eta,\gamma)}{\partial\eta^2}\right)\right)\end{aligned} \tag{3.24}$$

$$\begin{aligned}\mathcal{N}_s[s(\eta,\gamma),g(\eta,\gamma),f(\eta,\gamma)] &= Pr^{-1}\left(\frac{\partial^2 s(\eta,\gamma)}{\partial\eta^2}\right)-\left(\frac{\eta}{2}\right)\left(\frac{\partial s(\eta,\gamma)}{\partial\eta}\right)\\ -2\lambda s(\eta,\gamma) &+ (f(\eta,\gamma)+cg(\eta,\gamma))\left(\frac{\partial s(\eta,\gamma)}{\partial\eta}\right)\end{aligned} \tag{3.25}$$

$$\begin{aligned}\mathcal{N}_\Phi[\Phi(\eta,\gamma),g(\eta,\gamma),f(\eta,\gamma)] &= Pr^{-1}\left(\frac{\partial^2 \Phi(\eta,\gamma)}{\partial\eta^2}\right)-2\left(\frac{\partial f(\eta,\gamma)}{\partial\eta}\right)\Phi(\eta,\gamma)\\ &+ (f(\eta,\gamma)+cg(\eta,\gamma))\left(\frac{\partial \Phi(\eta,\gamma)}{\partial\eta}\right)\\ &+ \alpha\left[\left(\frac{\partial^2 f(\eta,\gamma)}{\partial\eta^2}\right)^2 + M\left(\frac{\partial f(\eta,\gamma)}{\partial\eta}\right)^2\right]\\ &- 2\lambda\Phi(\eta,\gamma)-\left(\frac{\eta}{2}\right)\lambda\Phi(\eta,\gamma)\end{aligned} \tag{3.26}$$

$$\begin{aligned}\mathcal{N}_\theta[\theta(\eta,\gamma),g(\eta,\gamma),f(\eta,\gamma)] &= Pr^{-1}\left(\frac{\partial^2 \theta(\eta,\gamma)}{\partial\eta^2}\right)-2c\left(\frac{\partial g(\eta,\gamma)}{\partial\eta}\right)\theta(\eta,\gamma)\\ &+ (f(\eta,\gamma)+cg(\eta,\gamma))\left(\frac{\partial \theta(\eta,\gamma)}{\partial\eta}\right)\\ &+ \beta\left[\left(\frac{\partial^2 g(\eta,\gamma)}{\partial\eta^2}\right)^2 + M\left(\frac{\partial g(\eta,\gamma)}{\partial\eta}\right)^2\right]\\ &- 2\lambda\theta(\eta,\gamma)-\left(\frac{\eta}{2}\right)\lambda\theta(\eta,\gamma),\end{aligned} \tag{3.27}$$

with appropriate boundary conditions rewritten from (3.18) as,

$$f(\eta;\gamma)|_{\eta=0} = g(\eta;\gamma)|_{\eta=0} = 0,\quad \left.\frac{\partial f(\eta;\gamma)}{\partial\eta}\right|_{\eta=0} = \left.\frac{\partial g(\eta;\gamma)}{\partial\eta}\right|_{\eta=0} = 0,$$

$$\left.\frac{\partial f(\eta;\gamma)}{\partial\eta}\right|_{\eta=\infty}=\left.\frac{\partial g(\eta;\gamma)}{\partial\eta}\right|_{\eta=\infty}=1; s(\eta;\gamma)|_{\eta=0}=1; \Phi(\eta;\gamma)|_{\eta=0}=0,$$

$$\theta(\eta;\gamma)|_{\eta=0}=s(\eta;\gamma)|_{\eta=\infty}=\Phi(\eta;\gamma)|_{\eta=\infty}=\theta(\eta;\gamma)|_{\eta=\infty}=0\text{''}. \tag{3.28}$$

### 3.4.2 Higher-order deformation problem

For $\ell^{th}$-order deformation equations, differentiate (3.22) $\ell$-times with respect to $\gamma$, and divide by $\ell!$. Setting $\gamma=0$, one may get

$$L_X[X_\ell(\eta)-\Omega_\ell X_{\ell-1}(\eta)] \;=\; c_X\mathscr{R}_\ell^X(\eta). \tag{3.29}$$

The boundary conditions can be redefined as

$$\begin{aligned}&f_\ell(0)=g_\ell(0)=0,\ f'_\ell(0)=\ g'_\ell(0)=0,\ f'_\ell(\infty)=\ g'_\ell(\infty)=1\\ &s_\ell(0)=1,\Phi_\ell(0)=\theta_\ell(0)=0,\ s_\ell(\infty)=\Phi_\ell(\infty)=\theta_\ell(\infty)=0.\end{aligned} \tag{3.30}$$

In (3.29), the term $\mathscr{R}_\ell^X(\eta)$ denotes $\mathscr{R}_f^\ell(\eta)$, $\mathscr{R}_g^\ell(\eta)$, $\mathscr{R}_s^\ell(\eta)$, $\mathscr{R}_\Phi^\ell(\eta)$ and $\mathscr{R}_\theta^\ell(\eta)$. These are the remainder terms from the linear operators which are given by,

$$\begin{aligned}\mathscr{R}_\ell^f(\eta) \;&=\; f'''_{\ell-1}(\eta)+\sum_{j=0}^{\ell-1}[f_{\ell-1-j}f''_j-f'_{\ell-1-j}f'_j]+\lambda[1-f'_{\ell-1}(\eta)\\ -\left(\frac{\eta}{2}\right)f''_{\ell-1}(\eta)] \;&+\; c\sum_{j=0}^{\ell-1}[g_{\ell-1-j}f''_j]+(1+M[1-f'_{\ell-1}(\eta)])\end{aligned} \tag{3.31}$$

$$\begin{aligned}\mathscr{R}_\ell^g(\eta) \;&=\; g'''_{\ell-1}(\eta)+\sum_{j=0}^{\ell-1}[f_{\ell-1-j}g''_j]+\lambda\left[1-g'_{\ell-1}(\eta)-\left(\frac{\eta}{2}\right)g''_{\ell-1}(\eta)\right]\\ &+\; c\sum_{j=0}^{\ell-1}\left[g_{\ell-1-j}g''_j-g'_{\ell-1-j}g'_j\right]+(c+M[1-g'_{\ell-1}(\eta)])\end{aligned} \tag{3.32}$$

$$\begin{aligned}\mathscr{R}_\ell^s(\eta) \;&=\; Pr^{-1}s''_{\ell-1}(\eta)+\sum_{j=0}^{\ell-1}[f_{\ell-1-j}\,s'_j(\eta)]+c\sum_{j=0}^{\ell-1}[g_{\ell-1-j}\,s'_j(\eta)]\\ &+\; \left(\frac{\eta}{2}\right)s'_{\ell-1}(\eta)-2\lambda s_{\ell-1}(\eta)\end{aligned} \tag{3.33}$$

$$\begin{aligned}\mathscr{R}_\ell^\Phi(\eta) \;&=\; Pr^{-1}\Phi''_{\ell-1}(\eta)+\sum_{j=0}^{\ell-1}[f_{\ell-1-j}\,\Phi'_j(\eta)]+c\sum_{j=0}^{\ell-1}[g_{\ell-1-j}\,\Phi'_j(\eta)]\\ &-\; \left(\frac{\lambda\eta}{2}\right)\Phi_{\ell-1}(\eta)+\alpha\left[\sum_{j=0}^{\ell-1}[f''_{\ell-1-j}f''_j+Mf'_{\ell-1-j}f'_j]\right]\\ &+\; 2\sum_{j=0}^{\ell-1}[f'_{\ell-1-j}\,\Phi_j(\eta)]-2\lambda\Phi_{\ell-1}(\eta)\end{aligned} \tag{3.34}$$

$$
\begin{aligned}
\mathscr{R}_\ell^\theta(\eta) &= Pr^{-1}\theta''_{\ell-1}(\eta)+\sum_{j=0}^{\ell-1}[f_{\ell-1-j}\,\theta'_j(\eta)]-2\lambda\,\theta_{\ell-1}(\eta)-\left(\frac{\lambda\eta}{2}\right)\theta_{\ell-1}(\eta)\\
&+ c\sum_{j=0}^{\ell-1}[g_{\ell-1-j}\,\theta'_j(\eta)]-2c\sum_{j=0}^{\ell-1}[g'_{\ell-1-j}\,\theta_j(\eta)]\\
&+ \beta\left[\sum_{j=0}^{\ell-1}[g''_{\ell-1-j}g''_j+Mg'_{\ell-1-j}g'_j]\right]. \qquad (3.35)
\end{aligned}
$$

Here the function $\Omega_\ell$ denotes the characteristic function defined as

$$
\Omega_\ell=\begin{cases} 0 & \text{if } \ell\le 1\\ 1 & \text{if } \ell>1. \end{cases} \qquad (3.36)
$$

Expanding $X(\eta;\gamma)$ with respect to $\gamma$ using Taylor's series, we get

$$
X(\eta;\gamma)=X_0(\eta)+\sum_{\ell=1}^{\infty}X_\ell(\eta)\gamma^\ell, \text{ where } X_\ell(\eta)=\frac{1}{\ell!}\frac{\partial^\ell X(\eta;\gamma)}{\partial\gamma^\ell}\bigg|_{\gamma=0}. \qquad (3.37)
$$

The auxiliary parameters are selected as $\gamma=0$ and $\gamma=1$ from (3.22), one may write

$$
X(\eta;0)=X_0(\eta),\;\; X(\eta;1)=X(\eta). \qquad (3.38)
$$

Thus as $\gamma$ increases from 0 to 1 and $X(\eta;\gamma)$ varies from the initial guess $X_0(\eta)$ to the solution $X(\eta)$ of the governing equations respectively. The auxiliary parameters are suitable chosen so that the series solutions converge for $\gamma=1$ and the particular solution is given by

$$
X(\eta)=X_0(\eta)+\sum_{\ell=1}^{\infty}X_\ell(\eta), \qquad (3.39)
$$

Therefore, we get the general approximate analytical solutions $f_\ell, g_\ell, s_\ell, \Phi_\ell, \theta_\ell$ in terms of special solutions $f_\ell^*, g_\ell^*, s_\ell^*, \Phi_\ell^*, \theta_\ell^*$ as,

$$
\begin{aligned}
f_\ell(\eta) &= f_\ell^*(\eta)+C_1+C_2e^\eta+C_3e^{-\eta},\;\; g_\ell(\eta)=g_\ell^*(\eta)+C_4+C_5e^\eta+C_6e^{-\eta},\\
s_\ell(\eta) &= s_\ell^*(\eta)+C_7e^\eta+C_8e^{-\eta},\;\; \Phi_\ell(\eta)=\Phi_\ell^*(\eta)+C_9e^\eta+C_{10}e^{-\eta},\\
\theta_\ell(\eta) &= \theta_\ell^*(\eta)+C_{11}e^\eta+C_{12}e^{-\eta}. \qquad (3.40)
\end{aligned}
$$

By solving (3.40) one after the other in the order $\ell=1,2,3,...$ by means of the symbolic computation software Mathematica, it is shown that the solution for the profiles can be expressed as an infinite series of any desired order. The approximate analytical solutions computed for $f,\ g,\ s,\ \Phi$ and $\theta$ for $\ell=1,2,3,...$ are given in **Appendix-B**.

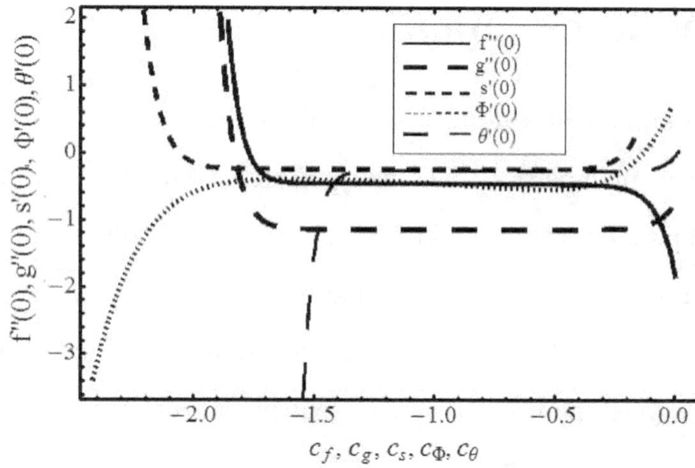


Figure 3.2: $c_f$, $c_g$, $c_s$, $c_\Phi$ and $c_\theta$-curves.

It is customary in HAM analysis to plot $c_X$-curves to identify the interval of optimal convergence control parameters (i.e, $c_f$, $c_g$, $c_s$, $c_\Phi$ and $c_\theta$) within which any values can be chosen to obtain convergent solutions. From Figure. 3.2 it is shown that choosing unique value from the ranges of $c_f \in [-1.6, -0.2]$, $c_g \in [-1.6, -0.1]$ does not affect the values of surface shear stress rates and it is $c_s \in [-1.5, -0.3]$, $c_\Phi \in [-1.9, -0.4]$ and $c_\theta \in [-1.4, -0.5]$ for surface heat transfer rates. The $c_X$ curves have been drawn for $20^{th}$ order of HAM solution described by Seshadri *et al.* (2015).

In all of the figures, we use $Pr = 0.72$, $\lambda = -1.0$ and $c = -0.5$, $M = 0.5$ and $\alpha = \beta = 0.2$ unless it is mentioned otherwise.

### 3.4.3 The error estimation at high orders

Use eq. (1.17) to compute the average squared residual errors of (3.12)-(3.16). At the $\ell^{th}$-order, the optimal values of $c_X$ are computed by the minimum of the squared residual $E_X$ of the governing equations, corresponding to (1.18). The average squared residual errors $E_X$, with the CPU time (Sec.) at different orders of approximation for $\ell$ are shown in Table 3.1. The averaged squared residual error decreases rapidly and the optimal values of the convergence control parameters are found to be $c_f = -0.609214$, $c_g = -0.59523$ and $c_s = -0.86576$, $c_\Phi = -1.31155$ and $c_\theta = -0.71554$. Thus the convergence control parameter used in HAM can greatly accelerate the convergence of series solution.

## 3.5 Numerical solution

Though several numerical results are available in the literature, to compare present results for different parametric values and performed numerical computation with the simple and still popular technique RKFM. The numerical solution of the governing eqs. (3.12)-(3.16) subject to the boundary conditions (3.18) have been obtained using the RKFM. It was necessary to adopt a shooting technique to get the missing slopes $f''(0)$, $g''(0)$, $-s'(0)$, $-\Phi'(0)$ and $-\theta'(0)$ for various physical parameters. The numerical results and approximate analytical results agree very well in all the calculations done in earlier studies.

## 3.6 Results Analysis

The approximate analytical solutions are obtained in the form of general series for the flow variables $f$, $g$, $s$, $\Phi$ and $\theta$. The approximate analytical solutions for the velocity and temperature are obtained in the form of a power series solution using computational software **Mathematica**. The expressions for $f$, $g$, $s$, $\Phi$ and $\theta$ are obtained up to $10^{th}$ degree polynomial. It is to be mentioned here that, though computations could be done easily up to $20^{th}$ order of deformations equations, to retain the results up to seven decimal places accuracy and stopped at the $5^{th}$ order.

Here the effect of various parameters such as unsteady parameter $\lambda$, magnetic parameter $M$, ratio of the velocity gradient $c$ and viscous dissipation parameters $\alpha$, $\beta$ and Prandtl number $Pr$ on velocity and temperature profiles as well as on skin friction coefficients and heat transfer rate discussed. Computations have been carried out for several combinations of parameters $\lambda$, $M$, $c$, $\alpha$, $\beta$ and $Pr$, and all results are presented here in the form of Tables 3.1-3.4 and Figures. 3.3-3.50.

For the special case of $M = \lambda = 0$ (in the absence of magnetic and unsteady parameter), Table 3.2 presents the values of skin friction results for steady case $(f''(0), g''(0))$ with that of Kumari *et al.* (2002) for nodal and saddle point regions. It was found to be in very good agreement from the $10^{th}$ order approximation itself. The comparison of heat transfer results for steady case $-s'(0)$ is presented in Table 3.3. Here, the values of the heat transfer coefficients in terms of local Nusselt number are small for $Pr = 0.7$ in comparison to the values for $Pr = 10.0$. This means that the values of the local Nusselt number increases with an increase in Prandtl number.

It is seen from Table 3.4 that the skin friction and heat transfer rates ($f''(0)$, $-s'(0)$) for various values of $c$ and $M$ are compared in steady case ($\lambda = 0$) with that of Kumari *et al.* (2002). It is found that the values of local skin friction and heat transfer coefficients in terms of local Nusselt number are small for $c = 0$ in comparison to the values for $c = 1.0$. This means that the values of the local Nusselt number increases with an increase in $c$ corresponding with that of magnetic values.

The Figures. 3.3-3.24 show the effect of the study parameters on the velocity, temperature profiles and 3.25-3.50 show variation of shear stresses and heat transfer rates.

The effect of magnetic parameter $M$ on the velocity profiles $f'(\eta)$ and $g'(\eta)$ in $x$- and $y$-directions and temperature profiles $s(\eta)$, $\phi(\eta)$ and $\theta(\eta)$ are plotted in Figures. 3.3-3.7. It is observed that there is an overshoot in the velocity profiles as magnetic parameter $M$ increases from 0.5 to 4.0. Overshoot in profiles means there is a sudden increase and an immediate decrease in the flow velocity near the surface. This is due to the fact that, the imposition of magnetic field creates a drag like force called Lorentz force in the flow field that has the tendency to slow down the flow near the surface at the same time increasing fluid temperature. As the magnetic field increases, the velocity profile increases and the temperature profile increases, but the temperature profiles are thinner for higher values of $M$. The temperature in the absence of viscous dissipation $s(\eta)$ gradually reaches the free stream values, but the behaviour of temperature profiles in the presence of viscous dissipation and Ohmic heating are significantly different in the sense that it increases sharply close to the boundary layer, attains a maximum value and starts decreasing rapidly to attain its free stream values.

The effect of unsteady parameter $\lambda$ on the velocity profiles $f'(\eta)$ and $g'(\eta)$ in $x$-and $y$-directions and temperature profiles $s(\eta)$, $\phi(\eta)$ and $\theta(\eta)$ are plotted in 3.8-3.12. It is observed that the $\lambda$ increases from 0.5 to 4.0, the velocity profile decrease and the temperature profile decrease at without viscous dissipation and the temperature profiles have no appreciable changes at with viscous dissipation and Ohmic heating.

The effect of ratio of the velocity gradient parameter $c$ on the velocity profiles $f'(\eta)$ and $g'(\eta)$ in $x$-and $y$-directions and temperature profiles $s(\eta)$, $\phi(\eta)$ and $\theta(\eta)$ are plotted in 3.13-3.17. It is observed that there is an overshoot in the velocity profiles as $c$

increases from 0.5 to 1.0. Overshoot in profiles means there is a sudden increase at nodal point region ( i.e, $0.5 \leq c \leq 1$), where the appreciable changes in the similarity solution of boundary layer equations compared to the solution near the nodal point region, while the corresponding flow near the saddle point region (i.e, $-1 \leq c < -0.5$) also increase in the flow velocity near the surface and similar effect seen at temperature profiles without viscous dissipation. Seen in 3.16-3.17 that the $c$ increases, temperature profiles have no appreciable changes at with viscous dissipation and Ohmic heating.

Figures. 3.18-3.20 depict the temperature profiles for different values of Prandtl number in the presence of the unsteady parameter. The 3.18-3.19 demonstrate the fact that an increase in the Prandtl number Pr results in a increase in the temperature profile due to the viscous dissipation parameters. The 3.20 demonstrate the fact that an increase in the Prandtl number results in a decrease in the temperature distribution and tends to zero as the space variable increases from the wall. That is, the thermal boundary layer thickness decreases as $Pr$ increases due to Ohmic heating.

The effect of viscous dissipation parameters $\alpha$ and $\beta$ are on the temperature profiles with viscous dissipation $\phi(\eta)$ and Ohmic heating $\theta(\eta)$ are plotted in 3.21-3.24. It is observed that there is no appreciable change in the temperature profiles as $\alpha$ and $\beta$ increases from 0.1 to 0.6.

The variation of surface shear stress rates in $x$-and $y$-directions (i.e, $f''(0)$ and $g''(0)$) and the heat transfer rate ($-s'(0)$, $-\Phi'(0)$ and $-\theta'(0)$) are presented in Figures. 3.25-3.50.

It is seen from 3.25-3.29 with the unsteady parameter $\lambda$ for different magnetic parameter $M$ that, the decrease in unsteady parameter $\lambda$ decreases the surface shear stress rates. It is to be noted that, the surface shear stress rates ($f''(0)$ and $g''(0)$) in $x$ and $y$-directions, for every $M$ curve becomes zero for a certain value of unsteady parameter $\lambda$. For example, as seen from 3.26, $g''(0)$ vanishes at $\lambda = -0.438, -2.189$ for $M = 0.5, 4.0$, respectively. Also, reverse flow occurs for negative values of $\lambda$. This means that the decelerating flow behaves like an adverse pressure gradient. Similar trend has been observed by Kumari *et al.* (2002). The boundary layer thickness increase with decreasing unsteady parameter, which means that the velocity in $z$-direction increases which in turn increases the heat transfer rate. Hence, as the unsteady parameter $\lambda$ decreases the heat transfer rate ($-s'(0), -\Phi'(0)$ and $-\theta'(0)$) increases as observed from 3.27-3.29.

The effect of ratio of the velocity gradient parameter $c$ with the unsteady parameter $\lambda$ on the shear stress rate ($f''(0)$ and $g''(0)$) in $x$ and $y$-directions, respectively and the surface heat transfer rate (i.e, $-s'(0), -\Phi'(0)$ and $-\theta'(0)$) are plotted in 3.30-3.34. It is observed that shear stress rate $f''(0)$, $g''(0)$ and heat transfer rate $-s'(0)$, $-\Phi'(0)$ and $-\theta'(0)$ rapidly increases with increasing by $c$ in the flow near stagnation point ( i.e, $0.5 \leq c \leq 1$) at the nodal point region and increases in $f''(0)$ and $-s'(0)$, while decreases in $g''(0)$, $-\Phi'(0)$ and $-\theta'(0)$ with decreasing by $c$ in the flow near stagnation point ( i.e, $-0.5 \leq c \leq -1$) at the saddle point region due to the unsteadiness.

It is seen from 3.35-3.39 with the magnetic parameter $M$ for different unsteady parameter $\lambda$ that, the increase in magnetic parameter $M$ increases the surface shear stress rates. It is to be noted that, the surface shear stress rates ($f''(0)$ and $g''(0)$) in $x$ and $y$-directions, for every $\lambda$ curve becomes zero for a certain value of magnetic parameter $M$. As the magnetic parameter $M$ increase the heat transfer rates ($-s'(0), -\Phi'(0)$ decrease and $-\theta'(0)$) is increases.

The effect of ratio of the velocity gradient parameter $c$ with the magnetic parameter $M$ on the shear stress rate ($f''(0)$ and $g''(0)$) in $x$ and $y$-directions, respectively and the surface heat transfer rate (i.e, $-s'(0), -\Phi'(0)$ and $-\theta'(0)$) are plotted in 3.40-3.44. It is observed that shear stress rate $f''(0)$, $g''(0)$ and heat transfer rate $-s'(0)$, $-\Phi'(0)$ and $-\theta'(0)$ rapidly increase with increasing by $c$ in the flow near stagnation point ( i.e, $0.5 \leq c \leq 1$) at the nodal point region and increases in $f''(0)$ and $g''(0)$, $-s'(0)$ and $-\Phi'(0)$ while decrease in $-\theta'(0)$ with decreasing by $c$ in the flow near stagnation point ( i.e, $-0.5 \leq c \leq -1$) at the saddle point region due to the magnetic parameter. Effect of the Prandtl number $Pr$ on the surface heat transfer rate (i.e, $-s'(0)$, $-\Phi'(0)$, $-\theta'(0)$), with $\lambda$ and $M$ are presented in 3.45-3.50. It observed from 3.45-3.48 that, the Prandtl number $Pr$ is increases from 0.7 to 10, the heat transfer rate increases, reverse trend is seen in 3.49-3.50.

## 3.7 Summary

The flow and heat transfer analysis is presented for a three-dimensional viscous fluid flow in the neighborhood of a stagnation point. An approximate analytical expression in the form of a series solution is derived for velocity and temperature using HAM. The coefficients of the series solution contain all the study parameters such as $c$, $M$, $Pr$, $\lambda$, $\alpha$ and $\beta$. The computer algebra software Mathematica is used to perform these semi-analytical calculations. The effect of various parameters such as unsteady parameter $\lambda$, magnetic parameter $M$ and ratio of the velocity gradient parameter $c$ are analyzed on velocity and temperature as well as on shear stress rates and heat transfer rates.

The following conclusions are drawn from the present study.

- The velocity and temperature profiles increase for the increase in the values of magnetic parameter, but the temperature profiles are thinner for higher values of magnetic parameter.

- The velocity and temperature profiles decrease for the increase in the values of unsteady parameter at without viscous dissipation and the temperature profiles have no appreciable changes at with viscous dissipation and Ohmic heating.

- The heat transfer and surface shear stress is found to increase with increasing the magnetic parameter, whereas the unsteady parameter decrease the heat transfer rate increase.

- The shear stress and heat transfer rates is rapidly increase with increasing by stretching ratio in the flow near stagnation point at the nodal point region, and increase in $f''(0)$ and $-s'(0)$, while decreases in $g''(0)$, $-\Phi'(0)$ and $-\theta'(0)$ with decreasing by stretching ratio $c$ in the flow near stagnation point at the saddle point region due to the unsteadiness.

- The percentage increase or decrease of a certain flow variable with respect to the change in a given parameter is well documented.

Table 3.1: The averaged squared residual error $E_X$ with the CPU time at different orders of approximations in HAM analysis.

| $l$ | CPU time(Sec.) | Minimum of Averaged Squared Residual Errors | | | | |
|---|---|---|---|---|---|---|
| | | $E_f$ | $E_g$ | $E_G$ | $E_\Phi$ | $E_\theta$ |
| 2 | 1.0 | $2.08642\times10^{-2}$ | $2.21558\times10^{-3}$ | $6.42071\times10^{-3}$ | $1.00611\times10^{-6}$ | $1.18235\times10^{-4}$ |
| 4 | 5.8 | $1.25201\times10^{-4}$ | $1.24501\times10^{-5}$ | $2.49866\times10^{-5}$ | $3.29999\times10^{-7}$ | $2.09782\times10^{-7}$ |
| 6 | 31.1 | $2.97143\times10^{-7}$ | $3.20537\times10^{-8}$ | $1.31442\times10^{-8}$ | $1.07162\times10^{-9}$ | $5.19336\times10^{-10}$ |
| 8 | 51.9 | $4.00527\times10^{-9}$ | $4.71582\times10^{-10}$ | $2.52719\times10^{-11}$ | $2.77611\times10^{-11}$ | $4.00001\times10^{-13}$ |
| 10 | 323.7 | $9.32769\times10^{-12}$ | $5.90002\times10^{-13}$ | $9.14281\times10^{-14}$ | $6.10022\times10^{-13}$ | $3.71102\times10^{-14}$ |
| 12 | 1281.8 | $2.62319\times10^{-14}$ | $6.00222\times10^{-15}$ | $1.71058\times10^{-16}$ | $8.29371\times10^{-17}$ | $7.33333\times10^{-18}$ |
| 14 | 1446.1 | $7.90133\times10^{-15}$ | $6.67216\times10^{-16}$ | $7.39669\times10^{-17}$ | $4.00222\times10^{-18}$ | $1.02761\times10^{-20}$ |
| 16 | 1582.8 | $2.83001\times10^{-17}$ | $5.07803\times10^{-19}$ | $1.40772\times10^{-20}$ | $7.76201\times10^{-21}$ | $6.99728\times10^{-21}$ |

Table 3.2: Comparison of skin friction results for steady case ( $f''(0)$, $g''(0)$) when $M=\lambda=0$ for nodal and saddle point regions.

| $c$ | $f''(0)$ | | | $g''(0)$ | | |
|---|---|---|---|---|---|---|
| | Kumari *et al.* (2002) | Present HAM | Present RKFM | Kumari *et al.* (2002) | Present HAM | RKFM |
| 0.00 | 1.2268 | 1.2268084 | 1.2268084 | 0.5848 | 0.5848333 | 0.5848333 |
| 0.25 | 1.2453 | 1.2453641 | 1.2453641 | 0.8378 | 0.8378750 | 0.8378750 |
| 0.50 | 1.2654 | 1.2654008 | 1.2654008 | 1.0142 | 1.0142396 | 1.0142396 |
| 0.75 | 1.2892 | 1.2892765 | 1.2892765 | 1.1723 | 1.1723170 | 1.1723170 |
| 1.00 | 1.3153 | 1.3153407 | 1.3153407 | 1.3153 | 1.3153347 | 1.3153347 |
| -0.2 | 1.2256 | 1.2256840 | 1.2256840 | 0.3350 | 0.3350904 | 0.3350904 |
| -0.4 | 1.2262 | 1.2262611 | 1.2262611 | 0.0459 | 0.0459610 | 0.0459610 |
| -0.6 | 1.2361 | 1.2361333 | 1.2361333 | -0.2664 | -0.2666421 | -0.2666421 |
| -0.8 | 1.2519 | 1.2519924 | 1.2519924 | -0.5485 | -0.5485740 | -0.5485740 |
| -1.0 | 1.2732 | 1.2732043 | 1.2732043 | -0.8110 | -0.8110879 | -0.8110879 |

Table 3.3: Comparison of heat transfer rates ($-s'(0)$) for different $Pr$, when $M = \lambda = 0.0$ for nodal and saddle point regions.

| $-s'(0)$ | | | | | | |
|---|---|---|---|---|---|---|
| $c$ | Kumari *et al.* (2002) | | Present HAM | | Present RKFM | |
| | Pr =0.7 | Pr =10.0 | Pr =0.7 | Pr =10.0 | Pr =0.7 | Pr =10.0 |
| 0.00 | 0.4957 | 1.3386 | 0.4959980 | 1.3387713 | 0.4959980 | 1.3387713 |
| 0.25 | 0.5358 | 1.4265 | 0.5369627 | 1.4262420 | 0.5369627 | 1.4262420 |
| 0.50 | 0.5798 | 1.5311 | 0.5784300 | 1.5320669 | 0.5784300 | 1.5320669 |
| 0.75 | 0.6233 | 1.6419 | 0.6235361 | 1.6438587 | 0.6235361 | 1.6438587 |
| 1.00 | 0.6656 | 1.7523 | 0.6659613 | 1.7526072 | 0.6659613 | 1.7526072 |
| -0.10 | — | — | 0.5463178 | 1.5901238 | 0.5463178 | 1.5901238 |
| -0.25 | — | — | 0.6109312 | 1.6432103 | 0.6109312 | 1.6432103 |
| -0.50 | — | — | 0.6961289 | 1.7074361 | 0.6961289 | 1.7074361 |
| -0.75 | — | — | 0.7233490 | 1.8498630 | 0.7233490 | 1.8498630 |
| -1.00 | — | — | 0.8073104 | 1.9103814 | 0.8073104 | 1.9103814 |

Table 3.4: Comparison of skin friction and heat transfer rates for steady case ( $f''(0)$, $-s'(0)$) when $Pr = 0.72$ at various values of $c$ and $M$.

| c | M | $f''(0)$ | | | $-s'(0)$ | | |
|---|---|---|---|---|---|---|---|
| | | Kumari *et al.* (2002) | Present HAM | RKFM | Kumari *et al.* (2002) | Present HAM | RKFM |
| 0.0 | 0.0 | 1.2268 | 1.2269340 | 1.2269340 | 0.4957 | 0.4959982 | 0.4959982 |
| 0.0 | 0.5 | 1.4132 | 1.4133836 | 1.4133836 | 0.5069 | 0.5070253 | 0.5070253 |
| 0.0 | 1.0 | 1.5795 | 1.5791185 | 1.5791185 | 0.5156 | 0.5158103 | 0.5158103 |
| 0.0 | 2.0 | 1.8664 | 1.8665012 | 1.8665012 | 0.5287 | 0.5282495 | 0.5282495 |
| 0.0 | 4.0 | 2.3397 | 2.3420600 | 2.3420600 | 0.5461 | 0.5462691 | 0.5462691 |
| 1.0 | 0.0 | 1.3153 | 1.3107777 | 1.3107777 | 0.6656 | 0.6658604 | 0.6658604 |
| 1.0 | 0.5 | 1.4827 | 1.4826013 | 1.4826013 | 0.6794 | 0.6794317 | 0.6794317 |
| 1.0 | 1.0 | 1.6403 | 1.6459755 | 1.6459755 | 0.6911 | 0.6919000 | 0.6919000 |
| 1.0 | 2.0 | 1.9176 | 1.9210201 | 1.9210201 | 0.7091 | 0.7107628 | 0.7107628 |
| 1.0 | 4.0 | 2.3796 | 2.3789651 | 2.3789651 | 0.7340 | 0.7341152 | 0.7341152 |

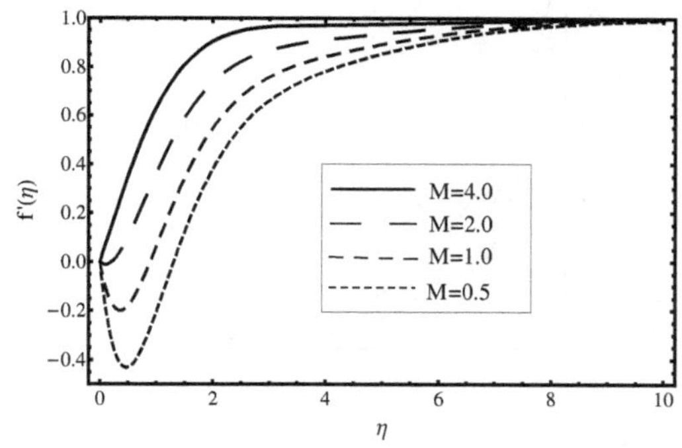


Figure 3.3: Effect of magnetic parameter on velocity profile in x-direction.

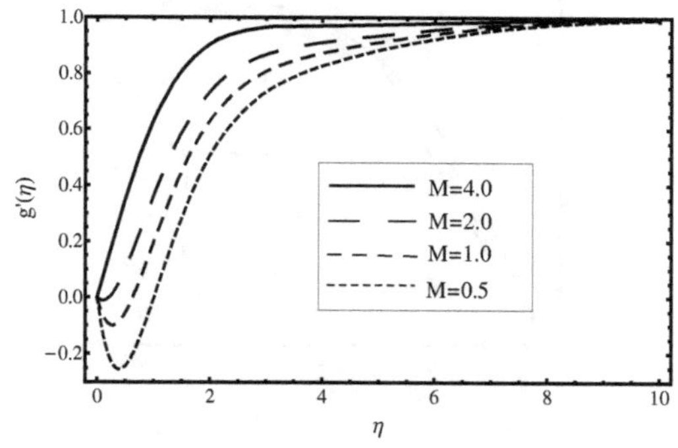


Figure 3.4: Effect of magnetic parameter on velocity profile in y-direction.

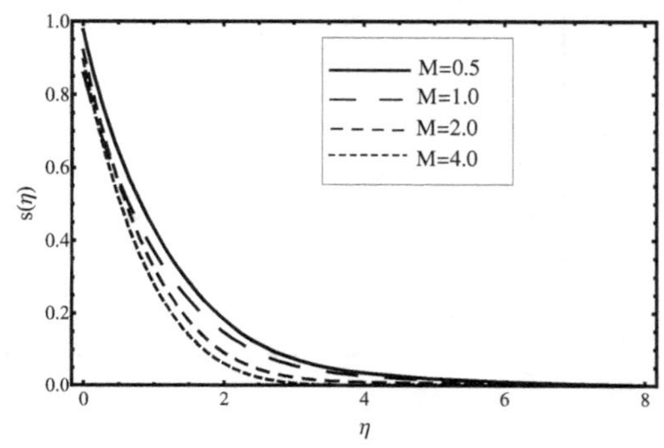


Figure 3.5: Effect of magnetic parameter on temperature profile without viscous dissipation.

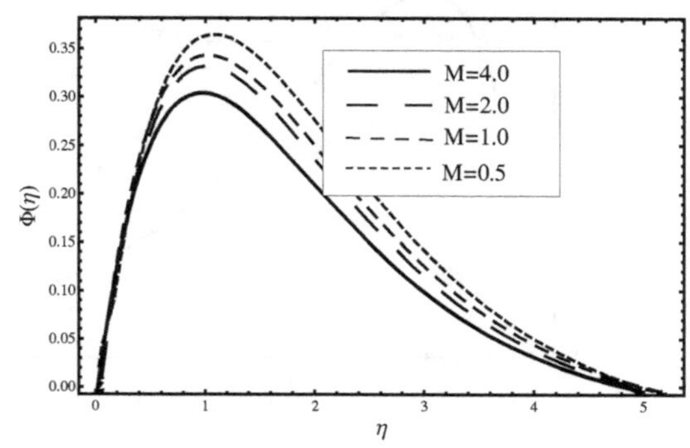


Figure 3.6: Effect of magnetic parameter on temperature profile with viscous dissipation.

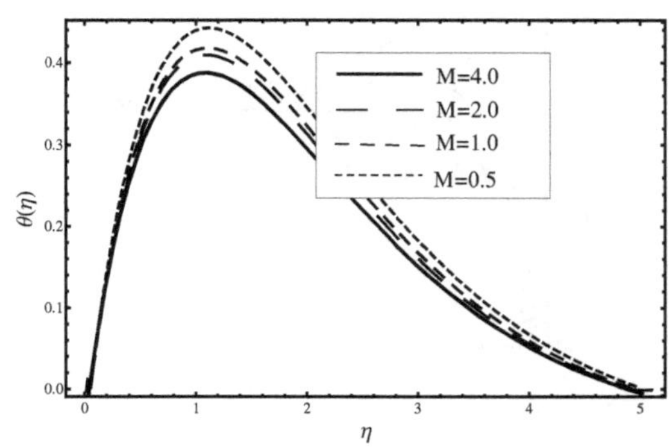


Figure 3.7: Effect of M on temperature profile with Ohmic heating.

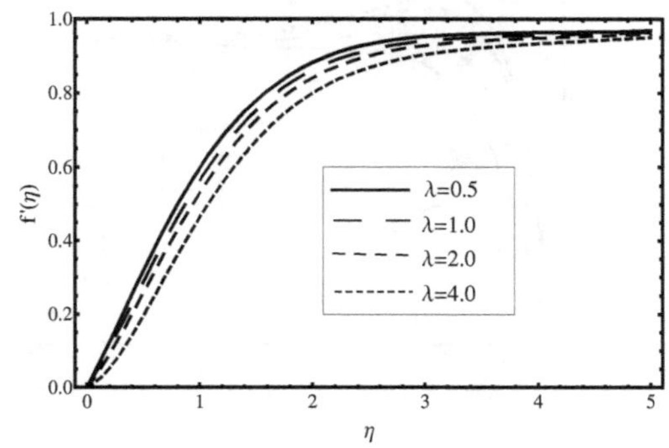


Figure 3.8: Effect of unsteady parameter on velocity profile in x-direction.

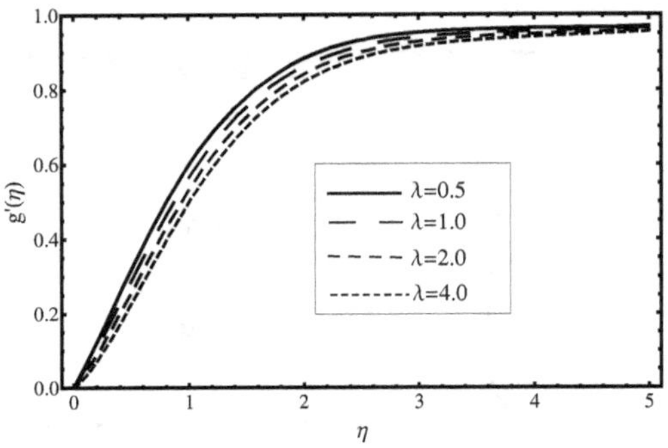


Figure 3.9: Effect of unsteady parameter on velocity profile in y-direction.

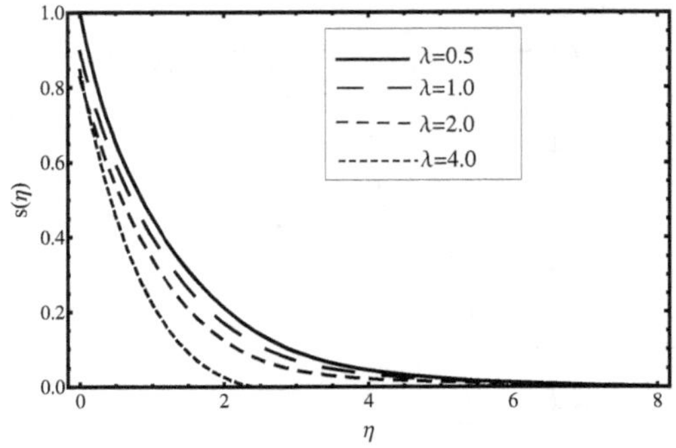


Figure 3.10: Effect of $\lambda$ on temperature profile without viscous dissipation.

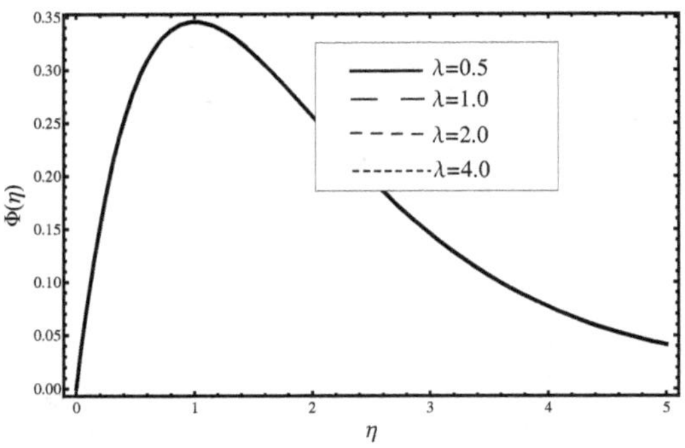


Figure 3.11: Effect of unsteady parameter on temperature profile with viscous dissipation.

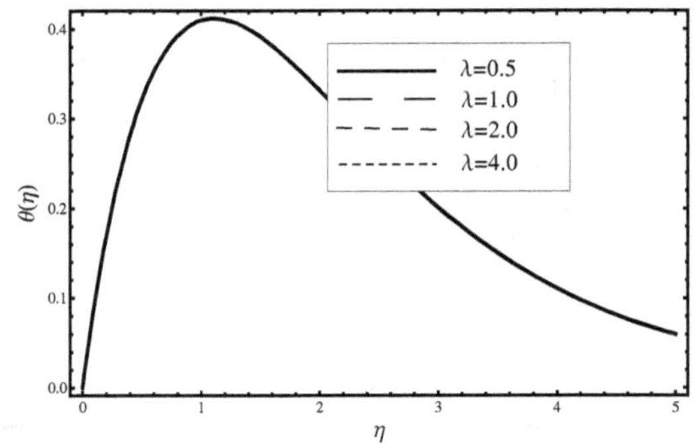


Figure 3.12: Effect of unsteady parameter on temperature profile with Ohmic heating.

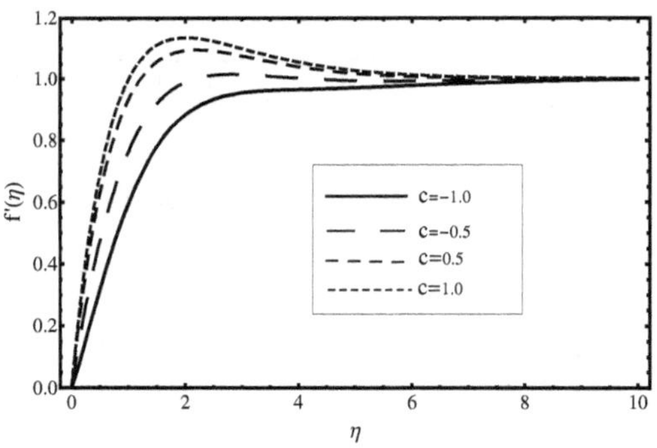


Figure 3.13: Effect of ratio of the velocity gradient parameter on velocity profiles in x-direction.

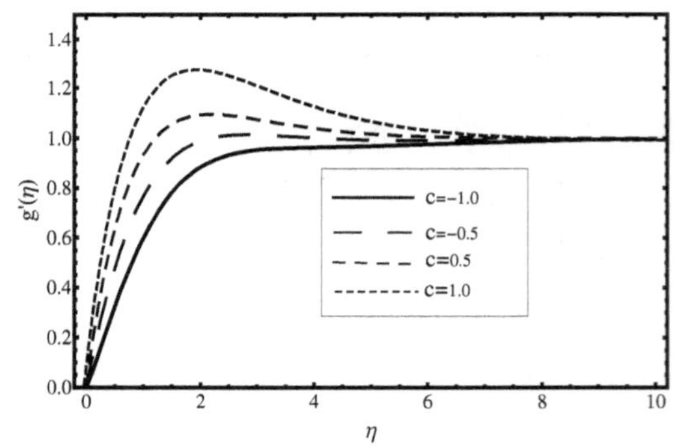


Figure 3.14: Effect of ratio of the velocity gradient parameter on velocity profiles in y-direction.

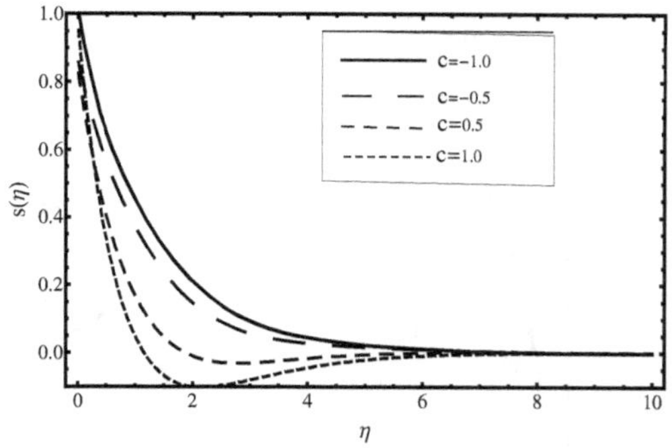


Figure 3.15: Effect of ratio of the velocity gradient parameter on temperature profile without viscous dissipation.

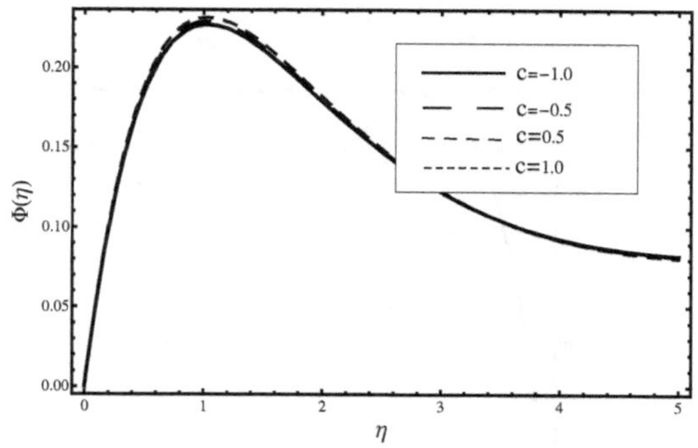


Figure 3.16: Effect of ratio of the velocity gradient parameter on temperature profile with viscous dissipation.

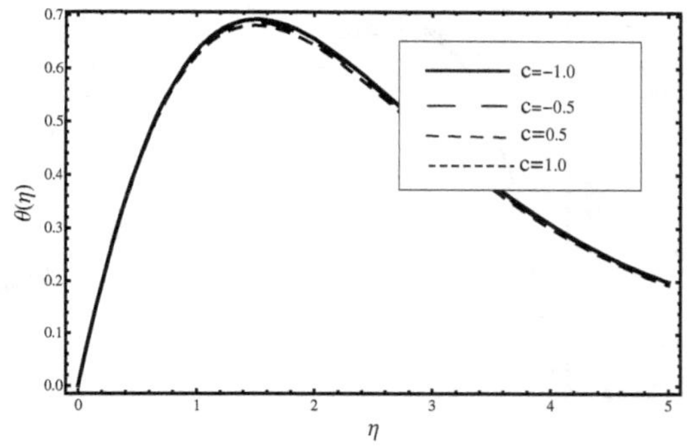


Figure 3.17: Effect of ratio of the velocity gradient parameter on temperature profile with Ohmic heating.

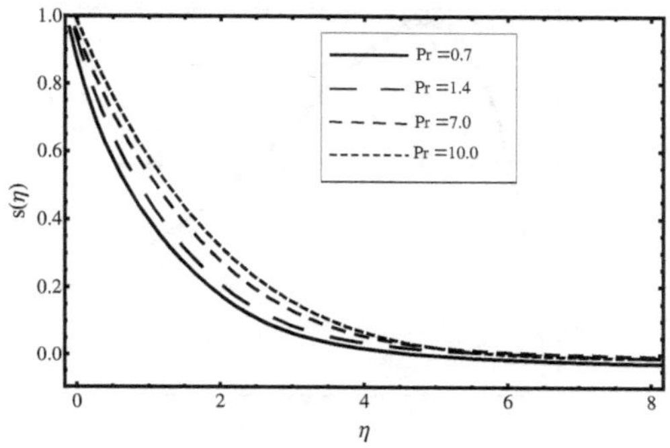


Figure 3.18: Effect of Prandtl number on temperature profile without viscous dissipation.

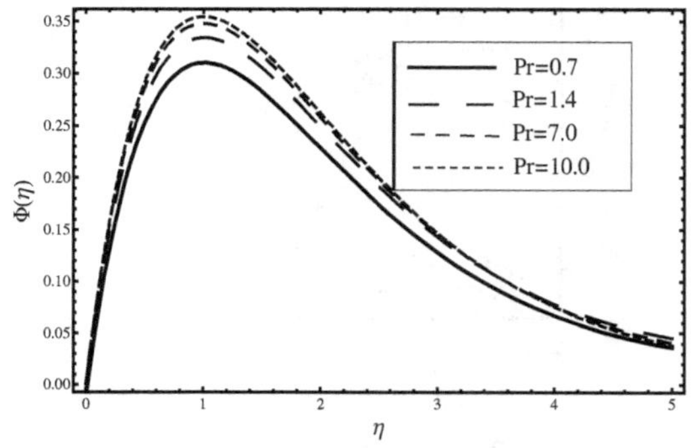


Figure 3.19: Effect of Pr on temperature profile with viscous dissipation.

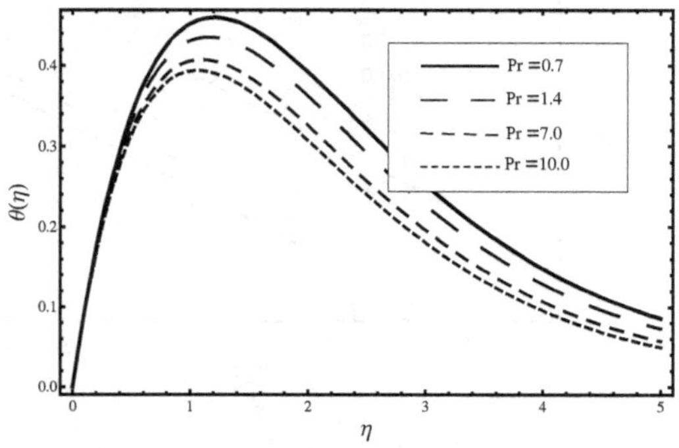


Figure 3.20: Effect of Prandtl number on temperature profile with Ohmic heating.

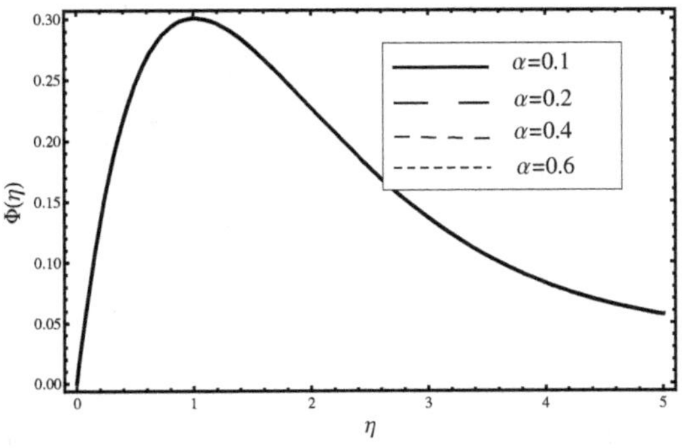


Figure 3.21: Effect of $\alpha$ on temperature profiles with viscous dissipation.

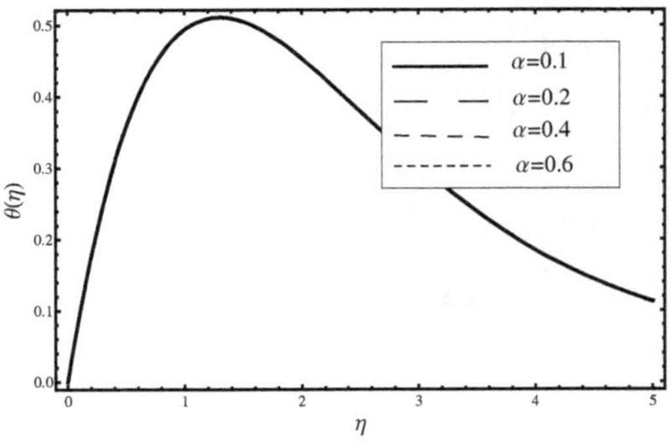


Figure 3.22: Effect of $\alpha$ on temperature profiles with Ohmic heating.

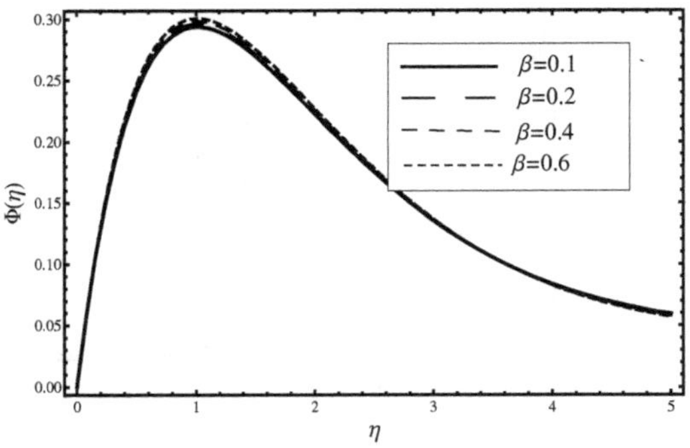


Figure 3.23: Effect of $\beta$ on temperature profiles with viscous dissipation.

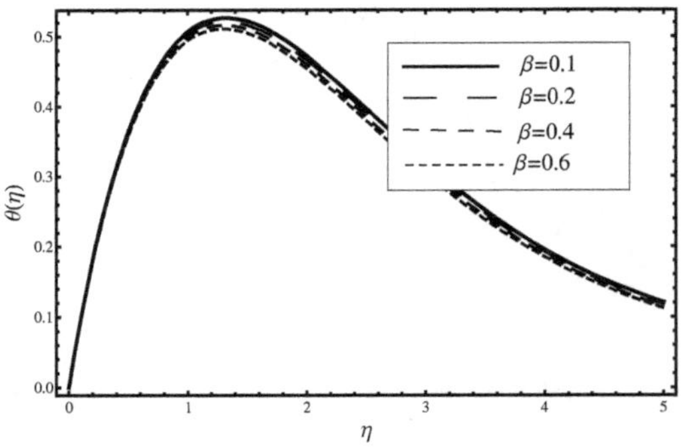


Figure 3.24: Effect of $\beta$ on temperature profiles with Ohmic heating.

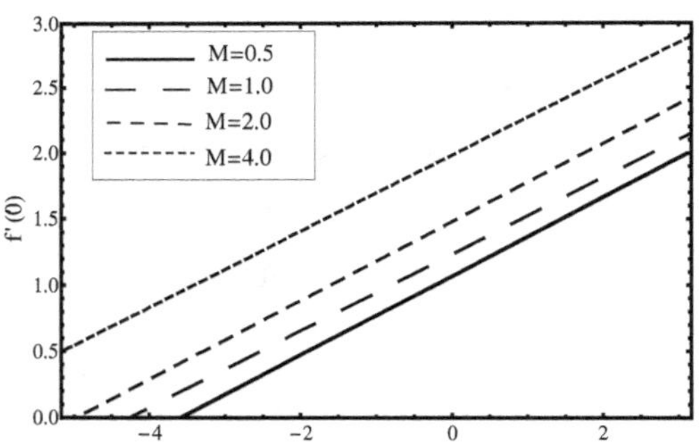


Figure 3.25: Effect of magnetic parameter on shear stress rate in x-direction.

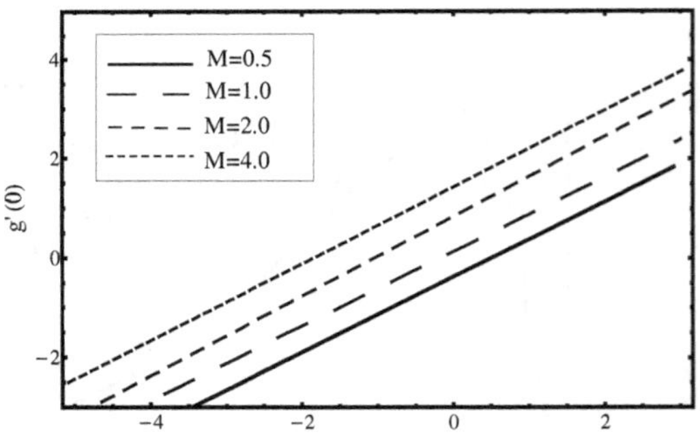


Figure 3.26: Effect of magnetic parameter on shear stress rate in y-direction.

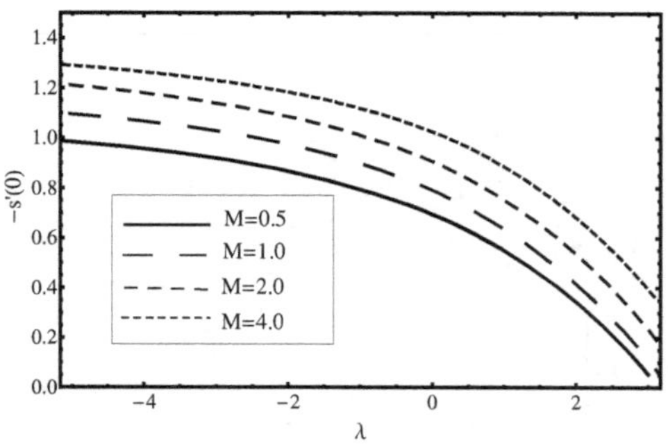


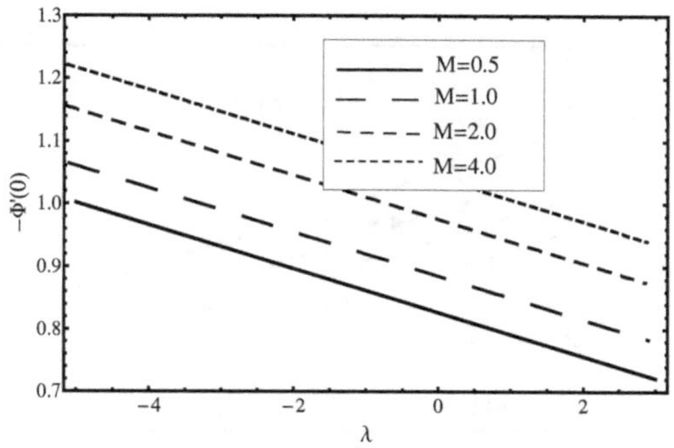


Figure 3.27: Effect of magnetic parameter on heat transfer rate without viscous dissipation.

Figure 3.28: Effect of magnetic parameter on heat transfer rate with viscous dissipation.

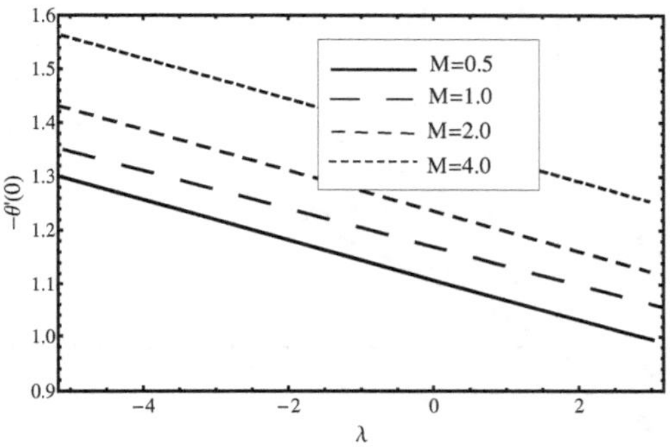


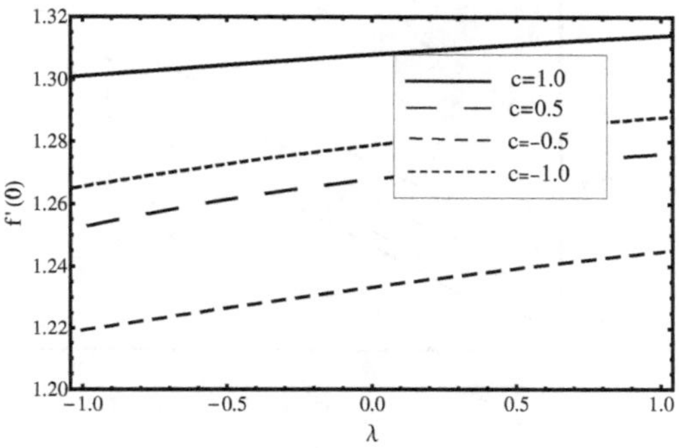


Figure 3.29: Effect of magnetic parameter on heat transfer rate with Ohmic heating.

Figure 3.30: Effect of the c on Shear stress rate in x-direction.

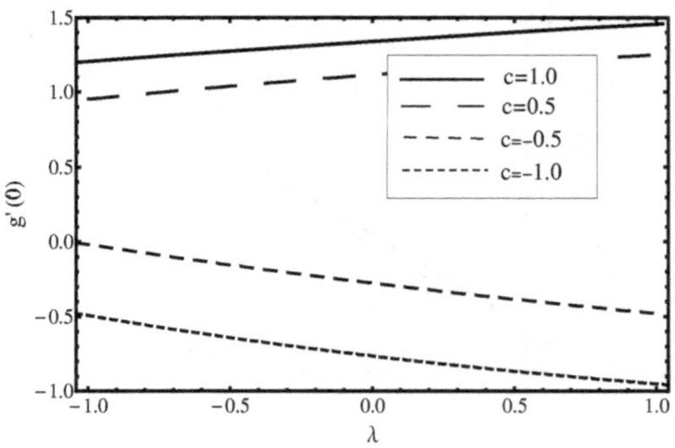


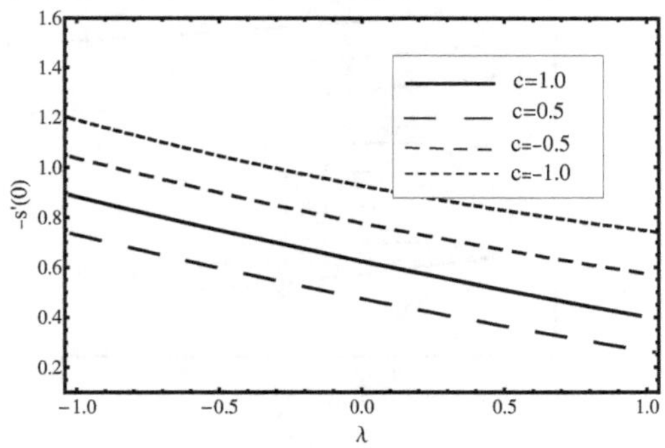


Figure 3.31: Effect of the c on Shear stress rate in y-direction.

Figure 3.32: Effect of the c on heat transfer rate without viscous dissipation.

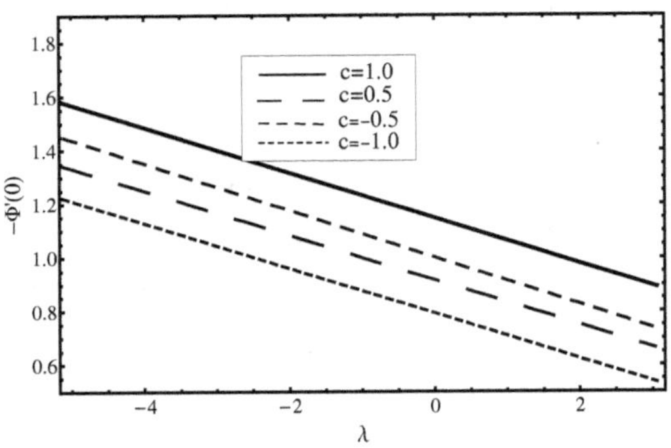


Figure 3.33: Effect of the c on heat transfer rate with viscous dissipation.

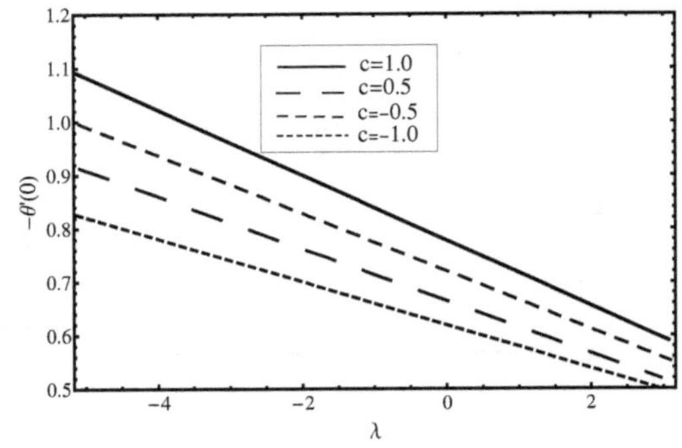


Figure 3.34: Effect of the c on heat transfer rate with Ohmic heating.

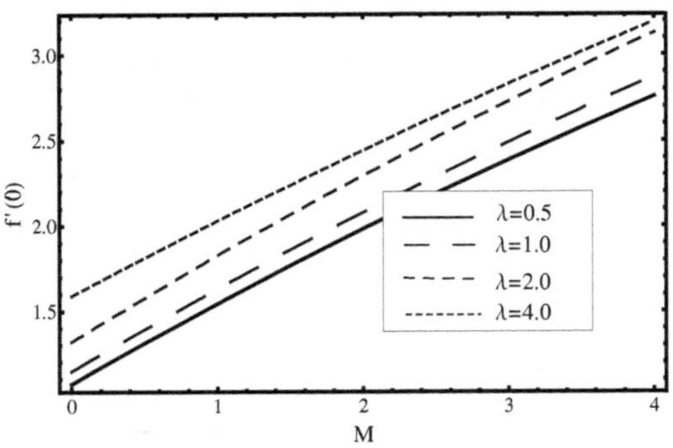


Figure 3.35: Effect of the $\lambda$ on Shear stress rate in x-direction.

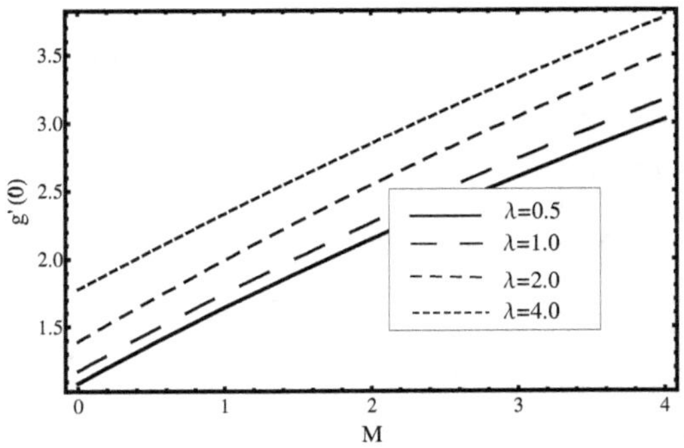


Figure 3.36: Effect of the $\lambda$ on Shear stress rate in y-direction.

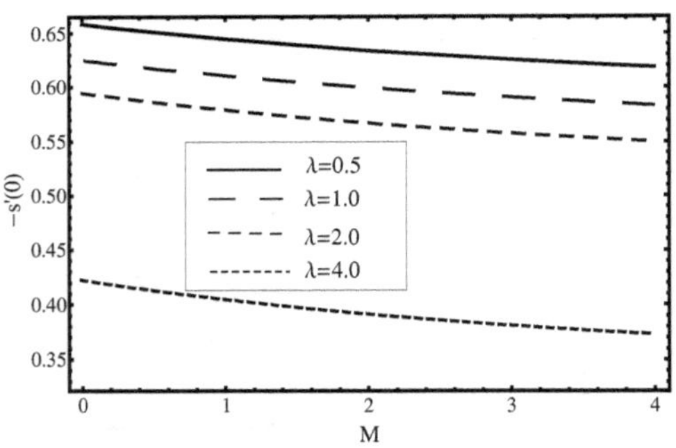


Figure 3.37: Effect of the $\lambda$ on heat transfer rate without viscous dissipation.

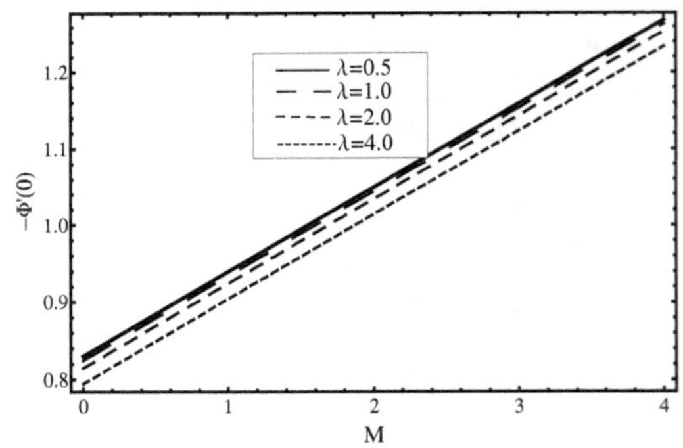


Figure 3.38: Effect of the $\lambda$ on heat transfer rate with viscous dissipation.

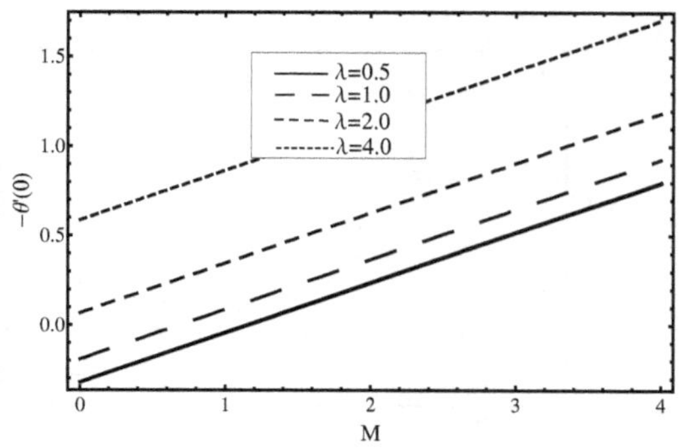


Figure 3.39: Effect of the $\lambda$ on heat transfer rate with Ohmic heating.

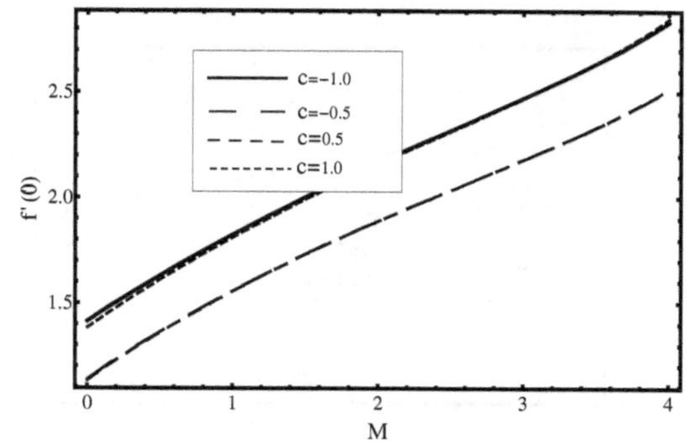


Figure 3.40: Effect of the c on Shear stress rate in x-direction.

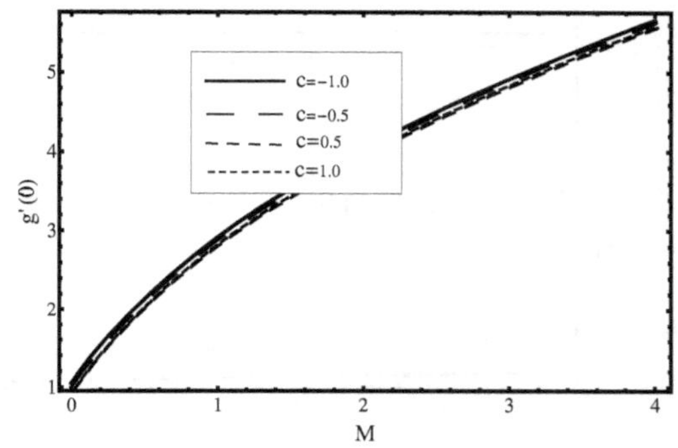


Figure 3.41: Effect of the c on Shear stress rate in y-direction.

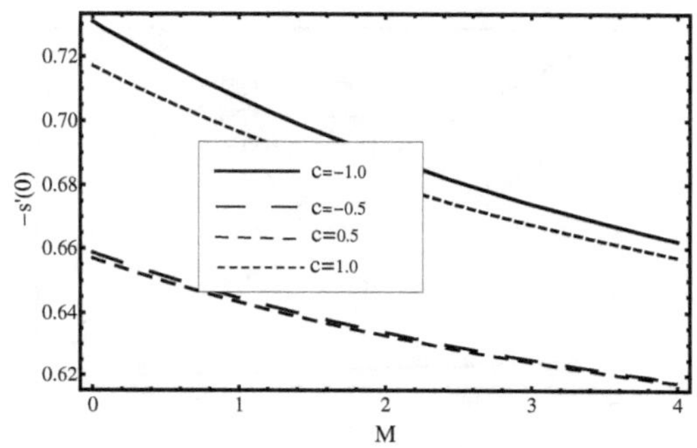


Figure 3.42: Effect of the $c$ on heat transfer rate without viscous dissipation.

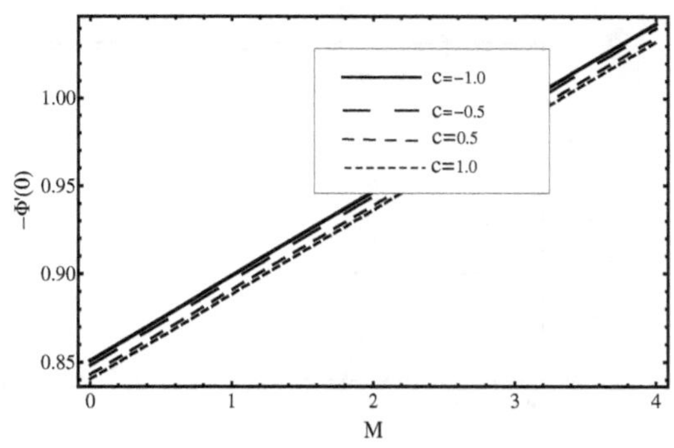


Figure 3.43: Effect of the $c$ on heat transfer rate with viscous dissipation.

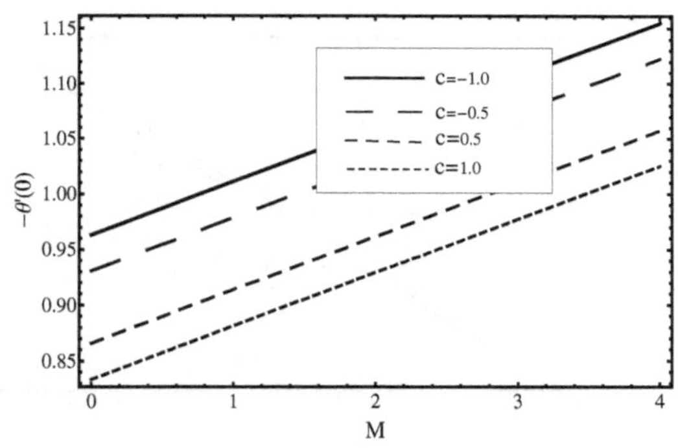


Figure 3.44: Effect of the $c$ on heat transfer rate with Ohmic heating.

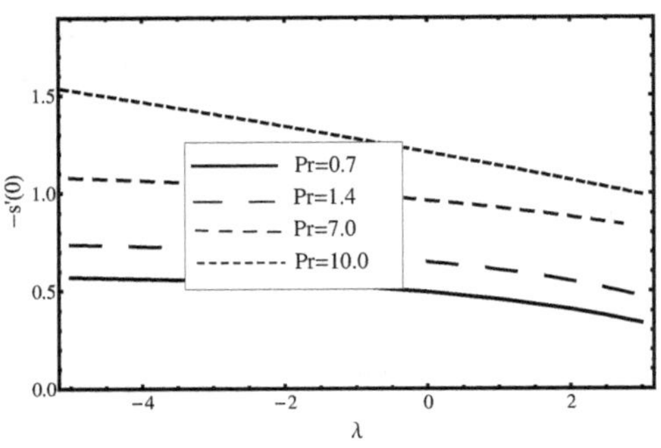


Figure 3.45: Effect of the Pr on heat transfer rate without viscous dissipation.

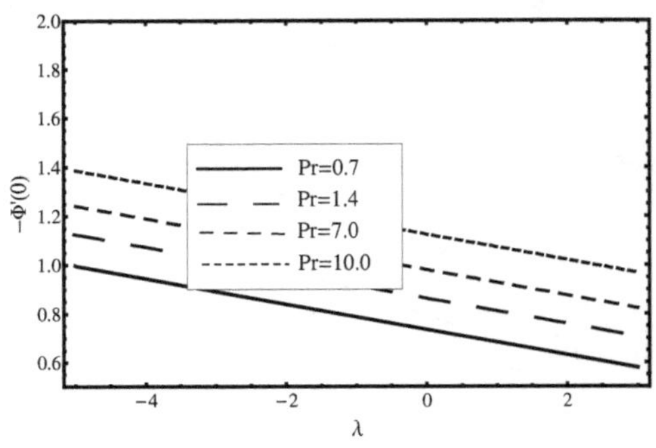


Figure 3.46: Effect of the Pr on heat transfer rate with viscous dissipation.

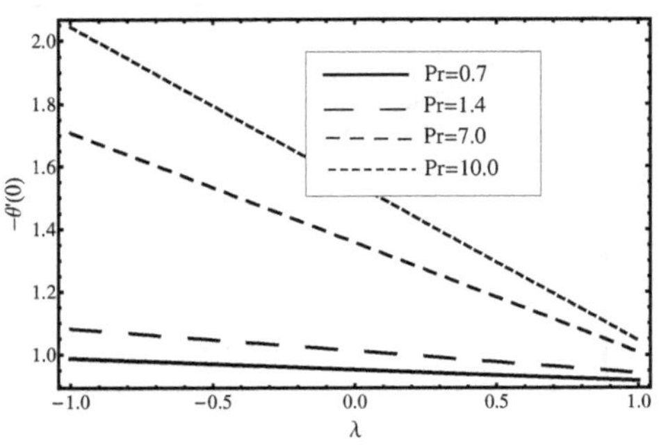


Figure 3.47: Effect of the Pr on heat transfer rate with Ohmic heating.

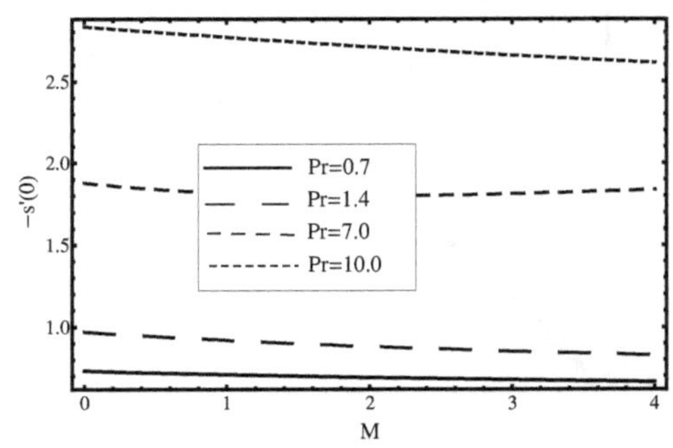


Figure 3.48: Effect of the Pr on heat transfer rate without viscous dissipation.

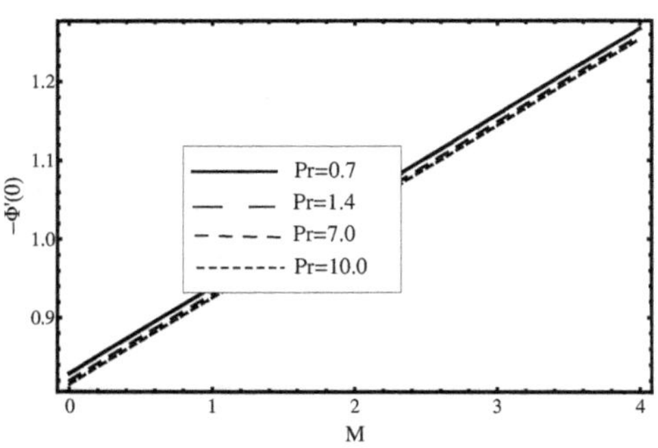


Figure 3.49: Effect of the Pr on heat transfer rate with viscous dissipation.

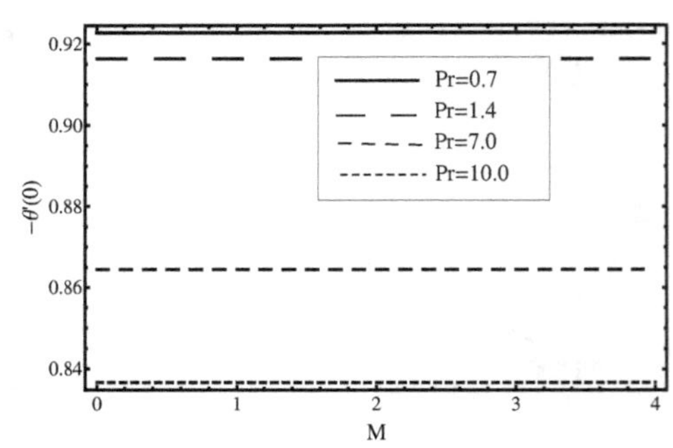


Figure 3.50: Effect of the Pr on heat transfer rate with Ohmic heating.

# Chapter 4

# Heat and mass transfer in a two-dimensional viscoelastic fluid flow due to a stretching surface

## 4.1 Abstract

In this chapter, an approximate analytical solution is derived for the flow velocity and temperature for the laminar, two-dimensional flow of non-Newtonian incompressible viscoelastic fluid due to a continuous stretching surface. The surface is stretched with a velocity proportional to the distance $x$ along the surface. The surface is assumed to have either power-law heat flux or power-law temperature distribution. The presence of source/sink and the effect of uniform suction and injection on the flow are considered for analysis. An approximate analytical solution has been obtained using HAM for various values of viscoelastic parameter, suction and injection rates. Optimal values of the convergence control parameters are computed for the flow variables. It was found that the computational time required for average residual error calculation is very very small compared to the computation time of exact squared residual errors. The effect of mass transfer parameter, viscoelastic parameter, source/sink parameter and the power law index on flow variables such as velocity, temperature profiles, shear stress, heat and mass transfer rates are discussed.

## 4.2 Introduction

In the previous two chapters we considered the newtonian fluids in which the viscous stresses arising from the flow are linearly proportional to the rate of change of its deformation at every point on the flow field. It is well known that, Newtonian fluids are the simplest mathematical models of fluids that account for viscosity. And, many common liquids and gases, such as water and air, can be assumed to be Newtonian for practical calculations under ordinary conditions.

But, the study of flow due to a non-Newtonian fluid is growing in prominence because, many fluids that we come across in everyday life are non-Newtonian in their behavior. Common non-Newtonian fluids include fluids that becomes stiffer when vigorously sheared (for ex. cornstarch) or the fluids that becomes thinner when sheared (for ex. non-drip paint). Other non Newtonian fluids include many polymer solutions and molten polymers, solid suspensions etc. Due to the importance and its applications, in the next two chapters we consider the study of non-Newtonian flows. Two engineering problems to study the flow, heat and mass transfer in a viscoelastic fluid flow due to stretching surfaces are considered for analysis.

The heat and mass transfer study over a continuously stretching surface is one of the important areas of current research. This finds its application over a broad spectrum of science and engineering disciplines, especially in the field of chemical engineering. Many chemical engineering processes like glass blowing and polymer extrusion involve cooling of a molten liquid being stretched into a cooling system. This aspect was considered by Abel *et al.* (2008). As polymer is a flexible substance, the filament surface may stretch during the course of blowing and hence the surface velocity deviates from being uniform as described by Char *et al.* (1988).

In these processes mechanical properties of the fluid play an important role in shaping the final product that would mainly depend on the cooling liquid used and the rate of stretching. Some of the polymer fluids such as Polyethylene oxide, poly-isobutylene solution in cetane are necessarily non Newtonian fluids. An utmost care has to be taken to control the rate of cooling these liquids when it is stretched to get the end product with desired characteristics. Rapid stretching would result in sudden solidification thereby making the final product more ductile where as too slow a cooling will result in the property of the product to be become more malleable. Hence the control of rate of cooling is very important in these processes.

The problem addressed here is a fundamental one that arises in many practical situations. To name some of them, drawing, annealing and tinning of copper wires, continuous stretching, rolling and manufacturing of plastic films and artificial fibres, materials manufactured by extrusion process and heat treated materials traveling between a feed roll and windup rolls or on conveyer belts, glass blowing, crystal growing, paper production as described by Seshadri *et al.* (1995).

Sakiadis (1961) was the first to study the boundary layer flow over a continuous moving surface in an ambient fluid. Due to the entrainment of ambient fluid, this boundary layer flow is quite different from the boundary layer flow over a stretching semi-infinite flat plate in a fluid with a free stream. Erickson *et al.* (1966) extended this problem to study the temperature distribution of the stretching surface in the boundary layer when the sheet is maintained at a constant temperature with suction or injection. Crane (1970) obtained an elegant analytical solution to the boundary layer equations for the problem of steady two-dimensional flows due to a stretching surface in a quiescent incompressible fluid.

Following that, several solution procedures such as analytical solutions, closed form solution, asymptotic solutions and numerical solutions on stretching surfaces for various cases of flow are available in the literature. The solution analysis for stretching surfaces in terms of finding approximate analytical solution procedure recently pick up popularity with the help of the HAM. The advantage of HAM is its independence on small physical parameters such as convergence control parameter and auxiliary parameters studied by Van *et al.* (2009). HAM can control and adjust the convergence region and rate of the homotopy solutions as envisaged by Liao (1997; 2003*b*).

To increase the efficiency of HAM, many authors have considered several analysis. Liao (2010) and Marinca *et al.* (2008), Zhao *et al.* (2013) and El-Tawil*et al.* (2013) have suggested an optimal HAM, optimal homotopy asymptotic method and modified HAM which improves the solution by reducing the CPU time as well as minimizing the residual errors.

The two-dimensional, magnetohydrodynamic non-Newtonian incompressible flow due to a stretching sheet was studied using HAM by Liao (2003*a*). Following this, several other studies using HAM are available in the open literature (Liao, 2003*c*; 2004) and Abbasbandy (2006) including one or more parameters such as magnetic effect, injection or suction.

Recently, Misra *et al.* (2010) studied the steady MHD flow of a viscoelastic fluid in a parallel channel in an uniform transverse magnetic field using perturbation analysis and numerical methods. Raftari *et al.* (2012) obtained the solution of the MHD viscoelastic fluid flow and heat transfer in a channel with a stretching wall using HAM. More researchers, Char *et al.* (1988), Seshadri *et al.* (1995), Sajid *et al.* (2011) and Hayat *et al.* (2012*a*), Shehzad *et al.* (2013*b*) have considered the heat transfer problem of viscoelastic fluid over a continuous stretching surface. Recently Prasad *et al.* (2010) have studied thermal radiation effects on viscoelastic fluid flow and heat transfer due to a stretching sheet using numerical method such as Runge-Kutta technique with Shooting method. Seshadri *et al.* (2013) employed the two-dimensional flow due to a stretching surface in a viscoelastic fluid with effect of heat and mass transfer using analytical method.

An excellent review of heat transfer papers published during 1999 and 2002 are given by Goldstein *et al.* (2001), (2005) in which the heat transfer studies due to several flows in different types of geometries under various conditions are discussed very lucidly.

After an extensive literature survey, it was realized that study of flow, heat and mass transfer of a viscoelastic fluid due to a stretching surface with important parameters such as power law variation of surface temperature or surface heat flux or presence of source and sink parameter as well as the influence of suction or injection on the flow have not been studied so far. Hence we consider the same in this chapter.

The aim of the present study is to consider the effect of the flow and heat transfer of a viscoelastic fluid over a continuous stretching surface placed in an ambient fluid. The effect of prescribed surface temperature or prescribed heat flux when the temperature has power law variation denoted by the parameter $\beta$ is considered in the presence of source or sink parameter. The governing partial differential equations have been reduced to a system of ordinary differential equations and an approximate analytical solution has been obtained using HAM.

## 4.3 Problem formulation and governing equations

This section deals with the steady laminar motion of a viscoelastic, incompressible fluid caused by the stretching of a surface in an ambient fluid. The flat surface is coincident with the plane $y = 0$, and the flow is confined to the region $y > 0$. Two equal and opposite forces are applied along the $x$-axis so that the wall is stretched but the origin remains fixed as shown in Figure. 4.1. The surface is stretched with a velocity proportional to

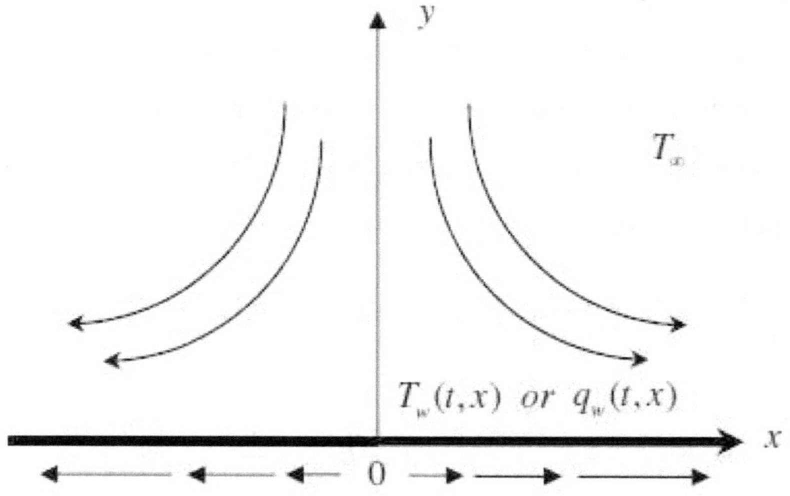


Figure 4.1: Sketch of two-dimensional coordinate system of flow.

the distance $x$ along the surface. The surface is assumed to have either power-law temperature distribution or power-law heat flux distribution. The fluid far away from the surface is kept at constant temperature.

The steady two-dimensional boundary layer equations governing the flow are

$$u_x + v_y = 0 \tag{4.1}$$

$$uu_x + vu_y = \nu u_{yy} - \lambda_1 \left[ (uu_{yy})_x + u_y v_{yy} + v u_{yyy} \right] \tag{4.2}$$

$$\rho C_p (uT_x + vT_y) = kT_{yy} + Q(T - T_\infty). \tag{4.3}$$

The boundary conditions for the problem when $x \geq 0$ are:

$$\begin{aligned} u &= Ax(A > 0),\ v = v_w,\ T = T_w \text{ or } -kT_y = q_w \text{ at } y = 0, \\ u &\to 0,\ T \to T_\infty \text{ as } y \to \infty. \end{aligned} \tag{4.4}$$

Since the problem is parabolic, the velocity $u$ and the temperature $T$ have to be prescribed at certain value of $x = x_0 (x_0 < 0)$ which are given by

$$u(x_0, y) = 0, \;\; T(x_0, y) = T_\infty. \tag{4.5}$$

Here $x$ and $y$ are distances along and perpendicular to the surface, respectively, $u$ and $v$ are the components of the velocity along the $x$-and $y$-directions, respectively, $T$ is the temperature, $Q$ is the source or sink parameter, $k$ is the thermal conductivity, $\lambda$ is the viscoelastic parameter, $\rho$ is the density, $\nu$ is the kinematic viscosity, $C_p$ is the specific heat at a constant pressure, $q_w$ is the surface heat flux, the subscripts $w$ and $\infty$ denote conditions at the surface and in the free stream, respectively.

The partial differential equations (4.1)-(4.3) under conditions (4.4) and (4.5) admit similarity solutions when the surface velocity $u_w = Ax (A > 0)$ and using the following similarity transformations

$$\eta = \left(\frac{A}{\nu}\right)^{1/2} y, \;\; u = Axf'(\eta), \;\; v = -(A\nu)^{1/2} f(\eta), \;\; T - T_\infty = (T_w - T_\infty) g(\eta),$$

$$T_w - T_\infty = (T_{w0} - T_\infty)\left(\frac{x}{L}\right)^\beta, \;\; T - T_\infty = \left(\frac{q_{w0}}{k}\right)\left(\frac{x}{L}\right)^\beta \left(\frac{\nu}{A}\right)^{1/2} G(\eta),$$

$$\lambda = \lambda_1 \frac{A}{\nu}, \;\; q_w = q_{w0}\left(\frac{x}{L}\right)^\beta, \;\; Pr = \frac{sC_p}{k}, \;\; s = \frac{Q\nu}{kA}, \;\; \alpha = -\frac{(\nu)_w}{(A\nu)^{1/2}}, \tag{4.6}$$

when these similarity transformations are applied on (4.1)-(4.3) and find that (4.1) is identically satisfied and (4.2) and (4.3) are reduced to

$$f''' + ff'' - (f')^2 = \lambda[2f'f''' - (f'')^2 - ff''''] \tag{4.7}$$

$$g'' + Prfg' - (Pr\beta f' - s)g = 0 \;\; (\text{ for the PST case}) \tag{4.8}$$

$$G'' + PrfG' - (Pr\beta f' - s)G = 0 \;\; (\text{ for the PHF case}). \tag{4.9}$$

The boundary conditions rewritten from (4.4)-(4.5) as,

$$f(0) = \alpha, \;\; f'(0) = 1, \;\; f'(\infty) = 0 \tag{4.10}$$

$$g(0) = 1, \;\; g(\infty) = 0 \quad (\text{ PST case}) \tag{4.11}$$

$$G(\infty) = 0, \;\; G'(0) = -1 \quad (\text{ PHF case}). \tag{4.12}$$

Here $\eta$ is the similarity variable, $f$ is the dimensionless stream function, $f'$ is the dimensionless velocity, $g$ and $G$ are the dimensionless temperatures, $Pr$ is the Prandtl number, $L$ is the characteristic length, $T_{w_0}$ and $q_{w_0}$ are constants, $\beta$ is the index in the power-law variation of wall temperature or heat flux, $s$ is the dimensionless source or sink parameter and prime denotes derivative with respect to $\eta$. $\alpha$ is the mass transfer parameter ($\alpha$ is a constant when $v_w$ is a constant). Also $\alpha \lesseqgtr 0$ according to whether there is suction or injection. The heat transfer coefficient of in terms of Nusselt number is expressed as

$$Nu = -\frac{(T_y)_w\, x}{T_w - T_\infty} = -(Re_x)^{1/2} g'(0) \text{ (PST case) and } Nu = \frac{(Re_x)^{\frac{1}{2}}}{G(0)} \text{ (PHF case)},$$

where $Re_x (= Ax^2/\nu)$ is the local Reynolds number.

## 4.4 Homotopy series solution

To apply the method of homotopy analysis, we choose the initial guesses and auxiliary linear operators as follows

$$f_0(\eta) = \alpha + 1 - e^{-\eta}, \; g_0(\eta) = e^{-\eta}, \; G_0(\eta) = e^{-\eta}. \tag{4.13}$$

$$L_f = \frac{d^3 f}{d\eta^3} - \frac{df}{d\eta}, \; L_g = \frac{d^2 g}{d\eta^2} - g, \; L_G = \frac{d^2 G}{d\eta^2} - G, \tag{4.14}$$

so that its solutions are simpler to evaluate analytically. They are given as

$$\begin{aligned} L_f\left[C_1 + C_2 e^{\eta} + C_3 e^{-\eta}\right] &= 0, L_g\left[C_4 e^{\eta} + C_5 e^{-\eta}\right] = 0, \\ L_G\left[C_6 e^{\eta} + C_7 e^{-\eta}\right] &= 0, \end{aligned} \tag{4.15}$$

where $C_i$ are arbitrary constants and can be obtained using (4.10)-(4.12).

### 4.4.1 Zeroth-order deformation problem

To obtain the HAM solution for the eqs. (4.7)-(4.9), let $\gamma \in [0,1]$ be an embedding parameter and $c_f$, $c_g$ and $c_G$ are the basic convergence control parameters. Then the zeroth order deformation equation and the non-linear operators become,

$$(1-\gamma) L_X[X(\eta,\gamma) - X_0(\eta)] = \gamma c_X \mathcal{N}_X[X(\eta,\gamma)], \tag{4.16}$$

where, $X = f,\ g$ and $G$ and $X_0 = f_0, g_0$ and $G_0$.

$$\begin{aligned}
\mathcal{N}_f[f(\eta,\gamma)] &= \frac{\partial^3 f(\eta,\gamma)}{\partial\eta^3} + f(\eta,\gamma)\frac{\partial^2 f(\eta,\gamma)}{\partial\eta^2} - \left(\frac{\partial f(\eta,\gamma)}{\partial\eta}\right)^2 \\
&- \lambda\left(2\frac{\partial f(\eta,\gamma)}{\partial\eta}\frac{\partial^3 f(\eta,\gamma)}{\partial\eta^3} - \left(\frac{\partial^2 f(\eta,\gamma)}{\partial^2\eta}\right)^2\right) \\
&+ \lambda\left(f(\eta,\gamma)\frac{\partial^4 f(\eta,\gamma)}{\partial\eta^4}\right) \qquad (4.17)
\end{aligned}$$

$$\begin{aligned}
\mathcal{N}_g[g(\eta,\gamma), f(\eta,\gamma)] &= \frac{\partial^2 g(\eta,\gamma)}{\partial\eta^2} + Pr\left(f(\eta,\gamma)\frac{\partial g(\eta,\gamma)}{\partial\eta}\right) \\
&- g(\eta,\gamma)\left(Pr\beta\frac{\partial f(\eta,\gamma)}{\partial\eta} - s(\eta,\gamma)\right) \qquad (4.18)
\end{aligned}$$

$$\begin{aligned}
\mathcal{N}_G[G(\eta,\gamma), f(\eta,\gamma)] &= \frac{\partial^2 G(\eta,\gamma)}{\partial\eta^2} + Pr\left(f(\eta,\gamma)\frac{\partial G(\eta,\gamma)}{\partial\eta}\right) \\
&- G(\eta,\gamma)\left(Pr\beta\frac{\partial f(\eta,\gamma)}{\partial\eta} - s(\eta,\gamma)\right), \qquad (4.19)
\end{aligned}$$

with appropriate boundary conditions rewritten from (4.10)-(4.12) as,

$$f(\eta;\gamma)|_{\eta=0} = \alpha,\ \left.\frac{\partial f(\eta;\gamma)}{\partial\eta}\right|_{\eta=0} = 1,\ \left.\frac{\partial f(\eta;\gamma)}{\partial\eta}\right|_{\eta=\infty} = 0 \qquad (4.20)$$

$$g(\eta;\gamma)|_{\eta=0} = 1, g(\eta;\gamma)|_{\eta=\infty} = 0, \qquad \text{(PST case)} \qquad (4.21)$$

$$G(\eta;\gamma)|_{\eta=\infty} = 0,\ \left.\frac{\partial G(\eta;\gamma)}{\partial\eta}\right|_{\eta=0} = -1 \quad \text{(PHF case)}. \qquad (4.22)$$

### 4.4.2 Higher-order deformation problem

For obtaining the $\ell^{th}$-order deformation equations, differentiate (4.16) $\ell$-times with respect to $\gamma$, and divide by $\ell!$. Setting $\gamma = 0$, we get

$$L_X[X_\ell(\eta) - \Omega_\ell X_{\ell-1}(\eta)] = c_X \mathcal{R}_\ell^X(\eta). \qquad (4.23)$$

The boundary conditions can be redefined as

$$\begin{aligned}
f_\ell(0) &= \alpha,\ f_\ell'(0) = 1,\ f_\ell'(\infty) = 0, \\
g_\ell(0) &= 1,\ g_\ell(\infty) = 0 \qquad \text{(PST case)} \\
G_\ell(\infty) &= 0,\ G_\ell'(0) = -1 \quad \text{(PHF case)}, \qquad (4.24)
\end{aligned}$$

In (4.23), the term $\mathscr{R}_X^\ell(\eta)$ denotes $\mathscr{R}_\ell^f(\eta)$, $\mathscr{R}_\ell^g(\eta)$ and $\mathscr{R}_\ell^G(\eta)$. These are the remainder terms from the linear operators which are given by

$$\begin{aligned}\mathscr{R}_\ell^f(\eta) &= f'''_{\ell-1}(\eta)+\sum_{j=0}^{\ell-1}[f_{\ell-1-j}f''_j - f'_{\ell-1-j}f'_j] \\ &- \lambda\sum_{j=0}^{\ell-1}[2f'_{\ell-1-j}f'''_j + f''_{\ell-1-j}f''_j + f_{\ell-1-j}f''''_j]\end{aligned} \tag{4.25}$$

$$\mathscr{R}_\ell^g(\eta) = g''_{\ell-1}(\eta)+Pr\sum_{j=0}^{\ell-1}[f_{\ell-1-j}g'_j] - \beta Pr\sum_{j=0}^{\ell-1}[f'_{\ell-1-j}g_j] + sg_{\ell-1}(\eta) \tag{4.26}$$

$$\mathscr{R}_\ell^G(\eta) = G''_{\ell-1}(\eta)+Pr\sum_{j=0}^{\ell-1}[f_{\ell-1-j}G'_j] - \beta Pr\sum_{j=0}^{\ell-1}[f'_{\ell-1-j}G_j] + sG_{\ell-1}(\eta), \tag{4.27}$$

where $\Omega_\ell$ defines as

$$\Omega_\ell = \begin{cases} 0 & \text{if } \ell \le 1 \\ 1 & \text{if } \ell > 1. \end{cases} \tag{4.28}$$

Expanding $X(\eta;\gamma)$ with respect to $\gamma$ using Taylor's series, we get

$$X(\eta;\gamma) = X_0(\eta)+\sum_{\ell=1}^{\infty}X_\ell(\eta)\gamma^\ell, \quad X_\ell(\eta) = \frac{1}{\ell!}\frac{\partial^\ell X(\eta;\gamma)}{\partial\gamma^\ell}\bigg|_{\gamma=0}. \tag{4.29}$$

The auxiliary parameters are selected as $\gamma = 0$ and $\gamma = 1$ from (4.16), we get

$$X(\eta;0) = X_0(\eta), \quad X(\eta;1) = X(\eta). \tag{4.30}$$

Thus as $\gamma$ increases from 0 to 1 and $X(\eta;\gamma)$ varies from the initial guess $X_0(\eta)$ to the solution $X(\eta)$ of the governing equations respectively. The auxiliary parameters are selected so that the series solutions converge for $\gamma = 1$ and the particular solution is

$$X(\eta) = X_0(\eta)+\sum_{\ell=1}^{\infty}X_\ell(\eta). \tag{4.31}$$

Therefore, we get the general approximate analytical solutions $f_\ell,\ g_\ell,\ G_\ell$ in terms of special solutions $f_\ell^*,\ g_\ell^*,\ G_\ell^*$ are given by

$$f_\ell(\eta) = f_\ell^*(\eta)+C_1+C_2e^\eta+C_3e^{-\eta}, \tag{4.32}$$

$$g_\ell(\eta) = g_\ell^*(\eta)+C_4e^\eta+C_5e^{-\eta}, \tag{4.33}$$

$$G_\ell(\eta) = G_\ell^*(\eta)+C_6e^\eta+C_7e^{-\eta}. \tag{4.34}$$

By solving (4.32)-(4.34) one after the other in the order $\ell = 1,2,3,...$ by means of the symbolic computation software Mathematica. It is shown that the solution for the profiles can expressed as an infinite series of any desired order. The approximate analytical solutions computed for $f,\ g$ and $G$ for $\ell = 1,2,3,...$ are given in **Appendix-C**.

### 4.4.3 The error estimation at high orders

An optimal value of the convergence control parameter $c_X$, integrated in the whole region $[0,\infty)$ have the exact squared residual errors at $\ell^{th}$-order of approximations. we get

$$\Delta_\ell = \int_0^{+\infty}\left(N\left[\sum_{i=0}^{\ell} X_i(\eta)\right]\right)^2 d\eta \tag{4.35}$$

where $X = f$, $g$ and $G$.

At every $\ell^{th}$-order of approximation, $\Delta_\ell$ takes at most three convergence control parametric values for eq. (4.32) and at most two for (4.33) and (4.34). The convergence control parameters are represented by $c_f$, $c_g$ and $c_G$ for (4.7), (4.8) and (4.9), respectively. When $\Delta_\ell$ decreases to zero rapidly then the homotopy series solutions converges faster.

At the $\ell^{th}$-order, the optimal values of $c_X$ are computed by the minimum of the squared residual $\Delta_\ell$ of the governing equations, corresponding to (1.18).

Whenever, the (4.31) is known to be convergent series, the (4.32)-(4.34) represent the exact solution of governing equations. But, (4.35) requires too much CPU time to compute the exact squared residual errors even for the low order of approximation. It is observed that, it needs 42.31, 296.86 and 965.116 seconds of CPU time for $\ell = 2, 4$ and 6 respectively and therefore not very useful in practice.

The exact squared residual errors computed using (4.35) and convergence control parameters (i.e, $c_f$, $c_g$ and $c_G$) at the $10^{th}$, $16^{th}$ and $20^{th}$-order approximation are as shown in Figures. 4.2-4.4. The exact squared residual errors increase in the region of $c_f \in [-1.5, -0.9]$, decrease in the region of $c_g \in [-1.8, -1.0]$ and increase in the region of $c_G \in [-1.9, -0.6]$ as the order of approximation increases, which shows that the series solution converges for $c_f$, $c_g$ and $c_G$ at arbitrary values. The exact squared residual attains its minimum values at $c_f = -1.25846$, $c_g = -1.02823$ and $c_G = -1.0262$. These calculations not only give the efficiency region of the convergence control parameters but also their appropriate values to enable faster convergence of the solution series. The same analysis has been carried out for average squared residual errors using (1.17).

Table 4.1 gives the minimum of the average squared residual errors for $E_f$, $E_g$ and $E_G$ for different orders of approximation. The minimum value of these average squared residuals for the computation of series solutions for $f$, $g$ and $G$ respectively are found to be $(E_f)_{\ell=10} = 9.65429 \times 10^{-19}$, $(E_g)_{\ell=14} = 6.31826 \times 10^{-20}$ and $(E_G)_{\ell=10} = 9.26369 \times 10^{-16}$ at $c_f = -1.25846$, $c_g = -1.02823$ and $c_G = -1.0262$.

In particular, for the case of $\ell \leq 6$, it takes only 0.22801, 1.43008 and 4.01023 seconds of computing time to get optimal convergence control values (using eq. (1.17)) for $\ell = 2, 4$ and 6 respectively. This is much much smaller compared to the CPU time needed to compute exact residual errors (using (4.35) for the same set of $\ell = 2, 4$ and 6 which are found to be 42.31, 296.86 and 965.116 seconds, respectively. Hence by using (1.17) to calculate the average squared residuals use only 0.53% of CPU time for $\ell = 2$; 0.48% of CPU time for $\ell = 4$ and 0.41% of CPU time for $\ell = 6$ compared to exact squared residual errors computation using (4.35). It is found that, the CPU time required to compute errors using eq. (1.17) is much less than that of using (4.35). Hence, use only (1.17) to find the convergence control parameters for entire calculations.

The average squared residual errors at different orders of approximation for $f(\eta)$, $g(\eta)$ and $G(\eta)$ are shown as Figure. 4.5. The corresponding average squared residual decreases much more quickly with convergence control parameters $c_f = -1.25846$, $c_g = -1.02823$ and $c_G = -1.0262$. Therefore, the suitable choice of convergence control parameter can greatly accelerate the convergence of series solution in HAM.

In all of the figures, we use $Pr = 0.7$, $s = 0.1$, $\lambda = 0.2$, $\alpha = 0.1$ and $\beta = 0.5$ unless it is mentioned otherwise.

## 4.5 Results Analysis

The approximate analytical solutions are obtained in the form of general series for the flow variables $f$, $g$ and $G$. The approximate analytical solutions for the velocity and temperature are obtained in the form of a power series solution using computational software **Mathematica**. The expressions for $f$, $g$ and $G$ are evaluated up to tenth order to keep the results up to seven decimal places accuracy.

Here the effect of various parameters such as viscoelastic parameter $\lambda$, mass transfer parameter $\alpha$, heat flux parameter $\beta$, Prandtl number $Pr$ and effect of source/sink in PST and PHF cases are analysed. The influence of these parameters on velocity and temperature profiles as well as in shear stress rate and surface heat transfer rates discussed. Computations have been carried out for velocity and temperature profiles and for shear stress rates and heat transfer rates for several combinations of parameters $\lambda$, $\alpha$, $\beta$, $Pr$ and $s$, and all the results are reported in the form of Tables 4.1-4.4 and Figures. 4.6-4.34 in the following part of the chapter. It is found that, velocity and temperature profiles increases with the increase in viscoelastic parameter values. The heat transfer decreases as the injection and suction rates are raised. The effect of increasing viscoelastic parameter increase the heat transfer rates on the surface.

Table 4.2 illustrates the convergence of skin friction $-f''(0)$, surface heat transfer $-g'(0)$ and $-G'(0)$ after performing up to $35^{th}$-order approximation of functions $f$, $g$ and $G$ computed from deformation equations. Table 4.3 shows the comparison of numerical values (using Runge-Kutta Method) of skin friction results with that of Prasad *et al.* (2010) for the available values of the viscoelastic parameters and the results are found to be satisfactory.

It is seen from Table 4.4 that the heat transfer rates for different Prandtl numbers (and for two different values of mass transfer) for a fixed $\beta = 3.0$ is compared in the absence of viscoelastic parameter with that of Char *et al.* (1988). It is found that the values of the heat transfer coefficients in terms of local Nusselt number are small for $Pr = 0.01$ in comparison to the values for $Pr = 1.0$. This means that the values of the local Nusselt number increases with the increase in Prandtl number.

The Figures. 4.6-4.17 show the effect of the study parameters on the velocity, temperature profiles and 4.18-4.34 show the variation of shear stresses and heat transfer rate for the power law variation of both prescribed surface temperature (PST) and prescribed heat flux (PHF) cases.

The effect of viscoelastic parameter and mass transfer parameter on velocity and temperature profiles are plotted in Figures. 4.6 and 4.9. There is a slight undershoot in velocity profiles as $\lambda$ increases, but the increase in mass transfer parameter $\alpha$ makes the velocity profiles to converge faster to its free stream values. 4.7-4.8 and 4.10-4.17 depict the temperature profiles for the both PST and for PHF cases for different values of $\lambda$, $\alpha$, $s$, $\beta$ and $Pr$. It is seen from 4.7-4.8 that the viscoelastic parameter increases the thickness of the temperature boundary layer whereas the temperature boundary layer thins down for a higher mass transfer parametric values.

From 4.10 to 4.11 demonstrate that an increasing values suction ($\alpha < 0$), the profiles tend to approach to the free stream values faster where as in the case of injection ($\alpha > 0$) there is a slight overshoot in the temperature profiles close to the wall and then it gradually approaches to free stream values.

The temperature variation for PST and for PHF cases by for different source/sink parameter $s$ is presented in 4.12-4.13. There is a temperature overshoot as $s$ increases for both PST and PHF cases, but the values are higher for PHF compared to PST. The temperature variation for PST and PHF cases for different $\beta$ and Prandtl numbers $Pr$ are presented in 4.16-4.17. Temperature increase as $\beta$ and $Pr$ increases for both PST and PHF cases, but the values are higher for PHF compared to PST.

The influence of mass transfer parameter $\alpha$ and viscoelastic parameter $\lambda$ on shear stress rates plotted in 4.18. Here, the shear stress rate increases with the increase in the values of $\alpha$ and $\lambda$. But the rate of increase is rather slow for viscoelastic parameter compared to the mass transfer values. The effect of heat transfer rates for the both PST and PHF cases, for various values of $\alpha$, $s$, $\beta$ and $Pr$ and viscoelastic parameters $\lambda$ are plotted in 4.19-4.26. It is found that the heat transfer rate is not affected much by the change in the viscoelastic parameter for a given value of $\alpha$, $s$, $\beta$ and $Pr$. However, the heat transfer rate increases as the source/sink parameter increase and decrease as the parameters $\alpha$, $\beta$ and $Pr$ value increases for a given $\lambda$. The plots clearly depict that for a fixed value of any one these parameters $\alpha$ or $s$ or $\beta$ or $Pr$, the variation of the heat transfer rate for the change in viscoelastic parameter is negligible. But for a fixed $\lambda$, the change in the heat transfer rate with respect to each of these parameters is that doubling any one of its values results in at least 40% increase in the heat transfer values.

The effect of heat transfer rate for the both PST and PHF cases, for various values of $\alpha$, $s$, $\beta$ and $Pr$ are plotted in 4.27-4.34. The variation of heat transfer rates for the both PST and PHF cases versus $\beta$ for various values of viscoelastic parameter presented in 4.27-4.28 shows the increase in heat transfer rates for increase on $\lambda$ as well as $\beta$.

Figures. 4.29-4.34 present the heat transfer rate for the both PST and PHF for different values of $\alpha$, $s$ and $Pr$ with respect to the change in the power law index $\beta$. The heat transfer rate increases as the source/sink parameter and decreases but the trend is reversed when $\alpha$ and $Pr$ value increases for a given $\beta$. Thus by a suitable choice of the parametric values $\alpha$, $s$ and $Pr$, $\beta$, it is possible to control the skin friction and heat transfer values there by alter the rate of change of cooling of the stretching surface.

## 4.6 Summary

The flow, heat and mass transfer analysis is carried out on a viscoelastic flow over a continuous stretching surface in an ambient fluid. Using HAM, a series solution in the form of polynomials are derived for velocity $f$ and temperature $g$ and $G$ with the wall normal height $\eta$ as a variable of the polynomial. The coefficients of the polynomial contain all the other parameters such as $\lambda$, $\beta$, $s$ and $\alpha$. The computations have been carried out to retain at least up to $15^{th}$ order in $\eta$ in the polynomial expressions of $f$, $g$ and $G$ to get the results accurate up to seventh decimal place. The computer algebra software Mathematica is used to perform these semi-analytical calculations.

The effect of various parameters such as mass transfer parameters $\alpha$, viscoelastic parameters $\lambda$ are studied on flow velocities. The influence of power law variation $\beta$ on the surface temperatures and surface heat fluxes, the presence of source/sink parameter $s$ are analysed. The effect of Prandtl number $Pr$ on the temperature profiles and heat transfer rates are also studied. Thus the present study helps in identifying a suitable parameter that can be used to increase or decrease the heat transfer rate of the continuously stretching surface thereby enhancing the final product to a desired characteristics. Viscoelastic parameter, heat and mass transfer parameters helps in controlling the boundary layer thickness of both velocity and temperature profiles.

The following conclusions are drawn from the present study.

- The velocity profiles decreases for the increase in viscoelastic parameter and mass transfer parameter values whereas the trend is quite opposite for the temperature profiles. The undershoot that occurs in the velocity profiles for higher values of viscoelastic parameters can be suppressed by a suitable choice of mass transfer parameter.

- The temperature profiles increases for the increase in the values of mass transfer parameter and source/sink parameter where as it decreases for the increase in the values of power law index on temperature and Prandtl number.

- Similarly, the overshoot in temperature profiles that occur for higher values of source/sink parameter for PST and PHF cases can be controlled by increasing the injection or suction rate in the flow or by the slight change in the power law index.

- Also, higher Prandtl number fluids influence the thinner thermal boundary layer thereby reducing the heat transfer rates.

- The shear stress rates decreases for the increase in the values of viscoelastic parameter for any fixed value of mass transfer parameter.

- The heat transfer rates increases for the increase in mass transfer parameter, heat flux and Prandtl number, but decreases for the increase in viscoelastic parameter and source/sink parameter. Another observation is that the heat transfer rates show similar trend for both PST and PHF cases for the change of all the parameters but the heat transfer values for PHF case is always at a lower value compared to that of PST case.

Table 4.1: Minimum of the averaged squared residual error $E_f$, $E_g$ and $E_G$ with the CPU time at fixed $c_f = -1.25846$, $c_g = -1.02823$ and $c_G = -1.0262$.

| $\ell$ | Minimum of Averaged Squared Residual Errors | | | |
|---|---|---|---|---|
| | CPU time(Sec.) | $E_f$ | $E_g$ | $E_G$ |
| 2 | 0.22801 | $3.06471 \times 10^{-7}$ | $2.22635 \times 10^{-7}$ | $8.3716 \times 10^{-7}$ |
| 4 | 1.43008 | $1.82403 \times 10^{-10}$ | $1.26878 \times 10^{-10}$ | $2.49866 \times 10^{-10}$ |
| 6 | 4.01023 | $2.17438 \times 10^{-13}$ | $1.34723 \times 10^{-11}$ | $1.30498 \times 10^{-11}$ |
| 8 | 8.20247 | $4.06611 \times 10^{-16}$ | $1.42224 \times 10^{-12}$ | $2.82727 \times 10^{-12}$ |
| 10 | 13.8808 | $9.65429 \times 10^{-19}$ | $1.09374 \times 10^{-16}$ | $9.26369 \times 10^{-16}$ |
| 12 | 22.0793 | $2.60275 \times 10^{-21}$ | $1.16563 \times 10^{-18}$ | $1.26017 \times 10^{-18}$ |
| 14 | 32.2448 | $7.91939 \times 10^{-24}$ | $6.31826 \times 10^{-20}$ | $7.31169 \times 10^{-20}$ |
| 16 | 43.3805 | $2.75127 \times 10^{-26}$ | $5.07436 \times 10^{-22}$ | $1.25455 \times 10^{-21}$ |

Table 4.2: Convergence of HAM solution for different orders of approximation for $-f''(0)$, $-g'(0)$ and $-G'(0)$ when ( $\alpha = 0.1$, $\beta = 0.5$ and $s = 0.1$, $\lambda = 0.2$).

| $\ell$ | $-f''(0)$ | $-g'(0)$ | $-G'(0)$ |
|---|---|---|---|
| 1 | 1.1280000 | 0.6750000 | 0.4055992 |
| 5 | 1.1998968 | 0.6139803 | 0.4115234 |
| 10 | 1.2014585 | 0.6012477 | 0.4115303 |
| 15 | 1.2014756 | 0.6012218 | 0.4115304 |
| 20 | 1.2014757 | 0.6012215 | 0.4115304 |
| 25 | 1.2014758 | 0.6012213 | 0.4115304 |
| 30 | 1.2014758 | 0.6012213 | 0.4115304 |
| 35 | 1.2014758 | 0.6012213 | 0.4115304 |

Table 4.3: Comparison of shear stress rate $-f''(0)$ for various values of viscoelastic parameter when ( $\alpha = 0.0$, $\beta = 0.5$ and $s = 0.1$).

| $\lambda$ | $-f''(0)$ | |
|---|---|---|
| | Prasad *et al.* (2010) | Present HAM |
| 0.0 | — | 1.0000000 |
| 0.1 | 1.0663694 | 1.0658414 |
| 0.2 | 1.1113553 | 1.1116667 |
| 0.3 | 1.1909626 | 1.1904193 |
| 0.4 | — | 1.2773057 |
| 0.5 | — | 1.3798041 |

Table 4.4: Comparison of heat transfer rates($-g'(0)$) for different $Pr$, when ($s = 0.0$, $\lambda = 0.0$ and $\beta = 3.0$).

| $-g'(0)$ | | | | |
|---|---|---|---|---|
| $Pr$ | Char *et al.* (1988) | | Present HAM | |
| | $\alpha = 0.7$ | $\alpha = 2.0$ | $\alpha = 0.7$ | $\alpha = 2.0$ |
| 0.01 | 0.047667 | 0.034729 | 0.0474709 | 0.0347462 |
| 0.10 | 0.352134 | 0.326386 | 0.3519053 | 0.3261310 |
| 0.72 | 1.150099 | 1.854735 | 1.1508700 | 1.8546038 |
| 1.00 | 1.342679 | 2.429752 | 1.3421119 | 2.4266375 |

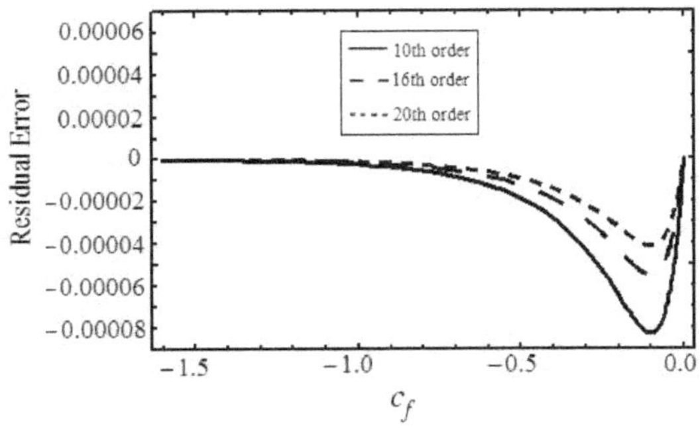


Figure 4.2: Exact residual error for the function $f(\eta)$.

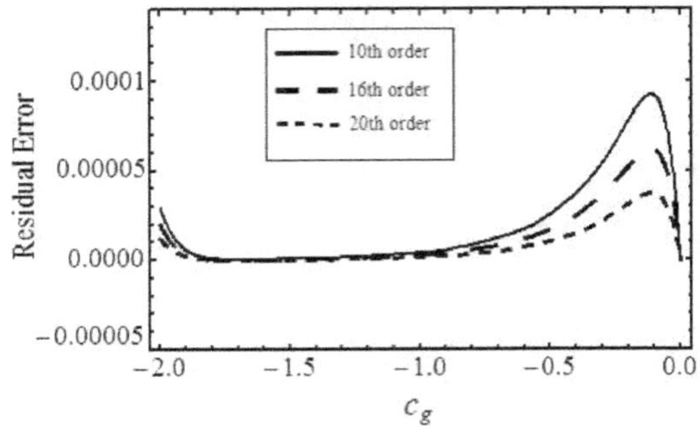


Figure 4.3: Exact residual error for the function $g(\eta)$.

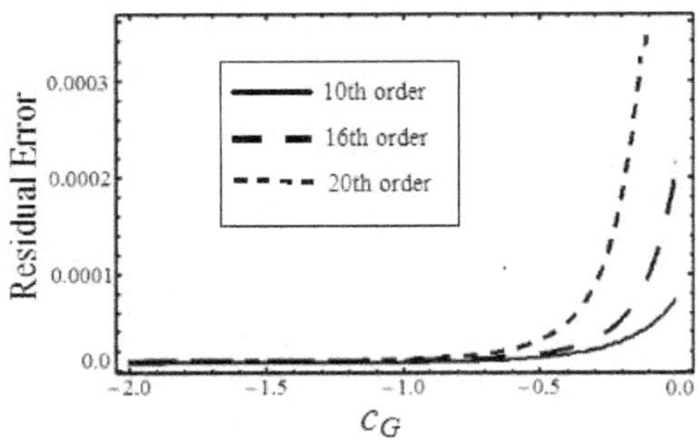


Figure 4.4: Exact residual error for the function $G(\eta)$.

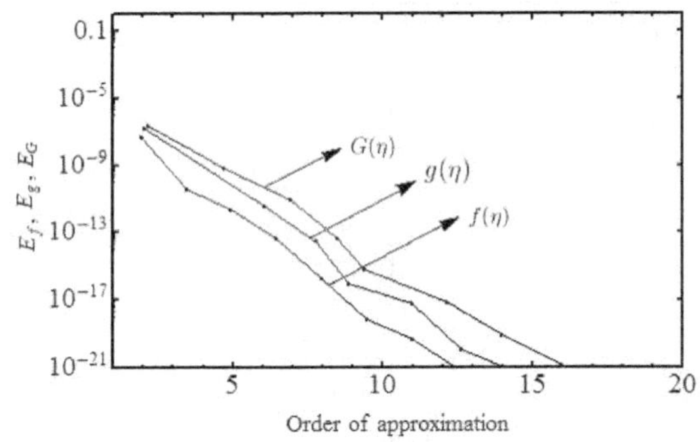


Figure 4.5: Averaged squared residual error at different order of approximations.

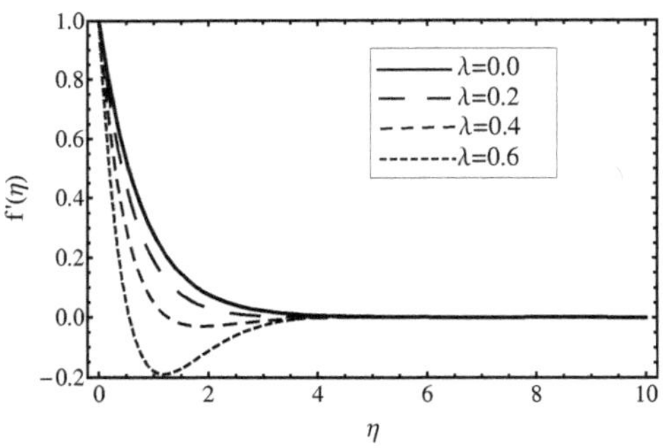


Figure 4.6: Effect of viscoelastic parameter on velocity profiles.

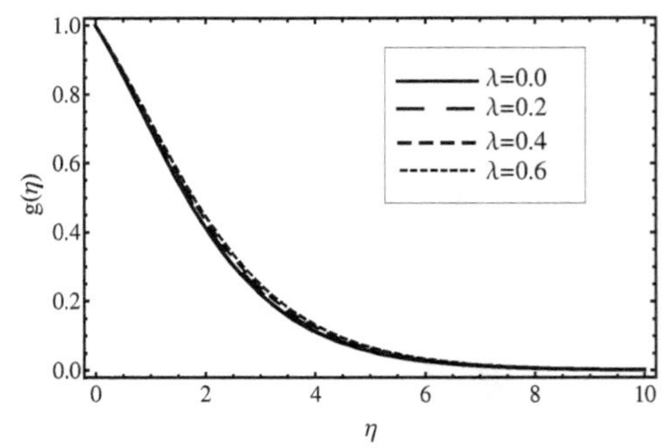


Figure 4.7: Effect of viscoelastic parameter on temperature profiles (PST case).

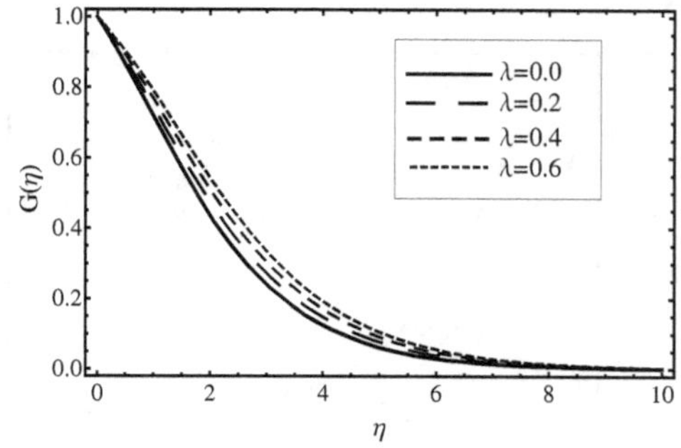


Figure 4.8: Effect of viscoelastic parameter on temperature profiles (PHF case).

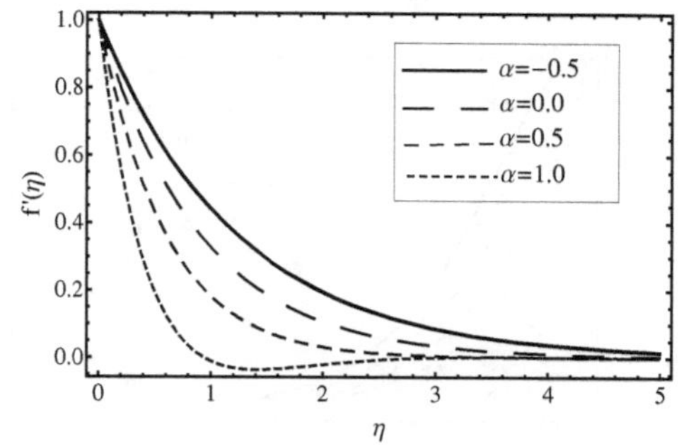


Figure 4.9: Effect of mass transfer parameter on velocity profiles.

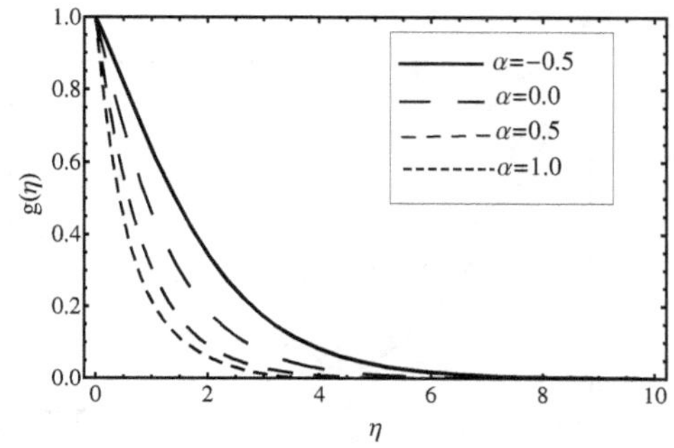


Figure 4.10: Effect of mass transfer parameter on temperature profiles (PST case).

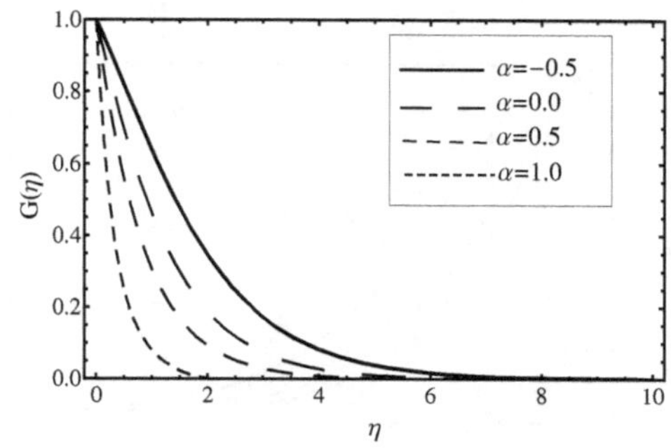


Figure 4.11: Effect of mass transfer parameter on temperature profiles (PHF case).

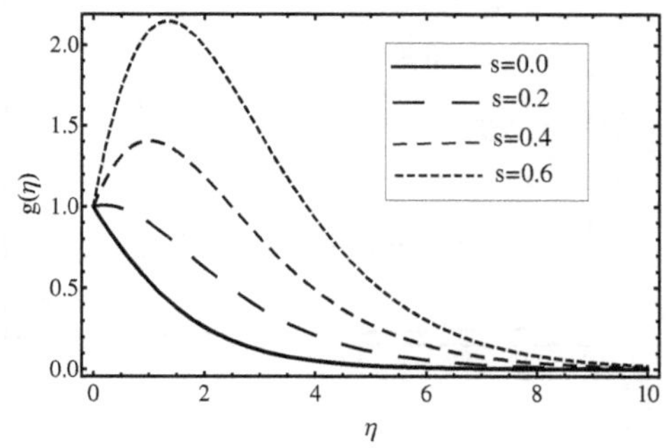


Figure 4.12: Effect of source/sink on heat transfer rate (PST case).

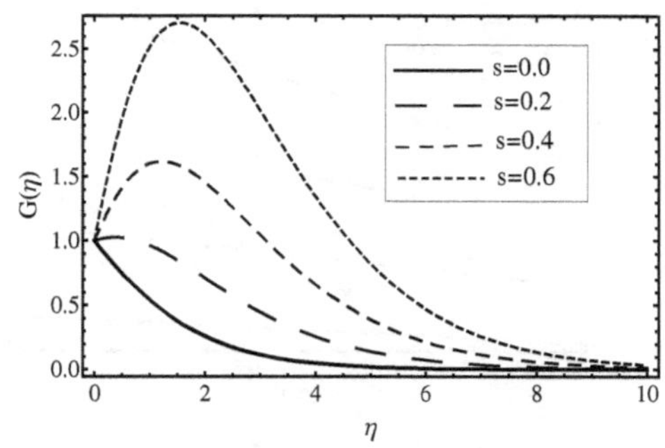


Figure 4.13: Effect of source/sink on heat transfer rate (PHF case).

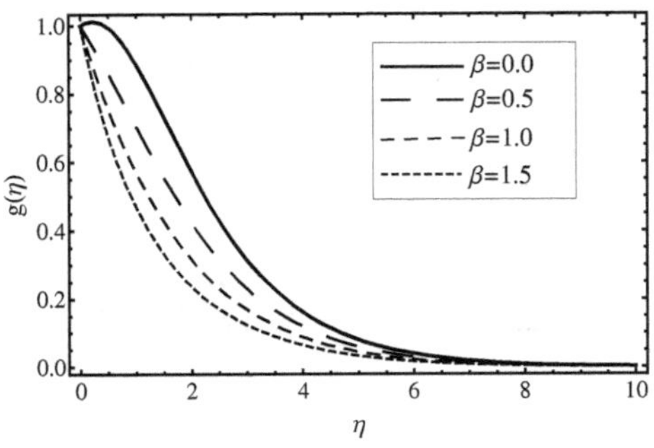


Figure 4.14: Effect of heat flux on heat transfer rate (PST case).

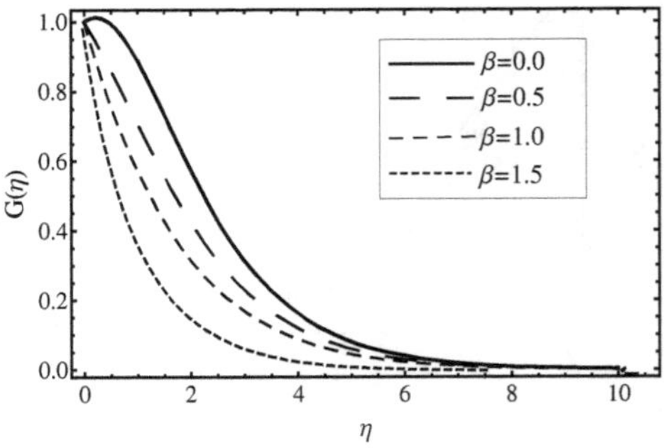


Figure 4.15: Effect of heat flux on heat transfer rate (PHF case).

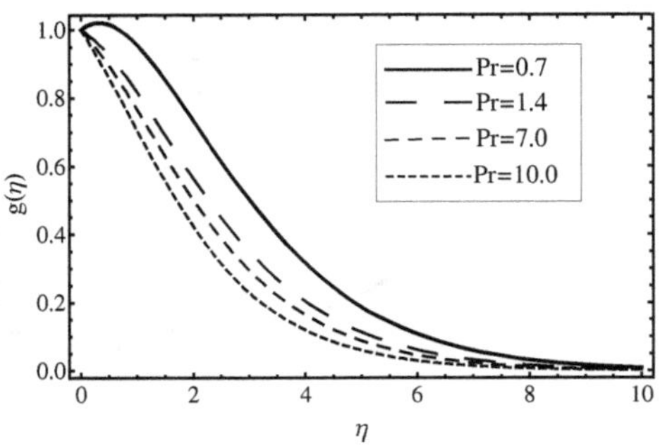


Figure 4.16: Effect of Prandtl number on temperature profile (PST case).

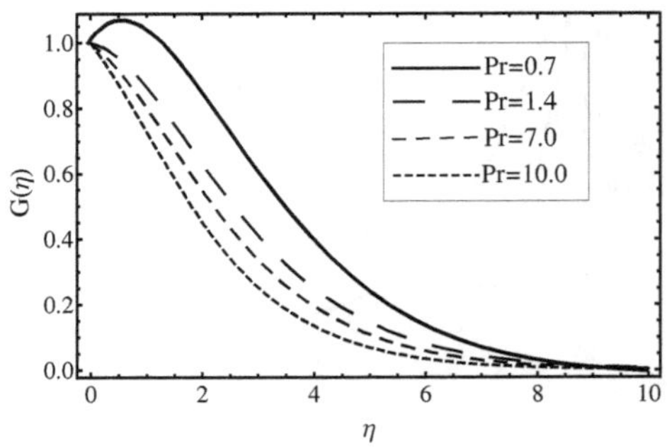


Figure 4.17: Effect of Prandtl number on temperature profile (PHF case).

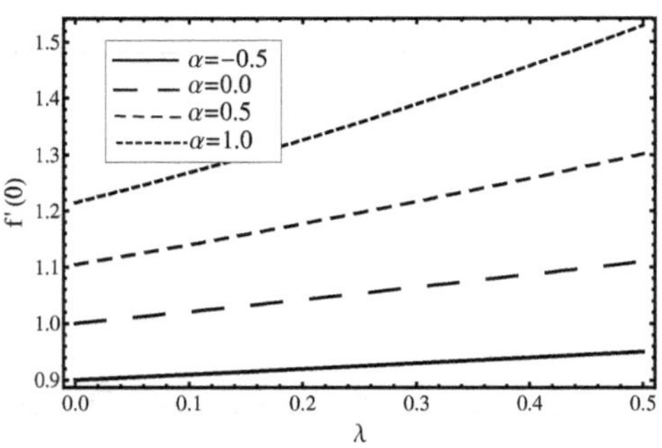


Figure 4.18: Effect of mass transfer on surface shear stress rate.

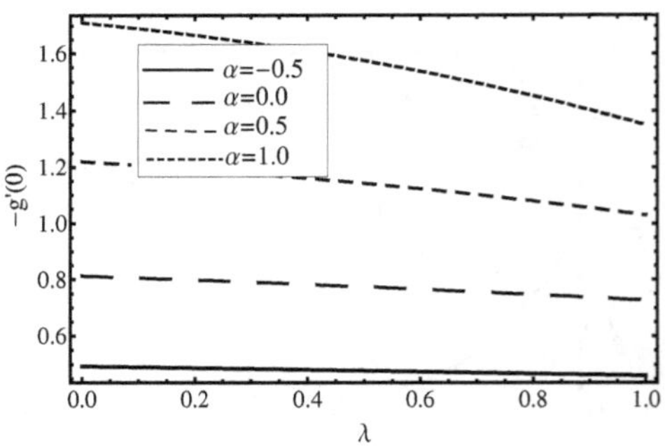


Figure 4.19: Effect of mass transfer on heat transfer rate (PST case).

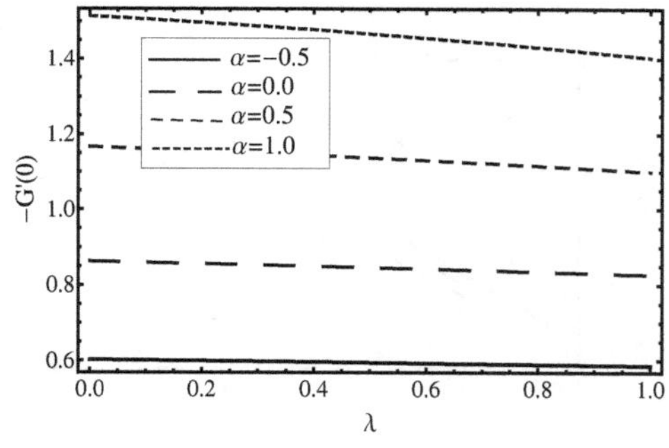


Figure 4.20: Effect of mass transfer on heat transfer rate (PHF case).

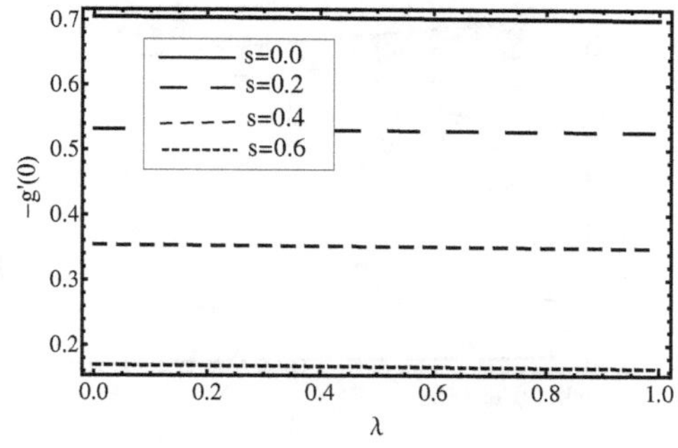


Figure 4.21: Effect of source/sink on heat transfer rate (PST case).

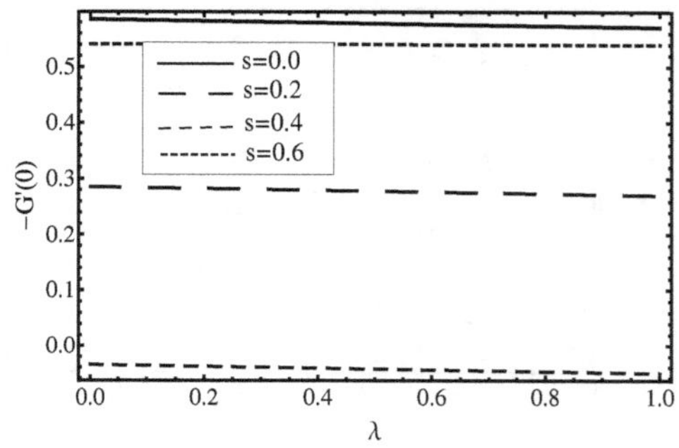


Figure 4.22: Effect of source/sink on heat transfer rate (PHF case).

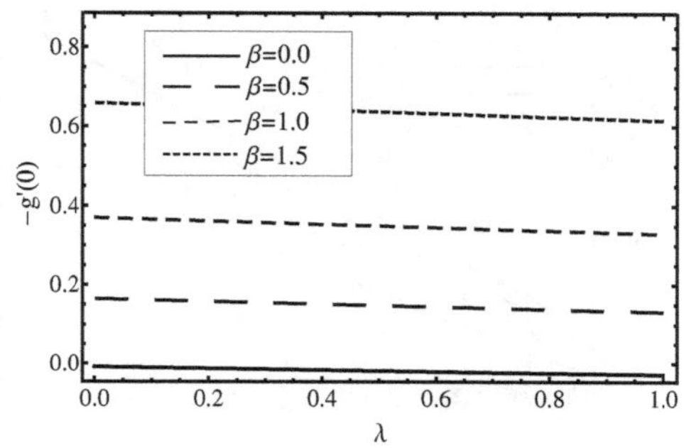


Figure 4.23: Effect of heat flux on heat transfer rate (PST case).

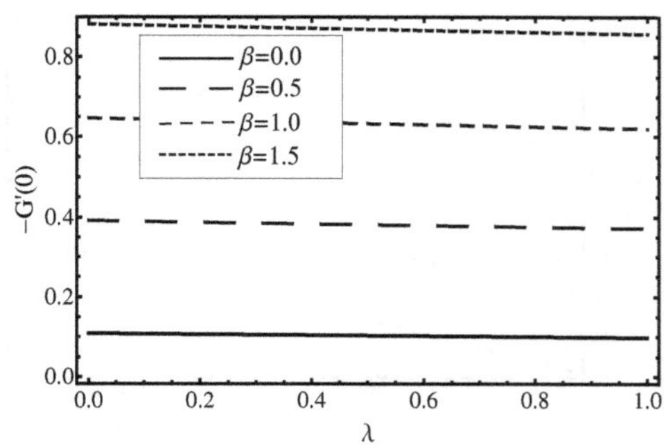


Figure 4.24: Effect of heat flux on heat transfer rate (PHF case).

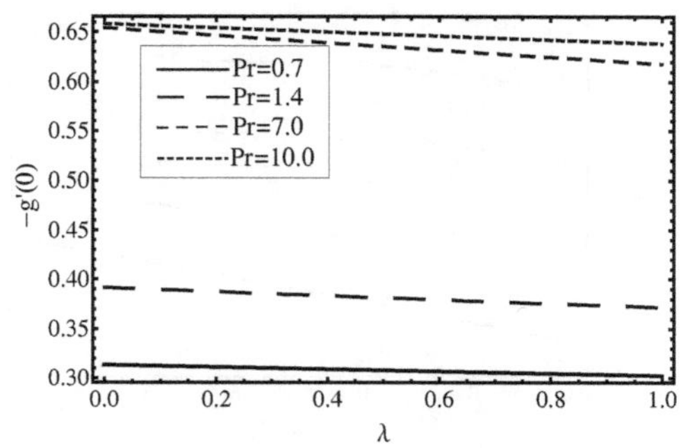


Figure 4.25: Effect of Prandtl number on heat transfer rate (PST case).

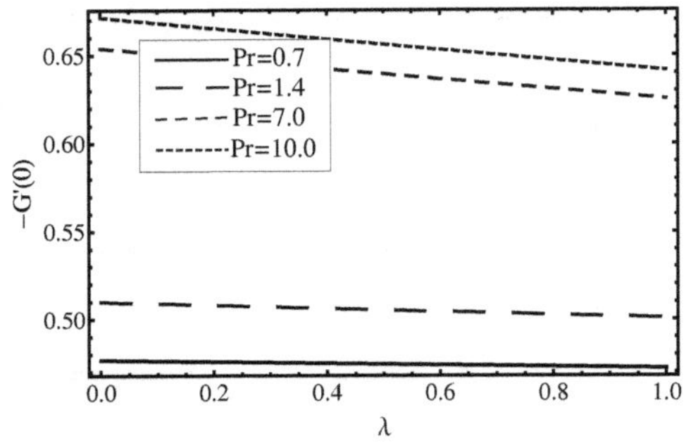


Figure 4.26: Effect of Prandtl number on heat transfer rate (PHF case).

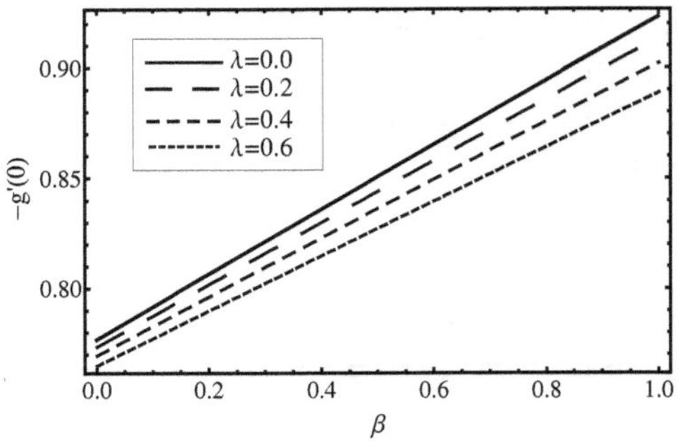


Figure 4.27: Effect of viscoelastic parameter on heat transfer rate (PST case).

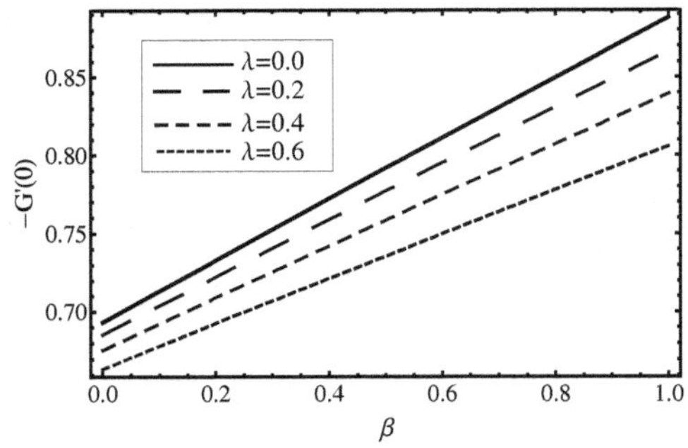


Figure 4.28: Effect of viscoelastic parameter on heat transfer rate (PHF case).

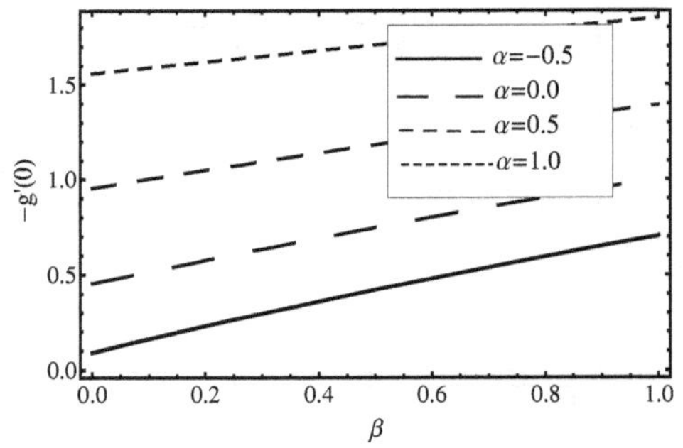


Figure 4.29: Effect of mass transfer on heat transfer rate (PST case).

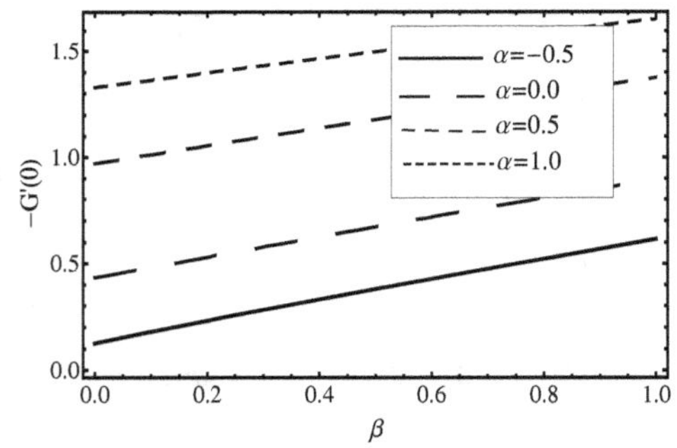


Figure 4.30: Effect of mass transfer on heat transfer rate (PHF case).

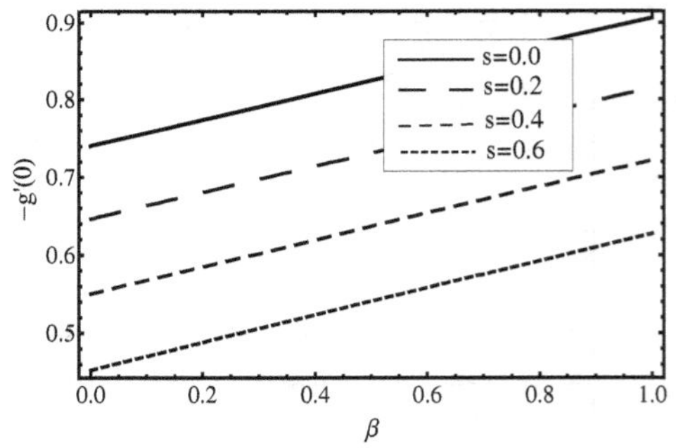


Figure 4.31: Effect of source/sink on heat transfer rate (PST case).

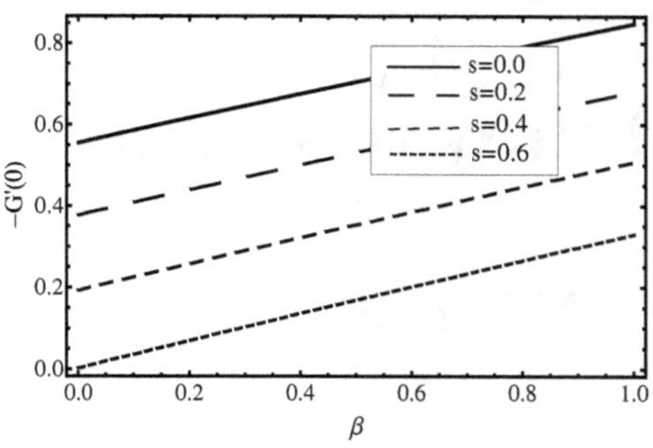


Figure 4.32: Effect of source/sink on heat transfer rate (PHF case).

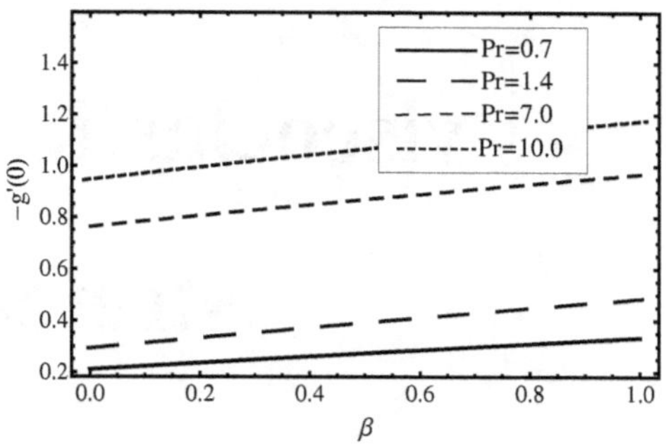


Figure 4.33: Effect of Prandtl number on heat transfer rate (PST case).

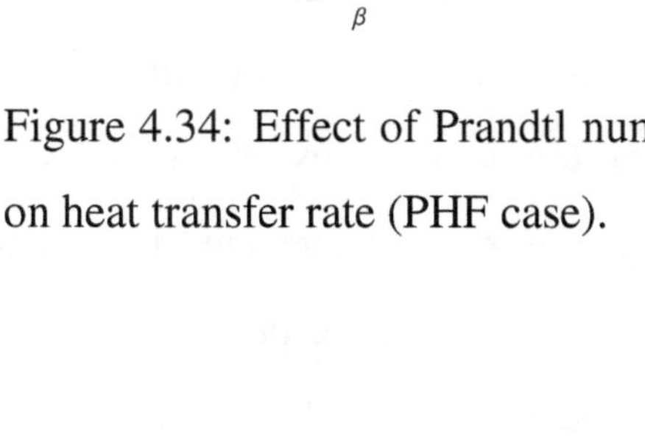


Figure 4.34: Effect of Prandtl number on heat transfer rate (PHF case).

# Chapter 5

# Heat transfer in a three-dimensional viscoelastic fluid flow due to a stretching surface

## 5.1 Abstract

In this Chapter, a steady three-dimensional viscoelastic fluid flow and heat transfer due to a stretching sheet with an applied magnetic field is considered for analysis. The fluid far away from the surface is ambient and the motion in the flow field is caused by the stretching surface in two lateral directions. The heat transfer analysis has been carried out for two heating processes, viz, the constant wall temperature (CWT) and the constant heat flux (CHF). An analytical solution in the form of series expansion for the velocity and temperature distribution is obtained employing HAM. The quantities of interest are velocity and temperature distribution as well as the skin-friction and the heat transfer coefficients. These are determined for various values of the parameters such as viscoelastic parameter, magnetic parameter, stretching ratio and the Prandtl number. The results obtained are presented in the form of graphs and tabulated data. It is observed that velocity and thermal boundary layer thicknesses decrease with increase in magnetic field. The influence of various parameters on the flow variables are discussed in detail.

## 5.2 Introduction

In several engineering and mechanical processes such as extrusion, melt spinning etc., the extruded material issues through a die. The ambient fluid condition is stagnant, but the flow is induced near the material surface being extruded due to entrainment of the fluid caused by stretching of a moving surface. In regions away from the slit, the flow may be assumed to be of boundary layer type. However, this is not true near the slit. Similar situations arise during the manufacture of plastic and rubber sheets. Another example that belongs to the above class of problems is the cooling of large metallic plate in a bath, which may be an electrolyte. Glass blowing, continuous casting and spinning of fibers also involve the flow due to a stretching surface. In all these cases, the quality of the final product depends largely on the skin friction and heat transfer rates at the surface.

In recent years, the non-Newtonian fluids with magnetic field find increasing applications in industry and technology. The non-Newtonian fluids characterized by a power law model have some limitations as they do not exhibit any elastic property such as normal stress differences in shear flows. The equations of motion of the viscoelastic fluid are one order higher than the Navier-Stokes or the boundary layer equations governing the Newtonian fluids and the boundary conditions are not sufficient to determine the solution completely. Since the elastic parameter occurs as a coefficient of the highest derivative in the differential equations governing the flow, the mathematical problem reduces to a singular perturbation problem.

Sarpakaya (1961) was the first researcher to investigate the magneto hydro dynamic flows of non-Newtonian fluids. Andersson (1992) and Ariel (1994) extended the above analysis to include the effect of the magnetic field. Dandapat *et al.* (1989) and Cortell (1994) have considered the heat transfer aspect of this problem for the constant wall temperature. Vajravelu *et al.* (1991) have investigated the effect of variable surface temperature and surface heat flux on the heat transfer of a stretching surface. The three-dimensional flow of Newtonian fluids over a stretching surface in two lateral directions without magnetic field was studied by Wang (1984). Unsteady three-dimensional stagnation flow over a viscoelastic fluid was considered by Seshadri *et al.* (1997).

Recently the three-dimensional flow of Jeffrey fluid with variable thermal conductivity and thermal radiation was examined analytically by Hayat *et al.* (2013). Nandappanavar *et al.* (2013) studied the heat transfer of viscoelastic fluid flow due to nonlinear stretching sheet with internal heat source. They obtained approximate analytical local similar solutions of the non-linear momentum equation for velocity distribution by transforming the equation into Riccati-type and then solving the same sequentially. The HAM solution for stagnation point flow of a non-Newtonian fluid an incompressible second grade fluid impinges on the wall was investigated by Hayat *et al.* (2012*a*).

The extension of Hayat *et al.* (2012*b*) by Shehzad *et al.* (2013*a*) presents the homotopy solution of boundary layer flow of Maxwell fluid with power law heat flux in the presence of heat source and hydromagnetics. HAM for MHD viscoelastic fluid flow and heat transfer in a channel with a stretching wall is examined by Raftari *et al.* (2012). The flow of the viscoelastic fluid over a linearly stretching surface in an otherwise ambient fluid was investigated by Rajagopal *et al.* (1984), who obtained the solution numerically for small values of the elastic parameter.

In all the above research papers, the combined effect of the three parameters such as applied magnetic field, stretching rate and the viscoelastic parameter on the velocity and temperature distribution and on skin friction and heat transfer rates have not been dealt with. Hence, the present analysis deals with the steady, three-dimensional flow and heat transfer of a viscoelastic fluid over a stretching surface in two lateral directions with a magnetic field applied normal to the surface.

## 5.3 Problem formulation and governing equations

In reality, most of the fluids considered in industrial applications are non-Newtonian in nature, especially of viscoelastic type than viscous type. Hence we consider the steady motion of a viscous incompressible electrically conducting viscoelastic fluid induced by the stretching of an infinite flat surface in two lateral directions $x$ and $y$. The surface is assumed to be highly elastic and is being stretched by the action of uniform but increasing forces. Let $a$ and $b$ be the rate of stretching in $x$-and $y$-directions, respectively. The fluid far away from the surface is ambient and the motion in the flow field is caused by stretching surface in two directions. The fluid is assumed to have constant properties and it is at rest at infinity. No slip conditions are imposed on the stretching

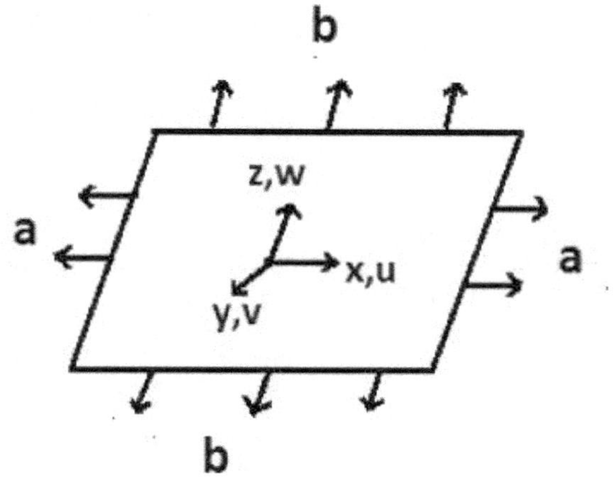


Figure 5.1: Sketch of three-dimensional coordinate system of flow.

surface. The temperature of the ambient fluid is kept constant as $T_\infty$. Both constant wall temperature (CWT) and the constant heat flux (CHF) cases are included in the analysis. For the CWT case, the surface temperature is kept constant while for the CHF case the temperature gradient in the $z$-direction at the surface is kept uniform.

It is assumed that the normal stress is of the same order of magnitude as the shear stress. Thus $\nu$ and $\lambda_1 (= \alpha_1/\rho)$ are of $o(\delta^2)$ where $\delta$ is the boundary layer thickness. The magnetic field $B$ is applied in $z$-direction. The magnetic Reynolds number $R_m = \mu_0 \sigma V L << 1$, where $\mu_0$ and $\sigma$ are the magnetic permeability and electrical conductivity, respectively and $V$ and $L$ are the characteristic velocity and length. Hence the induced magnetic field is small in comparison to the applied magnetic field and is therefore neglected. The electrical current flowing in the fluid will give rise to an induced magnetic field if the fluid were an insulator. Here we have taken the fluid to be electrically conducting. The viscous dissipation and ohmic heating terms in the energy equation are neglected as they are assumed to be small. Under the foregoing assumptions, the boundary layer equations, governing the flow and the heat transfer of a viscoelastic fluid over a stretching surface in two lateral directions, are given by Andersson (1992), Wang (1984) and Shehzad *et al.* (2013*a*) as follows

$$u_x + v_y + w_z = 0 \tag{5.1}$$

$$uu_x + vu_y + wu_z = \nu u_{zz} - \frac{\sigma B^2 u}{\rho} + \lambda_1 [(uu_{xzz} + vu_{yzz} + wu_{zzz}) - (u_{zz}u_x + v_{zz}u_y + w_{zz}u_z + 2u_z u_{xz} + 2v_z u_{yz} + 2w_z u_{zz})] \quad (5.2)$$

$$uv_x + vv_y + wv_z = \nu v_{zz} - \frac{\sigma B^2 v}{\rho} + \lambda_1 [(uv_{xzz} + vv_{yzz} + wv_{zzz}) - (u_{zz}v_x + v_{zz}v_y + w_{zz}v_z + 2u_z v_{xz} + 2v_z v_{yz} + 2w_z v_{zz})] \quad (5.3)$$

$$uT_x + vT_y + wT_z = \left(\frac{k}{\rho C_p}\right) T_{zz}. \quad (5.4)$$

The boundary conditions are given by

$$u(x,y,0) = u_w, v(x,y,0) = v_w, w(x,y,0) = 0,$$
$$u(x,y,\infty) = v(x,y,\infty) = u_z(x,y,\infty) = v_z(x,y,\infty) = 0, T(x,y,\infty) = T_\infty,$$

$$\begin{aligned} T(x,y,0) &= T_w \quad \text{for the CWT case,} \\ -k\left(\frac{\partial T}{\partial z}\right)_{z=0} &= q_w \quad \text{for the CHF case,} \end{aligned} \quad (5.5)$$

where $u_w = ax$, $v_w = by$. Here $x$, $y$ and $z$ are the orthogonal coordinate system and $u$, $v$ and $w$ are the velocity components along $x$, $y$ and $z$-directions, respectively. $\rho$ and $\nu$ are the density and kinematic viscosity, respectively. $\lambda_1 (= \alpha_1/\rho)$ is the viscoelastic parameter, $T$ is the temperature, $C_p$ is the specific heat at constant pressure, $k$ is the thermal conductivity, $q_w$ is the heat transfer rate at the surface, $a$ and $b$ are the velocity gradients at the wall in $x$-and $y$-directions, respectively, and the subscripts $x$, $y$ and $z$ denote derivatives with respect to $x$, $y$ and $z$ respectively, and the subscripts $w$ and $\infty$ denote conditions at the wall and in the ambient fluid, respectively.

The partial differential equations. (5.1)-(5.4) under conditions (5.5) admit similarity solutions, when the following transformations are applied.

$$\eta = \left(\tfrac{a}{\nu}\right)^{1/2} z, u = axf'(\eta), v = ays'(\eta), w = -(a\nu)^{1/2}(f+s), c = b/a,$$
$$M = \tfrac{\sigma B^2}{\rho a}, Pr = \mu C_p/k, \lambda = \lambda_1 a/\nu > 0,$$

$$\begin{aligned} T - T_\infty &= (T_w - T_\infty)\, g(\eta) \quad \text{for the CWT case,} \\ T - T_\infty &= (q_w/k)\left(\frac{\nu}{a}\right)^{1/2} G(\eta) \quad \text{for the CHF case.} \end{aligned} \quad (5.6)$$

It is verified that (5.1) is identically satisfied by the choice of $u$, $v$ and $w$ and (5.2)-(5.4) reduce to

$$
\begin{aligned}
f''' &+ (f+cs)f''-(f')^2-Mf'+\lambda[(f+cs)f^{IV}-2(f'+cs')f''' \\
&+ (f''-cs'')f'']=0 \qquad (5.7)
\end{aligned}
$$

$$
\begin{aligned}
s''' &+ (f+cs)s''-c(s')^2-Ms'+\lambda[(f+cs)s^{IV}-2(f'+cs')s''' \\
&+ (cs''-f'')s'']=0 \qquad (5.8)
\end{aligned}
$$

$$
\begin{aligned}
g''+Pr(f+cs)g' &= 0 \quad \text{for the CWT case,} \qquad (5.9)\\
G''+Pr(f+cs)G' &= 0 \quad \text{for the CHF case.} \qquad (5.10)
\end{aligned}
$$

The boundary condition corresponding to (5.5) can be rewritten as

$$
\begin{aligned}
f(0) &= s(0)=0,\ f'(0)=1,\ s'(0)=c,\ f'(\infty)=s'(\infty)=0\\
g(0) &= 1 \qquad \text{for the CWT case,}\\
G'(0) &= -1 \qquad \text{for the CHF case.} \qquad (5.11)
\end{aligned}
$$

For Newtonian fluids ($\lambda = 0$) and the boundary conditions $f''(\infty) = s''(\infty) = 0$ are not required.

Here $\eta$ is the transformed similarity variable, $f'$ and $s'$ are the dimensionless velocity components along $x$ and $y$-directions, respectively, $g$ and $G$ are the dimensionless temperatures for CWT and CHF cases, respectively, $c$ is the ratio of velocity gradients also known as stretching parameter, $M$ is the magnetic parameter, $\mu$ is the coefficient of viscosity, $Pr$ is the Prandtl number, $\lambda$ is the dimensionless viscoelastic parameter and prime denotes derivative with respect to $\eta$. Eqs. (5.7)-(5.10) under conditions (5.11) for $\lambda = 0$ represent the three-dimensional flow of Newtonian fluids and for $\lambda > 0$ they represent the flow of non-Newtonian fluids.

Also, (5.7)-(5.8) for $\lambda = M = 0$ reduces to Cortell (1994). For $c = 0$, (5.7)-(5.9) reduce to the two-dimensional flow over a stretching surface and for this case $s = 0$. Further, for $c = 1$ these equations represent axisymmetric flow and in this case $s = f$. For $c = 0$, (5.7) is identical to that of Andersson (1992).

The skin friction coefficients in $x$-and $y$-directions can be expressed as

$$
\begin{aligned}
C_{fx} &= (1-\lambda)\mu\left(\frac{\partial u}{\partial z}\right)_{z=0}/\rho u_w^2 = (1-\lambda)Re_x^{-1/2}f''(0), \qquad (5.12a)\\
C_{fy} &= (1-\lambda)\mu\left(\frac{\partial v}{\partial z}\right)_{z=0}/\rho u_w v_w = (1-\lambda)Re_x^{-1/2}s''(0). \qquad (5.12b)
\end{aligned}
$$

The heat transfer coefficient in terms of the Nusselt number are derived as

$$Nu = -k\left(\frac{\partial T}{\partial z}\right)_{z=0} x/k(T_w - T_\infty) = -Re_x^{1/2} g'(0) \text{ for the CWT case,}$$

$$\text{and } Nu = Re_x^{1/2}/G(0) \quad \text{for the CHF case,}$$

where $Re_x(= ax^2/\nu)$ is the local Reynolds number.

## 5.4 Homotopy series solutions

In order to obtain an analytical solution of the non-dimensional eqs. (5.7)-(5.10) satisfying the boundary conditions (5.11) we employ HAM. It is mainly an analytic approach to solution procedure but very tedious to solve manually and is solvable only using Computer Algebra System. We use Mathematica software to solve the system by means of HAM procedure to obtain the desired solutions. The main components involved in applying HAM procedure are $(i)$ selecting suitable initial profiles satisfying the boundary conditions of the problem and $(ii)$ selecting an appropriate auxiliary linear operator so that its solutions are simpler to evaluate analytically.

In the present problem, depending upon the boundary conditions (5.11), we choose the initial guesses and auxiliary linear operators as follows

$$f_0(\eta) = 1 - e^{-\eta}, \quad s_0(\eta) = c(1 - e^{-\eta}), \quad g_0(\eta) = G_0(\eta) = e^{-\eta} \tag{5.13}$$

$$L_f = \frac{d^3 f}{d\eta^3} - \frac{df}{d\eta}; \; L_s = \frac{d^3 s}{d\eta^3} - \frac{df}{d\eta}; \; L_g = \frac{d^2 g}{d\eta^2} - g; \; L_G = \frac{d^2 G}{d\eta^2} - G, \tag{5.14}$$

so as to obtain a simpler form of solution as

$$\begin{aligned} L_f\left[C_1 + C_2 e^{\eta} + C_3 e^{-\eta}\right] &= 0, \; L_s\left[C_4 + C_5 e^{\eta} + C_6 e^{-\eta}\right] = 0, \\ L_g\left[C_7 e^{\eta} + C_8 e^{-\eta}\right] &= 0, \; L_G\left[C_9 e^{\eta} + C_{10} e^{-\eta}\right] = 0, \end{aligned} \tag{5.15}$$

where $C_i$ are arbitrary constants and can be obtained using (5.11). It is to be mentioned here that the choice of initial profiles and linear operators are not unique for a given problem, but the faster convergence of the solution depends on the choice of those.

### 5.4.1 Zeroth-order deformation problem

To obtain the HAM solution for the eqs. (5.7)-(5.10), let $\gamma \in [0, 1]$ be an embedding parameter and $c_f$, $c_s$, $c_g$ and $c_G$ are the basic convergence control parameters. Then the zeroth order deformation equation and the non-linear operators become,

$$(1-\gamma)L_X[X(\eta,\gamma)-X_0(\eta)] = \gamma c_X \mathcal{N}_X[X(\eta,\gamma)], \tag{5.16}$$

where, $X = f,\ s,\ g$ and $G$ and $X_0 = f_0, s_0,\ g_0$ and $G_0$.

$$\begin{aligned}
\mathcal{N}_f[f(\eta,\gamma)] &= \frac{\partial^3 f(\eta,\gamma)}{\partial\eta^3} + (f(\eta,\gamma)+cs(\eta,\gamma))\frac{\partial^2 f(\eta,\gamma)}{\partial\eta^2} \\
&+ \lambda\left((f(\eta,\gamma)+cs(\eta,\gamma))\frac{\partial^4 f(\eta,\gamma)}{\partial\eta^4}\right) \\
&+ \lambda\left(\frac{\partial^2 f(\eta,\gamma)}{\partial\eta^2}(\frac{\partial^2 f(\eta,\gamma)}{\partial\eta^2} - c\frac{\partial^2 s(\eta,\gamma)}{\partial\eta^2})\right) \\
&- 2\lambda\left(\frac{\partial^3 f(\eta,\gamma)}{\partial\eta^3}(\frac{\partial f(\eta,\gamma)}{\partial\eta} + c\frac{\partial s(\eta,\gamma)}{\partial\eta})\right) \\
&- M\left(\frac{\partial f(\eta,\gamma)}{\partial\eta}\right) - \left(\frac{\partial f(\eta,\gamma)}{\partial\eta}\right)^2,
\end{aligned} \tag{5.17}$$

$$\begin{aligned}
\mathcal{N}_s[s(\eta,\gamma),f(\eta,\gamma)] &= \frac{\partial^3 s(\eta,\gamma)}{\partial\eta^3} + (f(\eta,\gamma)+cs(\eta,\gamma))\frac{\partial^2 s(\eta,\gamma)}{\partial\eta^2} \\
&+ \lambda\left((f(\eta,\gamma)+cs(\eta,\gamma))\frac{\partial^4 s(\eta,\gamma)}{\partial\eta^4}\right) \\
&- \lambda\left(\frac{\partial^2 s(\eta,\gamma)}{\partial\eta^2}(c\frac{\partial^2 s(\eta,\gamma)}{\partial\eta^2} - \frac{\partial^2 f(\eta,\gamma)}{\partial\eta^2})\right) \\
&- 2\lambda\left(\frac{\partial^3 s(\eta,\gamma)}{\partial\eta^3}(\frac{\partial f(\eta,\gamma)}{\partial\eta} + c\frac{\partial s(\eta,\gamma)}{\partial\eta})\right) \\
&- M\left(\frac{\partial s(\eta,\gamma)}{\partial\eta}\right) - c\left(\frac{\partial s(\eta,\gamma)}{\partial\eta}\right)^2,
\end{aligned} \tag{5.18}$$

$$\begin{aligned}
\mathcal{N}_g[g(\eta,\gamma),s(\eta,\gamma),f(\eta,\gamma)] &= \frac{\partial^2 g(\eta,\gamma)}{\partial\eta^2} + Pr(f(\eta,\gamma))\left(\frac{\partial g(\eta,\gamma)}{\partial\eta}\right) \\
&+ csPr(\eta,\gamma)\left(\frac{\partial g(\eta,\gamma)}{\partial\eta}\right),
\end{aligned} \tag{5.19}$$

$$\begin{aligned}
\mathcal{N}_G[G(\eta,\gamma),s(\eta,\gamma),f(\eta,\gamma)] &= \frac{\partial^2 G(\eta,\gamma)}{\partial\eta^2} + Pr(f(\eta,\gamma))\left(\frac{\partial G(\eta,\gamma)}{\partial\eta}\right) \\
&+ csPr(\eta,\gamma)\left(\frac{\partial G(\eta,\gamma)}{\partial\eta}\right).
\end{aligned} \tag{5.20}$$

Note that the nonlinear operator for CHF case is the same for the CWT case as they differ only in their boundary conditions.

The boundary conditions rewritten from (5.11) as,

$$f(\eta;\gamma)|_{\eta=0} = 0, \quad \left.\frac{\partial f(\eta;\gamma)}{\partial\eta}\right|_{\eta=0} = 1, \quad \left.\frac{\partial f(\eta;\gamma)}{\partial\eta}\right|_{\eta=\infty} = 0, \tag{5.21}$$

$$\left.\frac{\partial^2 f(\eta;\gamma)}{\partial \eta^2}\right|_{\eta=\infty} = 0, \quad s(\eta;\gamma)|_{\eta=0} = 0,$$

$$\left.\frac{\partial s(\eta;\gamma)}{\partial \eta}\right|_{\eta=0} = c, \quad \left.\frac{\partial s(\eta;\gamma)}{\partial \eta}\right|_{\eta=\infty} = 0, \quad \left.\frac{\partial^2 s(\eta;\gamma)}{\partial \eta^2}\right|_{\eta=\infty} = 0 \tag{5.22}$$

$$g(\eta;\gamma)|_{\eta=0} = 1, \quad g(\eta;\gamma)|_{\eta=\infty} = 0 \quad \text{for the CWT case,} \tag{5.23}$$

$$\left.\frac{\partial G(\eta;\gamma)}{\partial \eta}\right|_{\eta=0} = -1, \quad G(\eta;\gamma)|_{\eta=\infty} = 0 \quad \text{for the CHF case.} \tag{5.24}$$

### 5.4.2 Higher-order deformation problem

For obtaining the $\ell^{th}$-order deformation equations, differentiate eq. (5.16) $\ell$-times with respect to $\gamma$, and divide by $\ell!$. Setting $\gamma = 0$, we get

$$L_X[X_\ell(\eta) - \Omega_\ell X_{\ell-1}(\eta)] \;=\; c_X \mathscr{R}_\ell^X(\eta). \tag{5.25}$$

The boundary conditions can be redefined as

$$\begin{aligned}
f_l(0) &= 0,\ f'_\ell(0) = 1,\ f'_\ell(\infty) = 0,\ f''_\ell(\infty) = 0\\
s_\ell(0) &= 0,\ s'_\ell(0) = c,\ s'_\ell(\infty) = 0,\ s''_\ell(\infty) = 0\\
g_\ell(0) &= 1,\ g_\ell(\infty) = 0\ ,G'_\ell(0) = -1,\ G_\ell(\infty) = 0,
\end{aligned} \tag{5.26}$$

In (5.25), the term $\mathscr{R}_X^\ell(\eta)$ denotes $\mathscr{R}_\ell^f(\eta)$, $\mathscr{R}_\ell^s(\eta)$, $\mathscr{R}_\ell^g(\eta)$ and $\mathscr{R}_\ell^G(\eta)$. These are the remainder terms from the linear operators which are given by

$$\begin{aligned}
\mathscr{R}_\ell^f(\eta) &= f'''_{\ell-1}(\eta) + \sum_{j=0}^{\ell-1}[f_{\ell-1-j}f''_j - f'_{\ell-1-j}f'_j] + c\sum_{j=0}^{\ell-1}[s_{\ell-1-j}f''_j]\\
&+ \lambda\sum_{j=0}^{\ell-1}[f_{\ell-1-j}f''''_j + f''_{\ell-1-j}f''_j] + \lambda c\sum_{j=0}^{\ell-1}[s_{\ell-1-j}f''''_j - s''_{\ell-1-j}f''_j]\\
&- 2\lambda\sum_{j=0}^{\ell-1}[f'_{\ell-1-j}f'''_j] - 2\lambda c\sum_{j=0}^{\ell-1}[s'_{\ell-1-j}f'''_j] - Mf'_{\ell-1}(\eta),
\end{aligned} \tag{5.27}$$

$$\begin{aligned}
\mathscr{R}_\ell^s(\eta) &= s'''_{\ell-1}(\eta) + \sum_{j=0}^{\ell-1}[f_{\ell-1-j}s''_j - s'_{\ell-1-j}s'_j] + c\sum_{j=0}^{\ell-1}[s_{\ell-1-j}s''_j]\\
&+ \lambda\sum_{j=0}^{\ell-1}[f_{\ell-1-j}s''''_j + s''_{\ell-1-j}s''_j] + \lambda c\sum_{j=0}^{\ell-1}[s_{\ell-1-j}s''''_j + s''_{\ell-1-j}s''_j]\\
&- 2\lambda\sum_{j=0}^{\ell-1}[f'_{\ell-1-j}s'''_j] - 2\lambda c\sum_{j=0}^{\ell-1}[s'_{\ell-1-j}s'''_j] - Ms'_{\ell-1}(\eta).
\end{aligned} \tag{5.28}$$

$$\mathscr{R}_\ell^g(\eta) = g''_{\ell-1}(\eta) + Pr\sum_{j=0}^{\ell-1}[f_{\ell-1-j}g'_j] + cPr\sum_{j=0}^{\ell-1}[s_{\ell-1-j}g'_j] \tag{5.29}$$

$$\mathscr{R}_\ell^G(\eta) = G''_{\ell-1}(\eta) + Pr\sum_{j=0}^{\ell-1}[f_{\ell-1-j}G'_j] + cPr\sum_{j=0}^{\ell-1}[s_{\ell-1-j}G'_j], \tag{5.30}$$

where $\Omega_\ell$ defines as

$$\Omega_\ell = \begin{cases} 0 & \text{if } \ell \leq 1 \\ 1 & \text{if } \ell > 1. \end{cases} \tag{5.31}$$

Expanding $X(\eta;\gamma)$ with respect to $\gamma$ using Taylor's series, we get

$$X(\eta;\gamma) = X_0(\eta) + \sum_{\ell=1}^{\infty} X_\ell(\eta)\gamma^\ell, \; X_\ell(\eta) = \frac{1}{\ell!}\frac{\partial^\ell X(\eta;\gamma)}{\partial\gamma^\ell}\bigg|_{\gamma=0}. \tag{5.32}$$

The auxiliary parameters are selected as $\gamma = 0$ and $\gamma = 1$ from (5.16), we get

$$X(\eta;0) = X_0(\eta), \; X(\eta;1) = X(\eta). \tag{5.33}$$

Thus as $\gamma$ increases from 0 to 1 and $X(\eta;\gamma)$ varies from the initial guess $X_0(\eta)$ to the solution $X(\eta)$ of the governing equations respectively. Here, the auxiliary parameters are suitably chosen so that the series solution converges for $\gamma = 1$.

$$X(\eta) = X_0(\eta) + \sum_{\ell=1}^{\infty} X_\ell(\eta), \tag{5.34}$$

where $X = f^*, s^*, g^*$ and $G^*$.

Therefore, we get the general approximate analytical solutions $f_\ell, \; s_\ell, \; g_\ell, \; G_\ell$ in terms of special solutions $f_\ell^*, \; s_\ell^*, \; g_\ell^*, \; G_\ell^*$ are given by

$$f_\ell(\eta) = f_\ell^*(\eta) + C_1 + C_2e^\eta + C_3e^{-\eta} \tag{5.35}$$

$$s_\ell(\eta) = s_\ell^*(\eta) + C_4 + C_5e^\eta + C_6e^{-\eta} \tag{5.36}$$

$$g_\ell(\eta) = g_\ell^*(\eta) + C_7e^\eta + C_8e^{-\eta} \tag{5.37}$$

$$G_\ell(\eta) = G_\ell^*(\eta) + C_9e^\eta + C_{10}e^{-\eta}. \tag{5.38}$$

Equations. (5.7)-(5.8) are nonlinear equations and (5.9)-(5.10) are linear equation and these equations under conditions (5.11) constitute a boundary-value problem. Hence, we first linearize the non linear equations (5.7) and (5.8) using decriminalization technique. The resulting system of linear equations represents a linear boundary-value problem. It is well known that a linear boundary-value problem can always be reduced to an initial value problem.

By solving (5.35)-(5.38) one after the other in the order $\ell = 1,2,3,...$ by means of the symbolic computation software such as Mathematica, it is shown that the solution for the profiles can be expressed as an infinite series of any desired order. The approximate analytical solutions computed for $f$, $s$, $g$ and $G$ for $\ell = 1,2,3,...$ are given in **Appendix-D**.

### 5.4.3 Convergence of the Homotopy series

As it is done traditionally in all homotopy analysed, the optimal convergence control parameter $c_X$ is obtained by drawing $c_X$-curves with respect to $c_f$, $c_s$, $c_g$ and $c_G$ to find the uniformly convergent interval for $f$, $s$, $g$ and $G$. From these curves it is found that the admissible ranges of $c_f$, $c_s$, $c_g$ and $c_G$ are $-1.3 \leq c_f \leq -0.3$, $-1.2 \leq c_s \leq -0.2$, $-1.4 \leq c_g \leq -0.2$ and $-1.3 \leq c_G \leq -0.3$. The $c_X$-curves are shown in Figure. 5.2.

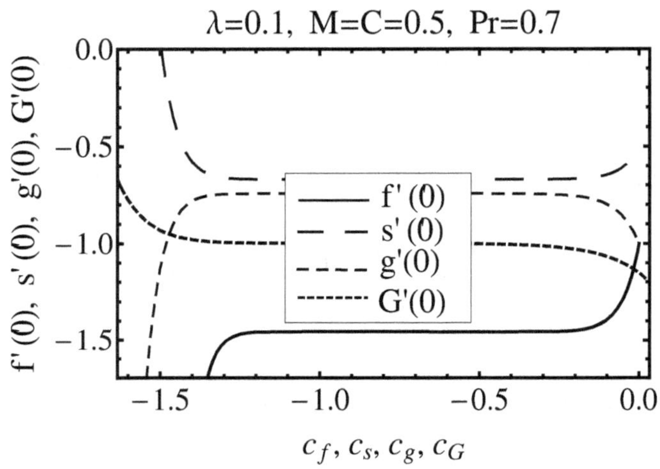


Figure 5.2: $c_f$, $c_s$, $c_g$ and $c_G$ curves at $\lambda = 0.1$, $M = C = 0.5$, $Pr = 0.7$.

### 5.4.4 The error estimation at high orders

Use eq. (1.17) for compute the average squared residual errors of (5.7)-(5.10). At the $\ell^{th}$-order, the optimal values of $c_X$ are computed by the minimum of the squared residual $E_X$ of the governing equations, corresponding to (1.18).

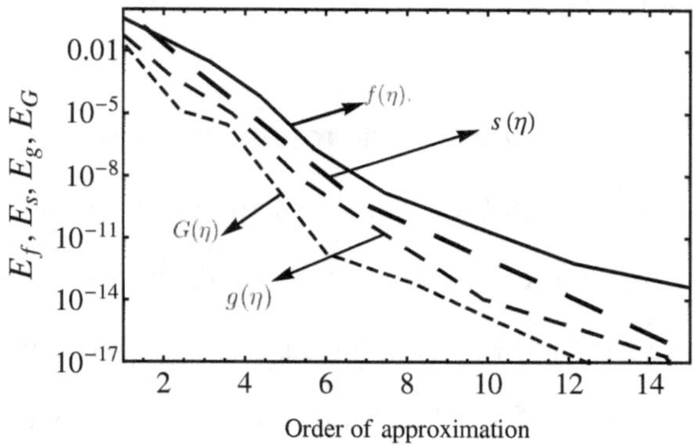


Figure 5.3: Average squared residual error at different order of approximations.

The average squared residual errors $E_X$, at different orders of approximation for $f(\eta)$, $s(\eta)$, $g(\eta)$ and $G(\eta)$ are shown in Figure. 5.3. The average squared residual errors decreases rapidly and the optimal values of the convergence control parameters are found to be $c_f = -0.93721$, $c_s = -0.71019$, $c_g = -0.70042$ and $c_G = -0.69422$. Thus the convergence control parameter used in HAM can greatly accelerate the convergence of series solution.

In all of the figures, use $Pr = 0.7$, $\lambda = 0.1$, $c = 0.5$ and $M = 0.5$ unless it is mentioned otherwise.

## 5.5 Results Analysis

The approximate analytical solutions are obtained in the form of general series for the flow variables $f$, $s$, $g$ and $G$. The computational software **Mathematica** is used for all algebraic and numerical calculations. The expressions for $f$, $s$, $g$ and $G$ are retained up to $10^{th}$ degree polynomial in the series solution. Though computations could be done easily up to $20^{th}$ order of deformations equations, to retain the results up to seven decimal places accuracy and stopped at the $10^{th}$ order.

Here the effect of various physical parameters such as magnetic parameter $M$, ratio of the velocity gradient $c$, Prandtl number $Pr$ and viscoelastic parameter $\lambda$ on velocity and temperature profiles as well as on shear stress rate and heat transfer rates for both constant wall temperature (CWT) and constant heat flux (CHF) cases are discussed. Computations have been carried out for several combinations of parameters $\lambda$, $M$, $c$

and $Pr$, and all results are presented here in the form of Tables 5.1-5.2 and Figures. 5.4-5.45.

In order to assess the accuracy of the results, we have compared present results for the Newtonian case ($\lambda = 0$) in the absence of magnetic parameter ($M = 0$) with Wang (1984) and Ariel (2003) which are presented in Table 5.1 for shear stress components in $x$ and $y$. The same for the heat transfer case is compared with Kumari *et al.* (2002) and Ibrahim (2008) in Table 5.2. It is found that present results are in good agreement with the existing results.

Figures. 5.4-5.17 show the effect of the study parameters on the velocity, temperature profiles and 5.18-5.45 show variation of shear stresses and heat transfer rate for both CWT and CHF cases.

In 5.4-5.7 show the influence of viscoelastic parameter $\lambda$ on the velocity and temperature profiles. It is observed that the boundary layer thickness decreases as the values of $\lambda$ increase from 0 to 1.5, whereas the thermal boundary layer thickens for the increasing values of viscoelastic parameter. There is a temperature over shoot for the higher values of $\lambda$ as seen from 5.6-5.7. The heat transfer coefficient for the CHF case is higher than that of the CWT case.

From 5.8-5.11 present the effect of magnetic parameter $M$ on velocity and temperature profiles and 5.12-5.15 shows the effect of the stretching ratio $c$. 5.16-5.17 shows the effect of Prandtl number on the temperature profiles for a fixed values of $M$, $\lambda$ and $c$. Here again increase in Prandtl number decreases the thermal boundary layer thickness in CWT and CHF cases.

The effect of viscoelastic parameter $\lambda$ on the shear stress and heat transfer rates plotted for various values of magnetic parameter $M$ in 5.18-5.21, respectively. Increase in $M$ increases the shear stress in both $x$-and $y$-directions, but the values are higher for $f''(0)$ compared to $s''(0)$. For a given value of $M$, the increase in $\lambda$, increases shear stress rates. But the effect is opposite for the heat transfer rates. That is to say that, as $\lambda$ increases heat transfer rate decreases for both CWT and CHF cases for all values of $M$. Thus the influence of $\lambda$ on shear stress rate is more pronounced compared to that on the heat transfer rate. The reason for this behavior is that $\lambda$ occurs explicitly in the momentum equations, but the effect of $\lambda$ on the energy equation is indirect.

Similar trend is seen in 5.38-5.41. The effect of viscoelastic parameter $\lambda$ on the shear stress and heat transfer rates plotted for various values of stretching ratio $c$ in 5.22-5.25, respectively. For a given value of $c$, the increase in $\lambda$ increases the shear stress rates and decreases the heat transfer rates in CWT and CHF cases.

The effect of the Prandtl number $Pr$ on the surface heat transfer rate (i.e, $-g'(0)$ and $-G'(0)$), with $\lambda$, $M$ and $c$ are presented in 5.26-5.27 and 5.36-5.37, respectively. It is observed from these figures that, the Prandtl number $Pr$ is increase from 0.7 to 10, the heat transfer rate increases in both CWT and CHF cases.

The variation of magnetic parameter $M$ on the shear stress rate and heat transfer rates plotted for various values of viscoelastic parameter $\lambda$ in 5.28-5.31. The shear stress rates and the heat transfer rates for a fixed $c$ and $M$ increase with increasing $\lambda$ values from 0 to 1.5, because increasing $\lambda$ implies thicker momentum and thermal boundary layers which reduce both the shear stress rates and the heat transfer rates in both CWT and CHF cases.

The effect of $M$ on the shear stress and heat transfer rates plotted for various values of stretching ratio $c$ in 5.32-5.35, respectively. For a given value of $c$, the increase in $M$ increases the shear stress rates and decreases the heat transfer rates in CWT and CHF cases. Similar effects are seen in 5.42-5.45.

## 5.6 Summary

This study presents the analysis of the flow and heat transfer of a three-dimensional viscoelastic fluid is studied in the presence of applied magnetic field. Using HAM, an approximate analytical solution is obtained in the form of Taylor's series expansion. The effects of various parameters such as the magnetic parameter $M$, the stretching ratio $c$, the viscoelastic parameter $\lambda$ and the Prandtl number $Pr$ on the velocity and temperature distributions as well as on skin friction and heat transfer coefficients are studied. Thus this analysis can help in identifying a suitable parameter from this study which can increase or decrease the velocity and temperature values as well as altering shear stress and heat transfer rates. In fact, from the values obtained through calculations, computations and plots, we can get the percentage increase in a flow variable with respect to doubling or halving a specific parameter values, there by we can get the desired value of the heat transfer rate or wall temperature or even shear stress rates.

The following conclusions are drawn from the present study.

- The velocity profiles decreases for the increase in viscoelastic parameter and magnetic parameter values whereas the trend is quite opposite for the temperature profiles.

- The skin friction and the heat transfer coefficient increase with the increasing viscoelastic parameter and the stretching parameter.

- The heat transfer coefficient for the constant heat flux case is higher than that of the constant wall temperature case.

- The shear stress rate and the heat transfer rate for a fixed stretching ratio and magnetic parameter increase with increasing the values of viscoelastic parameter. Another observation is that, for a given value of stretching ratio, the increase in magnetic parameter increases the shear stress rate and decrease the heat transfer rates in CWT and CHF cases.

- Thus the influence of viscoelastic parameter on shear stress rate is more pronounced compared to that on the heat transfer rate.

Table 5.1: Comparison of skin friction results for steady case ( $-f''(0)$, $-s''(0)$) when $Pr = 0.7$ and $M = \lambda = 0$.

| $c$ | $-f''(0)$ | | | $-s''(0)$ | | |
|---|---|---|---|---|---|---|
| | Wang (1984) | Ariel (2003) | Present | Wang (1984) | Ariel (2003) | Present |
| 0.00 | 1.00000 | 1.00000 | 1.00000 | 0.00000 | 0.00000 | 0.00000 |
| 0.10 | 1.02090 | 1.01702 | 1.00199 | 0.06684 | 0.07309 | 0.06477 |
| 0.20 | 1.04180 | 1.03458 | 1.00787 | 0.14873 | 0.15823 | 0.14047 |
| 0.30 | 1.06270 | 1.05247 | 1.01745 | 0.24336 | 0.25434 | 0.22766 |
| 0.40 | 1.08360 | 1.07052 | 1.03056 | 0.34920 | 0.36059 | 0.32671 |
| 0.50 | 1.10450 | 1.08866 | 1.04704 | 0.46520 | 0.47629 | 0.43777 |
| 0.60 | 1.12541 | 1.10679 | 1.06670 | 0.59052 | 0.60083 | 0.56090 |
| 0.70 | 1.14631 | 1.12488 | 1.08935 | 0.72453 | 0.73373 | 0.69608 |
| 0.80 | 1.16721 | 1.14879 | 1.11481 | 0.86668 | 0.87455 | 0.84324 |
| 0.90 | 1.18811 | 1.16076 | 1.14287 | 1.01653 | 1.02292 | 1.00234 |
| 1.00 | 1.20901 | 1.17351 | 1.17334 | 1.17372 | 1.17851 | 1.17334 |

Table 5.2: Comparison of heat transfer results for steady case $-g'(0)$ when $Pr = 0.7$.

| $c$ | $-g'(0)$ | | |
|---|---|---|---|
| | Kumari *et al.* (2002) | Ibrahim (2008) | Present |
| 0.00 | 0.4957 | 0.49587 | 0.494665 |
| 0.25 | 0.5358 | 0.53621 | 0.506619 |
| 0.50 | 0.5798 | 0.57967 | 0.540192 |
| 0.75 | 0.6233 | 0.62308 | 0.591103 |
| 1.00 | 0.6656 | 0.66538 | 0.654128 |

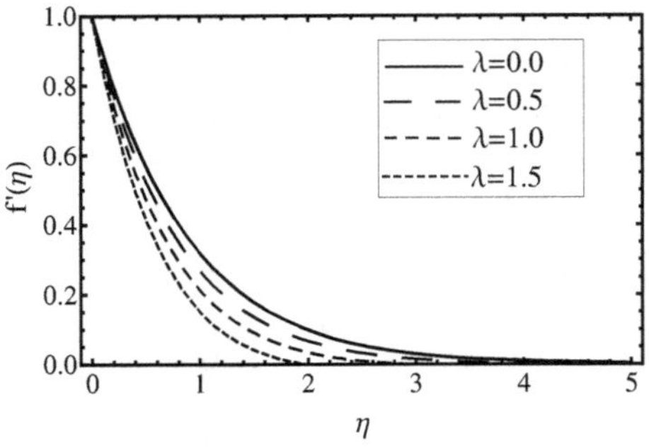


Figure 5.4: Influence of $\lambda$ on $f'(\eta)$.

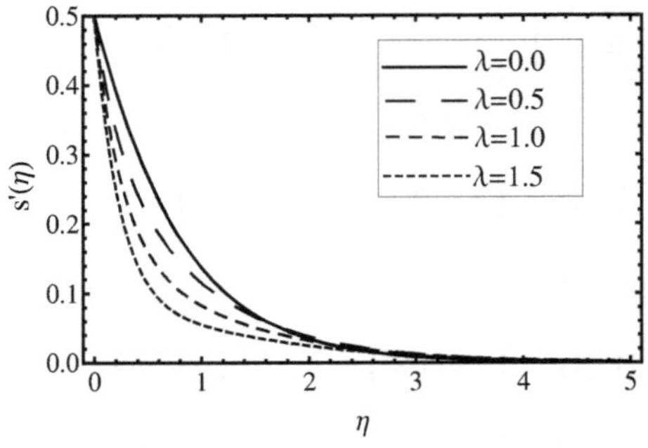


Figure 5.5: Influence of $\lambda$ on $s'(\eta)$.

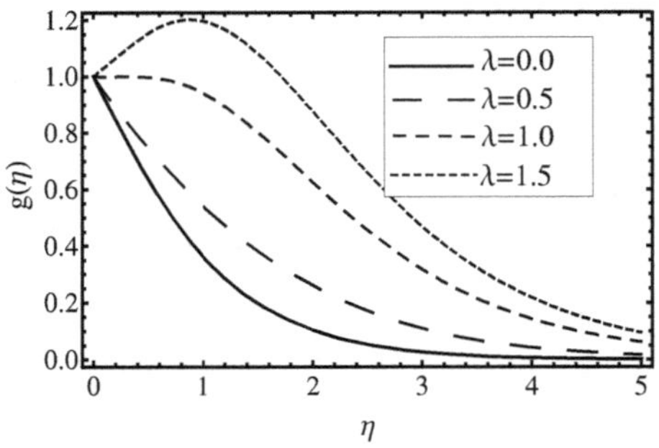


Figure 5.6: Influence of $\lambda$ on $g(\eta)$.

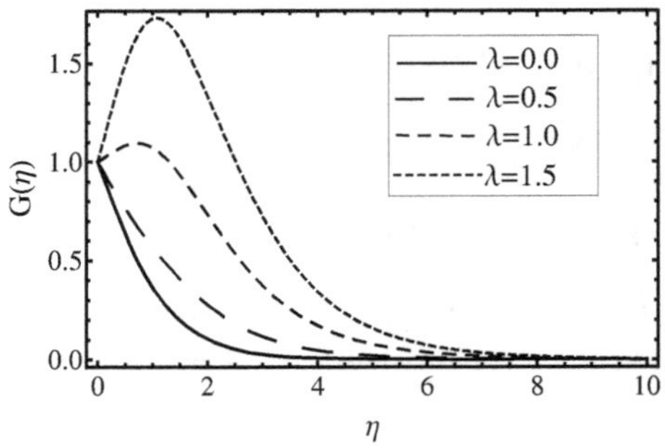


Figure 5.7: Influence of $\lambda$ on $G(\eta)$.

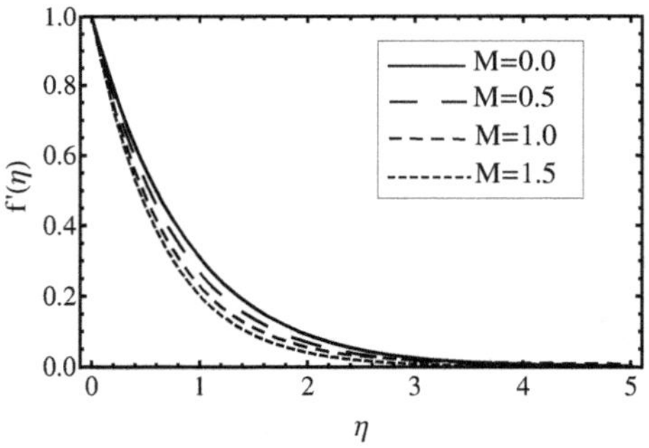


Figure 5.8: Influence of $M$ on $f'(\eta)$.

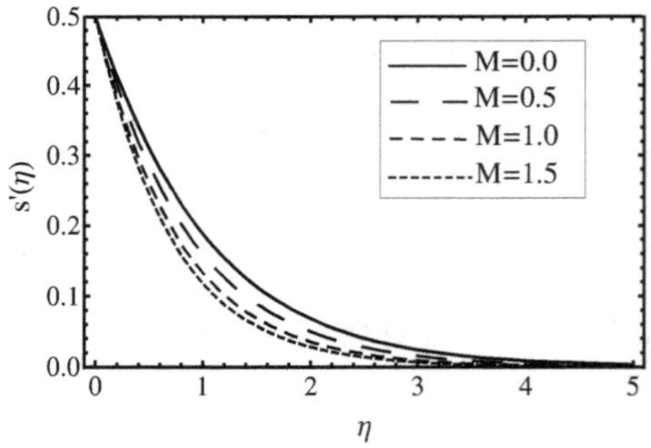


Figure 5.9: Influence of $M$ on $s'(\eta)$.

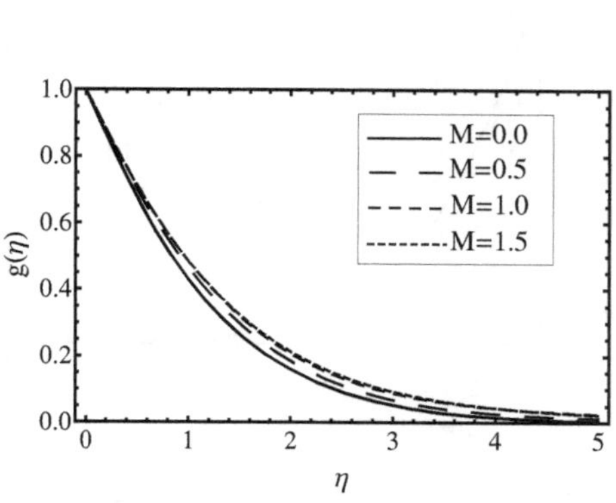


Figure 5.10: Influence of $M$ on $g(\eta)$.

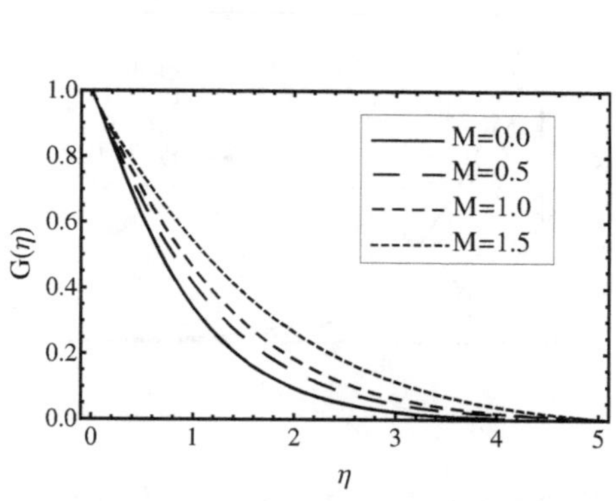


Figure 5.11: Influence of $M$ on $G(\eta)$.

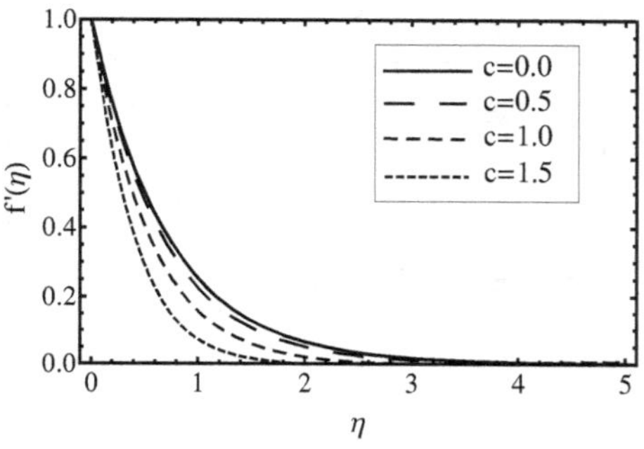


Figure 5.12: Influence of $c$ on $f'(\eta)$.

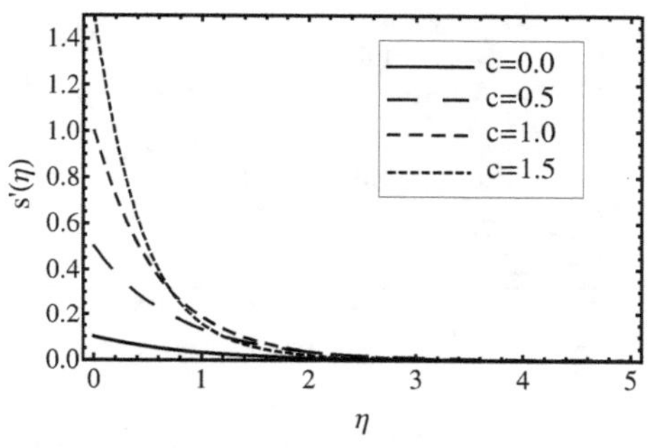


Figure 5.13: Influence of $c$ on $s'(\eta)$.

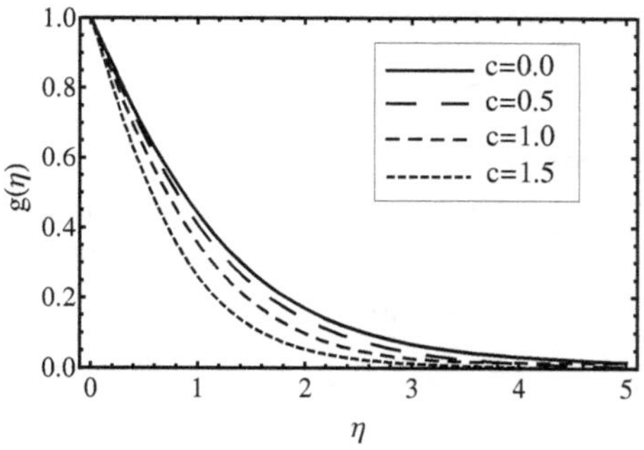


Figure 5.14: Influence of $c$ on $g(\eta)$.

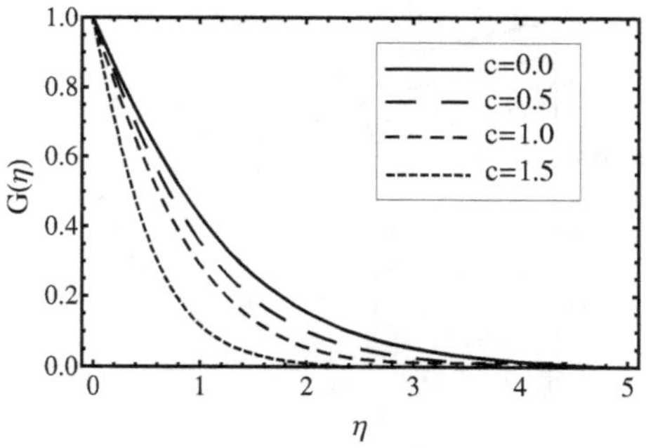


Figure 5.15: Influence of $c$ on $G(\eta)$.

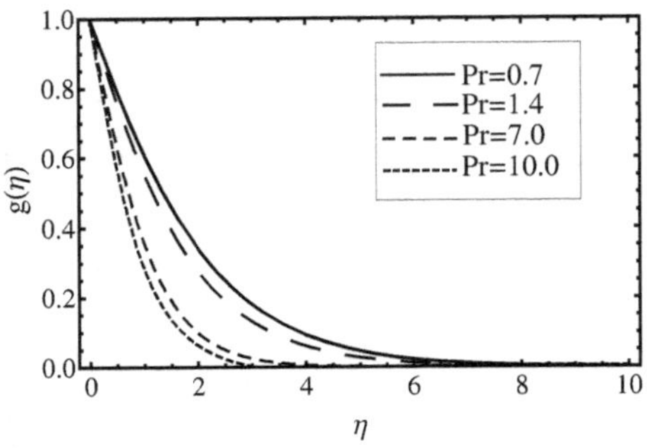


Figure 5.16: Influence of $Pr$ on $g(\eta)$.

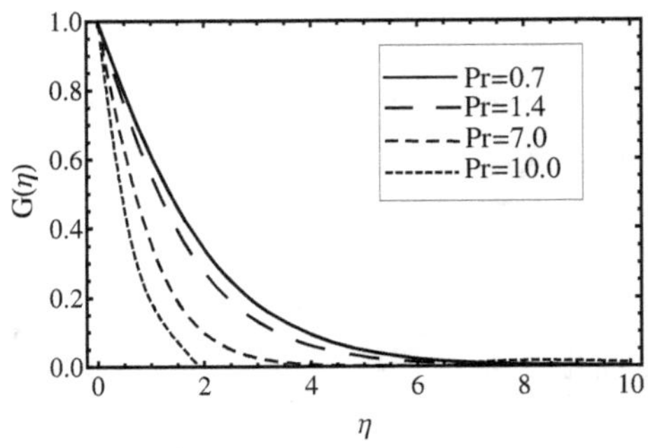


Figure 5.17: Influence of $Pr$ on $G(\eta)$.

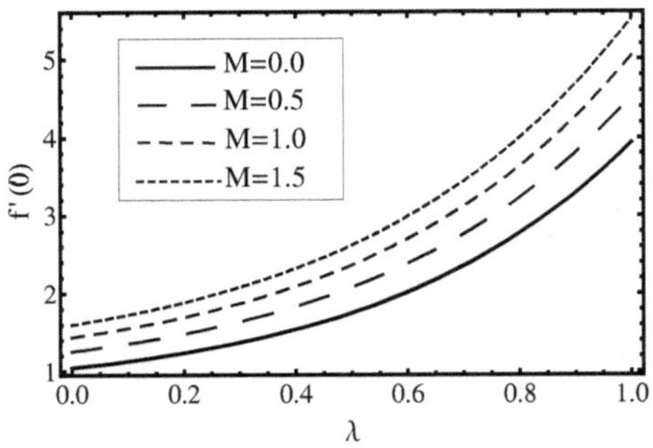


Figure 5.18: Effect of $\lambda$ on $f''(0)$ for different values of $M$.

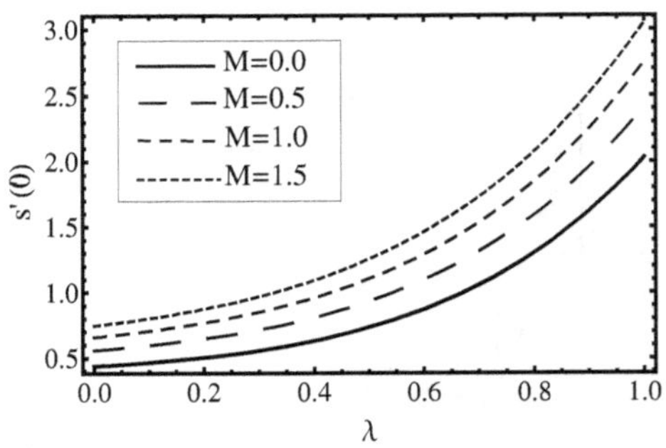


Figure 5.19: Effect of $\lambda$ on $s''(0)$ for different values of $M$.

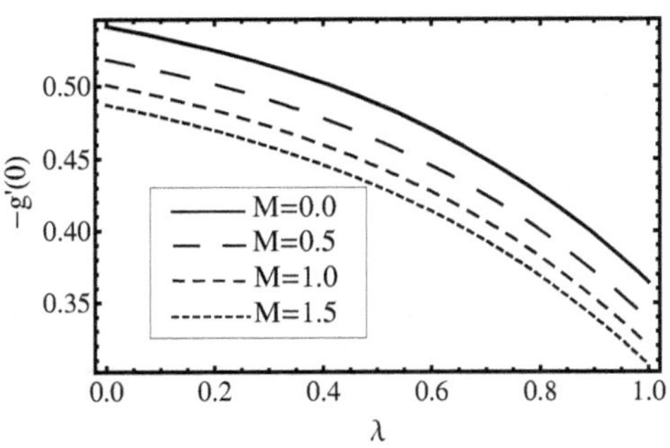


Figure 5.20: Effect of $\lambda$ on $-g'(0)$ for different values of $M$.

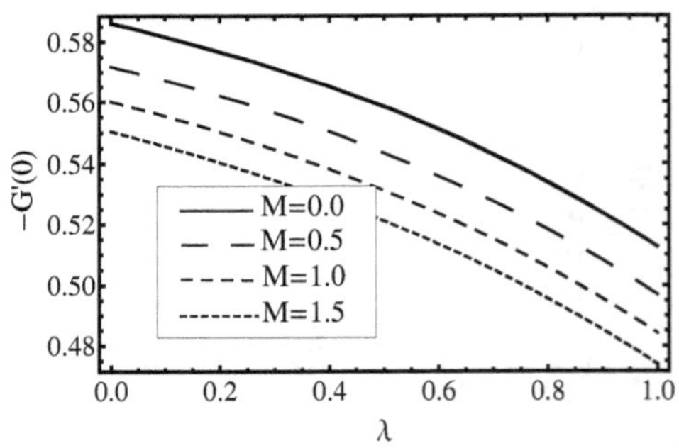


Figure 5.21: Effect of $\lambda$ on $-G'(0)$ for different values of $M$.

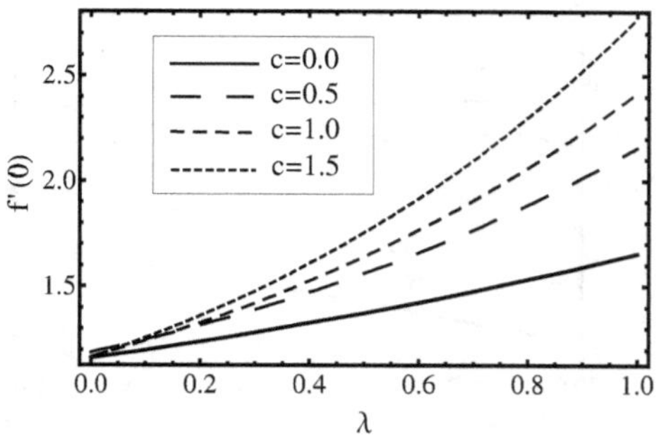


Figure 5.22: Effect of $\lambda$ on $f''(0)$ for different values of $c$.

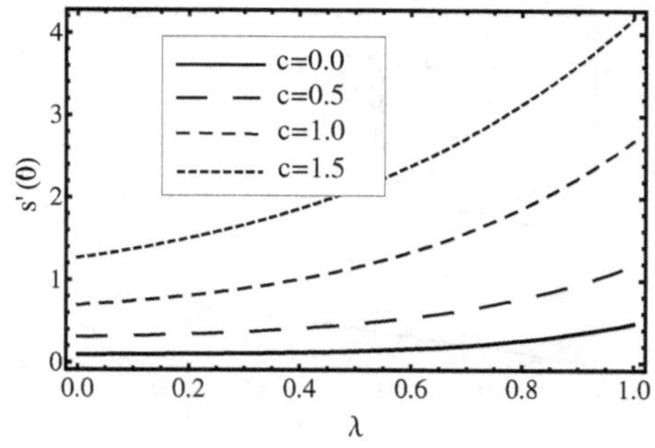


Figure 5.23: Effect of $\lambda$ on $s''(0)$ for different values of $c$.

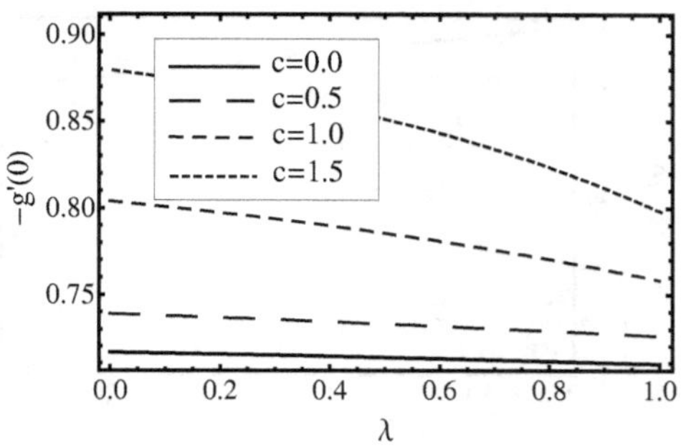


Figure 5.24: Effect of $\lambda$ on $-g'(0)$ for different values of $c$.

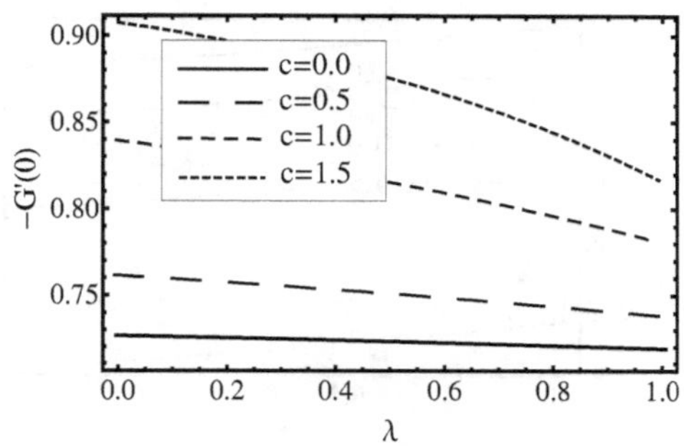


Figure 5.25: Effect of $\lambda$ on $-G'(0)$ for different values of $c$.

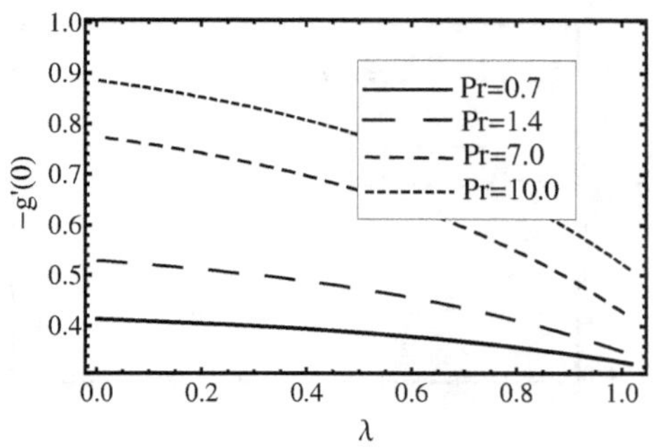


Figure 5.26: Effect of $\lambda$ on $-g'(0)$ for different values of $Pr$.

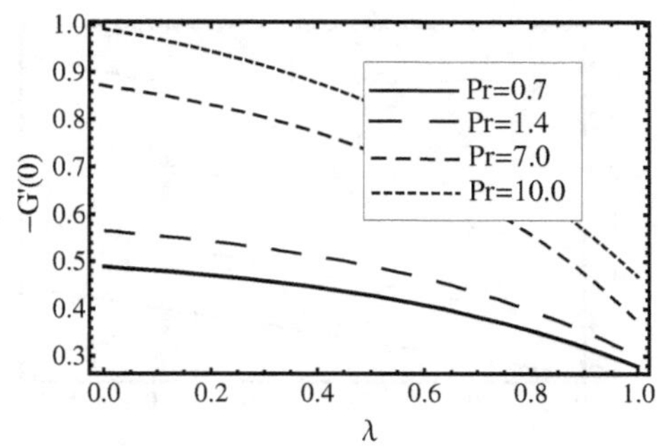


Figure 5.27: Effect of $\lambda$ on $-G'(0)$ for different values of $Pr$.

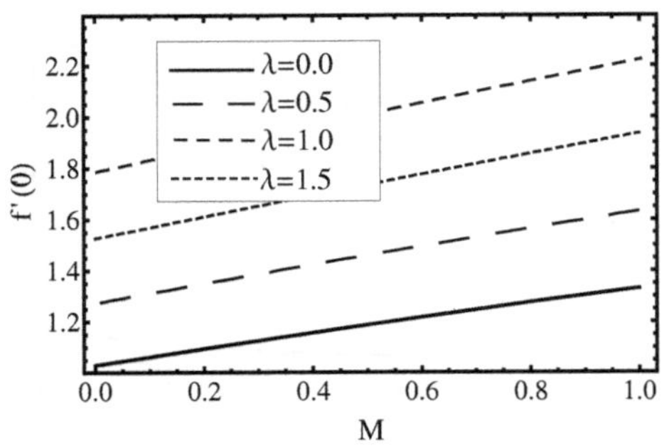


Figure 5.28: Effect of $M$ on $f''(0)$ for different values of $\lambda$.

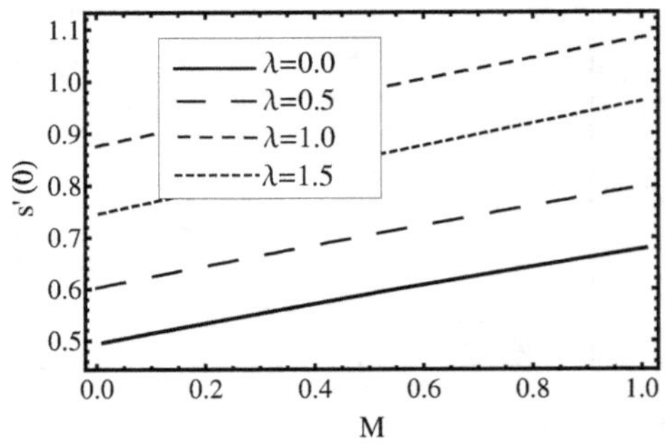


Figure 5.29: Effect of $M$ on $s''(0)$ for different values of $\lambda$.

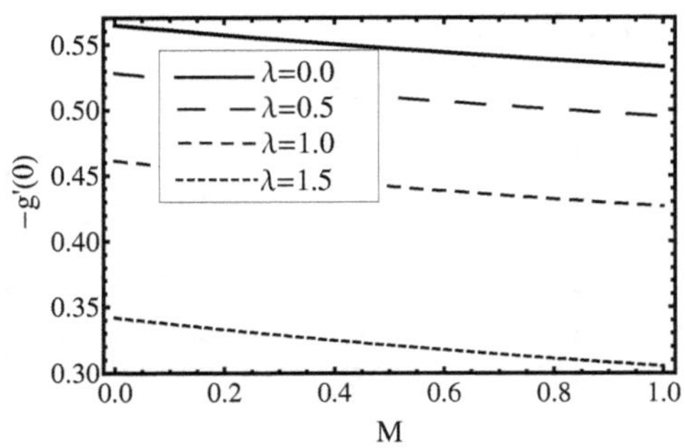


Figure 5.30: Effect of $M$ on $-g'(0)$ for different values of $\lambda$.

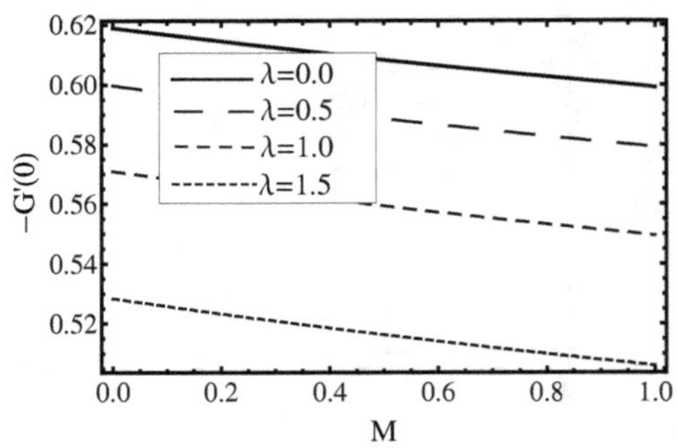


Figure 5.31: Effect of $M$ on $-G'(0)$ for different values of $\lambda$.

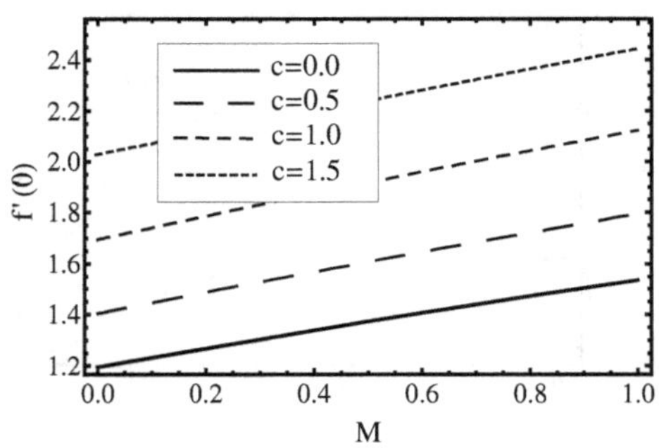


Figure 5.32: Effect of $M$ on $f''(0)$ for different values of $c$.

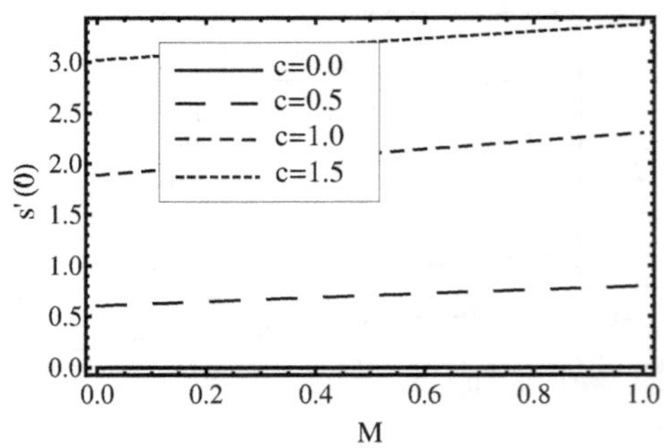


Figure 5.33: Effect of $M$ on $f''(0)$ for different values of $c$.

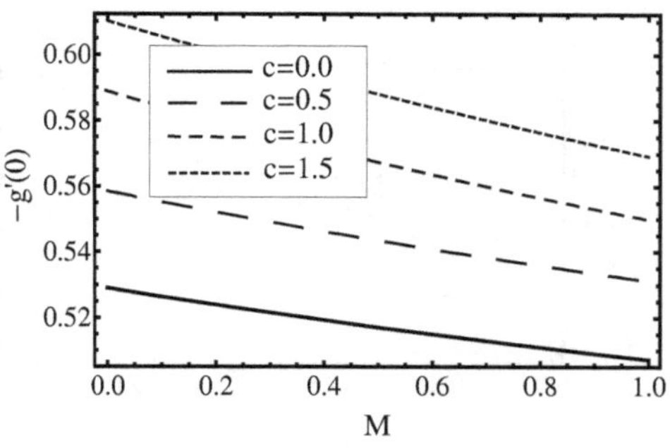


Figure 5.34: Effect of $M$ on $-g'(0)$ for different values of $c$.

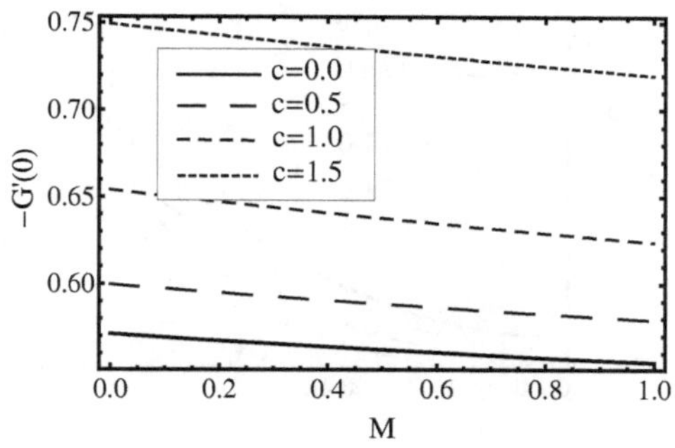


Figure 5.35: Effect of $M$ on $-G'(0)$ for different values of $c$.

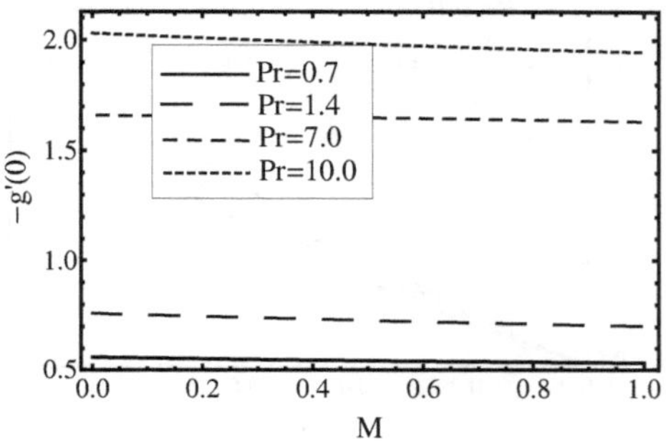


Figure 5.36: Effect of $M$ on $-g'(0)$ for different values of $Pr$.

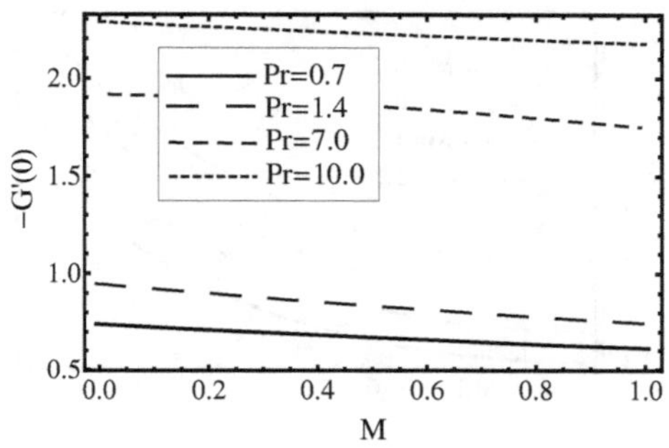


Figure 5.37: Effect of $M$ on $-G'(0)$ for different values of $Pr$.

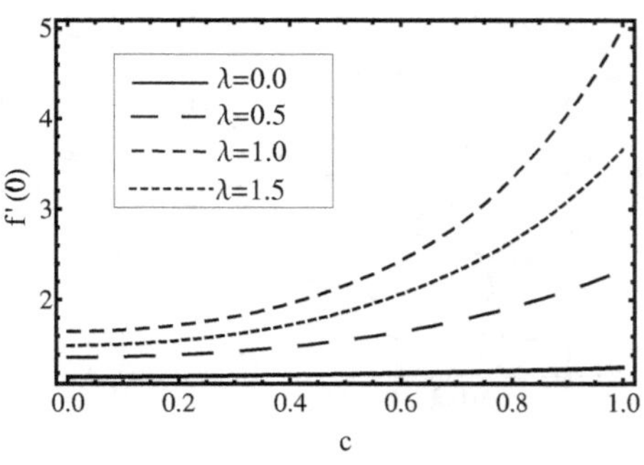


Figure 5.38: Effect of $c$ on $f''(0)$ for different values of $\lambda$.

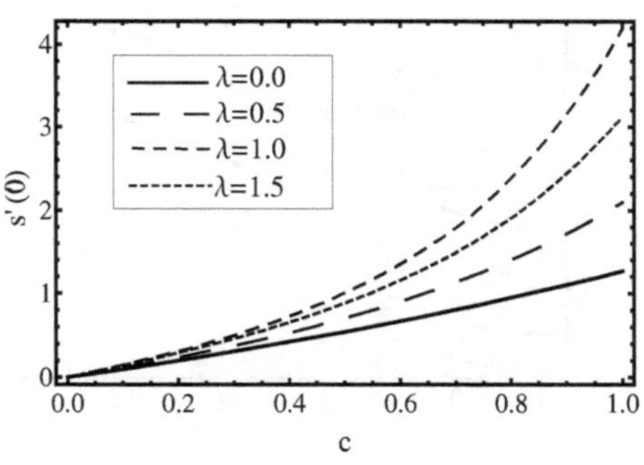


Figure 5.39: Effect of $c$ on $s''(0)$ for different values of $\lambda$.

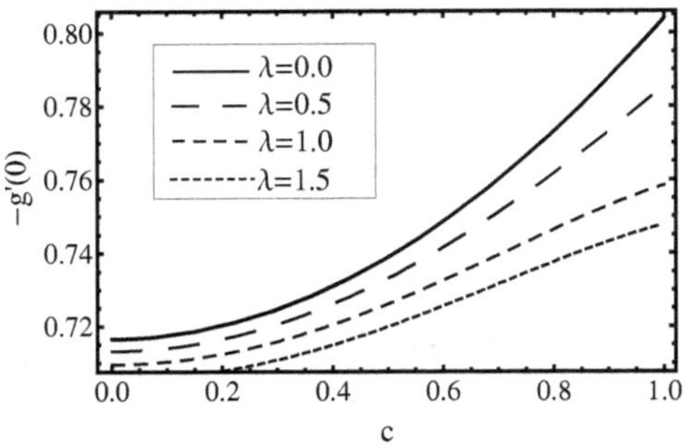


Figure 5.40: Effect of $c$ on $-g'(0)$ for different values of $\lambda$.

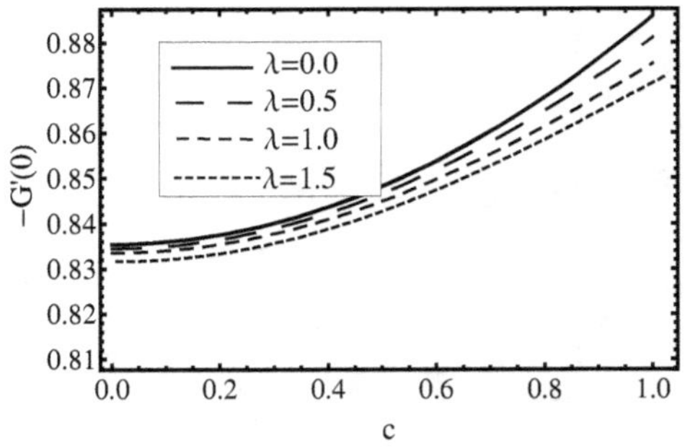


Figure 5.41: Effect of $c$ on $-G'(0)$ for different values of $\lambda$.

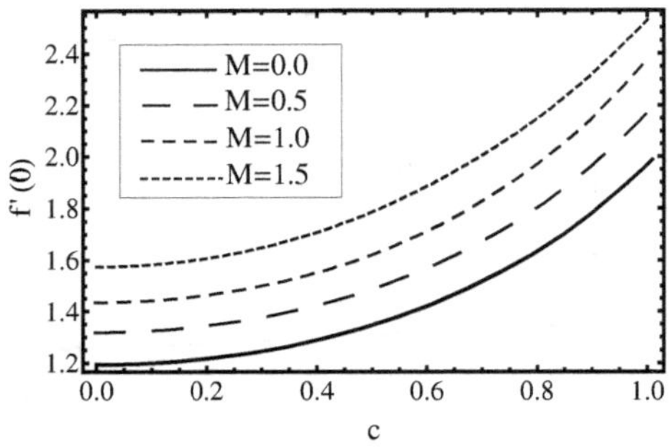


Figure 5.42: Effect of $c$ on $f''(0)$ for different values of $M$.

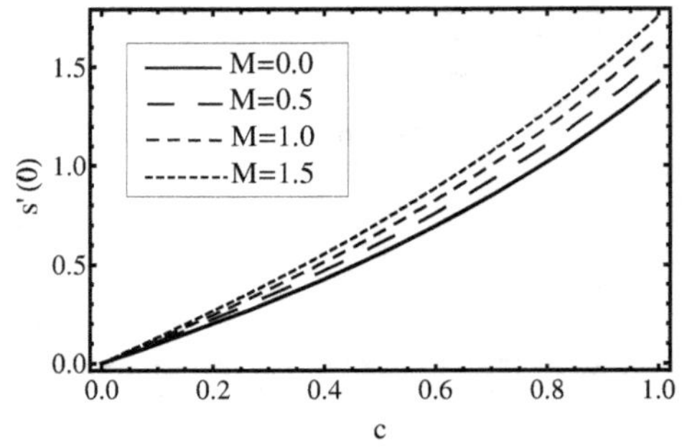


Figure 5.43: Effect of $c$ on $s''(0)$ for different values of $M$.

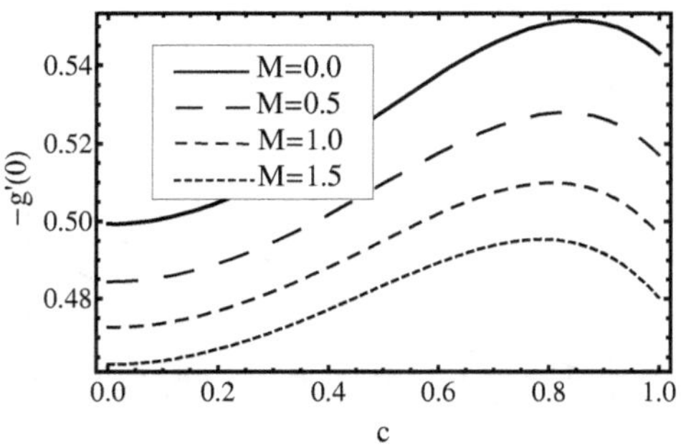


Figure 5.44: Effect of $c$ on $-g'(0)$ for different values of $M$.

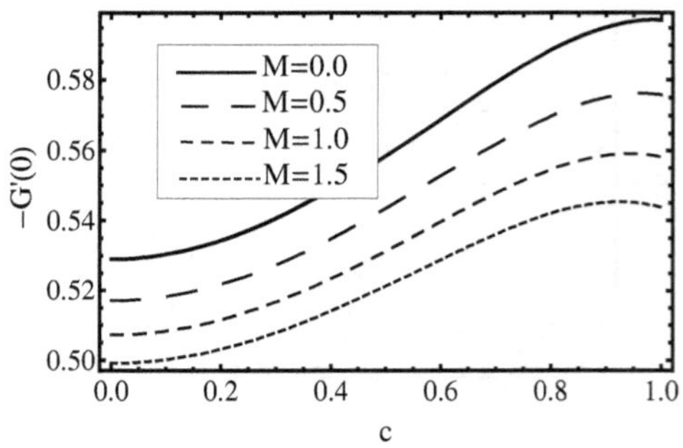


Figure 5.45: Effect of $c$ on $-G'(0)$ for different values of $M$.

# Chapter 6

# Mixed convection flow and heat transfer near the stagnation point on a heated vertical plate

## 6.1 Abstract

In all the earlier chapters, we considered different aspects of similarity boundary layer flows that are governed by a set of coupled nonlinear ordinary differential equations. But in this chapter, focus is on the non-similar boundary layer flows that are governed by non-linear partial differential equations. Non-similar boundary layer flows are more general, and thus are more important than similarity ones. Due to its complexity, very limited attempt has been made in solving non-similar flows by analytical procedure. Here, an advanced HAM is applied to study the flow and heat transfer in the stagnation region of a heated vertical plate in the presence of impulsive motion. The equations governing the two-dimensional flow and heat transfer are reduced to a system of non-similar, nonlinear partial differential equations. The governing non-similar equations are solved both analytically and numerically. An approximate analytical solution has been obtained for flow and heat transfer in the form of series solution using advanced HAM while the numerical results are computed using the KBM.

## 6.2 Introduction

The study of mixed convection flows (i.e. combination of forced and free convection flow) over different geometries have received much research interest due to its industrial and technical applications in solar central receivers, electronic devices, nuclear reactors and heat exchangers described by Seshadri *et al.* (2002). The mixed convection flow near the stagnation point is important when the buoyancy forces become large due to the temperature difference between the surface and the free stream. Consequently, both the flow and thermal fields are significantly affected by these buoyancy forces. The stagnation point flows often occur in several engineering processes and its applications are already highlighted in earlier chapters. During recent years, the subject of unsteady non-similar boundary layer studies near stagnation region has received considerable attention.

The importance of studying the unsteady non-similar boundary layer flow near stagnation region is that the heat transfer is maximum near the stagnation region. When the free stream velocity varies arbitrarily with time, unsteadiness is caused in the flow field. Hence the unsteadiness influences the flow and heat transfer to a great extent. Most of the earlier studies available in the literature were either the closed form solutions or semi analytical solutions or numerical solutions. The unsteady mixed convection flow near stagnation region of a heated vertical plate with thermal dissipation effects has been investigated by Alharbi *et al.* (2011). Beg *et al.* (2011) numerically studied the cross-diffusion effects on mixed convection, heat and species transfer in a boundary layer flow due to a inclined plate. Chamkha *et al.* (2001) studied buoyancy forces on the flow and heat transfer over a continuous moving vertical surface which moves with non-uniform velocity in an ambient fluid numerically studied.

The development of mixed convection flow near the stagnation region of a vertical surface embedded in a porous medium with anisotropy, permeability effect was studied by Bachok *et al.* (2010). The unsteady, mixed convection flow near the stagnation point on vertical plate in a two-dimensional flow was studied by Cheng *et al.* (2005). Various aspects of this problem were considered by several authors Kumari *et al.* (2004), Lok *et al.* (2006), Ramachandran *et al.* (1988), Devi *et al.* (1991), Harris *et al.* (2009) and Hassanien *et al.* (2009).

The two-dimensional non-similar boundary layer flow has been investigated extensively under various conditions by Farooq *et al.* (2014), Fan *et al.* (2013), Kousar *et al.* (2013), Liao (2006; 2009; 2012) and Nazar *et al.* (2004) and Saha *et al.* (2004), Nadeem *et al.* (2010), Mustafa *et al.* (2011), Nakhchi *et al.* (2012), Motsa (2014). Further Pal *et al.* (2011) solved the unsteady MHD, two-dimensional non-similar boundary layer flow due to stretching surface numerically using a RKFM.

Recently, Shafie (2013) studied the non-similar boundary layer flow considering the effect of thermophoresis and injection/suction in the stagnation point with micro polar fluid due to a moving plate and obtained solution by implicit finite difference method. Srinivasacharya *et al.* (2014) presented the natural convection flow of non-similar solution in the presence of thermophoresis and Brownian motion due to a doubly stratified porous medium and solved numerically using KBM. Two-dimensional unsteady, boundary layer flow near the stagnation region of a flat plate has been studied by Williams *et al.* (1980). Two-dimensional non similarity boundary layer flow near a stagnation region has been solved analytically by Xu *et al.* (2006) and You *et al.* (2010).

In several problems the flow may be unsteady which might be caused by the change in the free stream velocity or in the surface temperature (surface heat flux) or in both. When there is an impulsive change in the velocity field, the inviscid flow is developed instantaneously, but the flow in the viscous layer near the wall is developed slowly which becomes fully developed steady flow only after sometime. For small time the flow is dominated by the viscous forces and the unsteady acceleration, but for large time it is dominated by the pressure gradient and the convective acceleration in addition to the viscous forces. For small time the flow is generally independent of the conditions far upstream and at the leading edge and at the stagnation point, but, for large time the flow depends on these conditions. The mathematical problem for short time is governed by the Rayleigh type of equation and for large time by the Falkner-Skan type of equation.

The aim of this chapter is to study the development of flow and heat transfer near the stagnation region in the presence of buoyancy forces over to a vertical plate. The system of non-similar boundary layer equations to investigate its efficiency when dealing with strongly nonlinear, coupled partial differential equations (PDEs). The unsteadiness in the flow field is caused by impulsively creating motion in the free stream and at the same time suddenly raising the surface temperature (heat flux) above its surroundings. The problem is formulated in such a way that at $t = 0$ it is represented by the Rayleigh type of equation and for $t \to \infty$ it is represented by the Hiemenz type of equation.

Generally, HAM solutions are always represented as a power series form in which the coefficients contains the study parameters. In present analysis the various study parameters considered are the buoyancy parameter ($B$), unsteadiness in the flow ($t$) and Prandtl number ($Pr$). Also, computed the numerical solutions for the present governing equations using the KBM. The modified HAM presented in this chapter will be very useful for solving similar other non-linear boundary layer equations that arise in applied mathematics and computational fluid dynamics.

## 6.3 Problem formulation and governing equations

This section deals with the semi-infinite vertical plate which is placed in an ambient fluid with uniform temperature $T_\infty$. At $t = 0$ the ambient fluid is impulsively moved with a velocity $U_e$ and at the same time the surface temperature or heat flux of the plate is suddenly raised. Figure. 6.1 shows a flow field over a heated vertical surface where the upper half of the flow field is assisted by the buoyancy force, but the lower part experiences the buoyancy opposed flow. The reverse trend occurs if the plate is cooled below. The results illustrated here are valid for both cases. The surface of the plate is assumed to have an arbitrary temperature or it is subjected to an arbitrary heat flux. Under the above assumptions along with Boussinesq approximation, the unsteady laminar boundary layer equations governing the mixed convection flow are given by Ramachandran *et al.* (1988).

$$\begin{aligned} u_x + v_y &= 0 && (6.1)\\ u_t + uu_x + vu_y &= u_e(u_e)_x + \nu u_{yy} + g\alpha(T - T_\infty) && (6.2)\\ T_t + uT_x + vT_y &= \beta T_{yy}. && (6.3) \end{aligned}$$

The initial conditions for the problem when $t < 0$ are:

$$u(x,y) = v(x,y) = 0, \quad T(x,y) = T_\infty. \qquad (6.4)$$

The boundary conditions for the problem when $t \geq 0$ are:

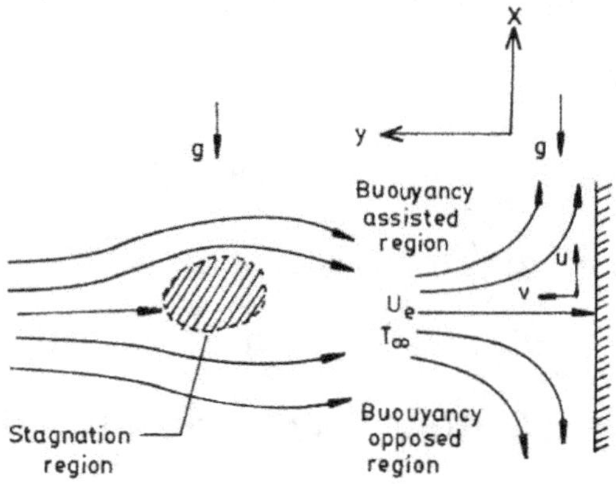


Figure 6.1: The coordinate system of flow model.

$$u(x,0)=v(x,0)=0,\;\; u(x,\infty)=U_e=ax,\;\; a>0$$
$$T(x,\infty)=T_\infty,\;\; T(x,0)=T_w(x)=bx^n,\;\; b>0,\;\; n\geq 0,$$

for the prescribed surface temperature (PST case);

$$-\kappa\frac{\partial T(x,0)}{\partial y}=q_w(x)=cx^n,\;\; c>0, \tag{6.5}$$

for the prescribed surface heat flux (PHF case). The indices $n=1$ and $n=0$ correspond the linear surface temperature and the constant surface temperatures, respectively.

Where $x$ and $y$ are distances along and normal to the surface, respectively, $u$ and $v$ are the components of the velocity along the $x$ and $y$ directions, respectively. $T$ is the temperature, $\kappa$, $\nu$ and $q_w$, $\alpha$, $g$ and $\beta$ are the thermal conductivity, kinematic viscosity and the surface heat transfer, coefficient of volumetric thermal expansion, the gravitational fluid acceleration and the thermal diffusivity, respectively. Subscripts $e$, $\infty$ and $w$ are the conditions at the edge of the boundary layer, at the free stream and in the surface, respectively. The subscripts $t$, $x$ and $y$ denote the derivatives with respect to the $t$, $x$ and $y$, respectively.

It may be noticed that, certain difficulties are encounter in formulating the boundary layer problem development in the presence of impulsive motion. Used the scale $Q=\frac{y}{\sqrt{\nu t}}$, $t^*=u_et/x$ for laser-time solution as well as for large-time solution for the scale $\eta=y\frac{u_e}{\sqrt{\nu x}}$. If the boundary layer problem is formulated in $(Q,t^*)$-system, the laser-time solution fits in properly, but the large-time solution does not fit. Therefore we have to find a scaling of the $y$ coordinate which behaves like $\frac{y}{\sqrt{\nu t}}$ for laser-time solution and as $y\frac{u_e}{\sqrt{\nu x}}$ for large-time solution. Consider here the time scale $\xi$ so that the region of time integration may become finite. Such transformations has been reported by Seshadri *et al.* (2002) as follows

$$\begin{aligned}
\eta &= (\frac{a}{\nu})^{1/2} y \xi^{-1/2}, \quad \text{where } \xi = 1 - e^{-t^*}, \quad t^* = at, \quad a > 0 \\
u(x,y,t) &= axf'(\eta,\xi) \text{ and } v = (a\nu)^{1/2}\xi^{1/2} f(\eta,\xi) \\
T(x,y,t) &= T_\infty + (T_w - T_\infty) g(\eta,\xi) \qquad \text{(PST Case)} \\
T(x,y,t) &= T_\infty + (\frac{a}{\nu})^{-1/2} (q_w/k) g(\eta,\xi) \quad \text{(PHF Case)} \\
Pr &= \frac{\nu}{\beta}, \quad Re_x = \frac{ax^2}{\nu}, \quad B_1 = \frac{Gr_x}{Re_x^2} \text{ and } B_2 = \frac{Gr_x^*}{Re_x^{5/2}} \\
Gr_x &= g\alpha(T_w - T_\infty)x^3/\nu^2 \text{ and } Gr_x^* = g\alpha q_w x^4/k\nu^2. \qquad (6.6)
\end{aligned}$$

Substituting eq. (6.6) into (6.1)-(6.3), find that (6.1) is identically satisfied and (6.2)-(6.3) are reduce to the following system of non-linear partial differential equations are as

$$f''' + 2^{-1}\eta(1-\xi)f'' + \xi(1 + ff'' - f'^2 + Bg) - \xi(1-\xi)\frac{\partial f'}{\partial \xi} = 0 \qquad (6.7)$$

$$g'' + 2^{-1}(1-\xi)\eta Prg' + Pr\xi(fg' - nf'g) - Pr\xi(1-\xi)\frac{\partial g'}{\partial \xi} = 0, \qquad (6.8)$$

where $B$ is a buoyancy parameter, $B = B_1$ and $B = B_2$ for PST case and PHF cases respectively. For $B_1(B_2) > 0$ and $B_1(B_2) < 0$ corresponding the buoyancy assisting flow and the buoyancy opposing flow, respectively.

$$\begin{aligned}
f(0,\xi) &= f'(0,\xi) = 0, \quad f'(\infty,\xi) = 1, \quad g(\infty,\xi) = 0, \\
g(0,\xi) &= 1 \text{ (PST case)}, \quad g'(0,\xi) = -1 \text{ (PHF case)}. \qquad (6.9)
\end{aligned}$$

Here $f'$ is the dimensionless velocity, $f$ and $g$ are the dimensionless stream function and dimensionless temperature, respectively, $B$ is the buoyancy parameter, $\eta$ is the pseudo-similarity variable and $Pr$ is the Prandtl number, $a$, $b$ and $c$ are the constants, $t$ and $t^*$ are the dimensional and dimensionless times, respectively, $Gr_x$ and $Gr_x^*$ are the Grashof numbers for the PST and PHF cases, respectively and prime denotes derivative with respect to $\eta$.

It may be noted that the buoyancy parameters $B_1$ and $B_2$ are the functions of stream wise distance $x$ unless the surface temperature $(T_w - T_\infty)$ and the surface heat flux $(q_w)$ vary linearly with $x$ (i.e., $n = 1$). For $n = 1$, $B_1$ and $B_2$ are constants. In particular, $b = c = \alpha g a^2$, then $B_1 = B_2 = 1$. Hence for the self-similar solution both $(T_w - T_\infty)$

and $(q_w)$ should vary linearly with x (i.e., $n = 1$). For $n \neq 1$, the equations are locally self-similar.

For the heat flux, the local Skin friction coefficient on the surface can be expressed as

$$C_f = 2\mu(\partial u/\partial y)_{y=0}/\rho U_e^2 = 2\xi^{-1/2}(Re_x)^{-1/2} f''(\xi,0), \ \xi > 0.$$

The heat transfer coefficient in terms of the Nusselt number for PST and PHF cases are expressed as

$$Nu = x(\partial T/\partial y)_{y=0}/(T_w - T_\infty) = -(Re_x)^{1/2} g'(\xi,0), \ \xi > 0 \text{ and}$$

$$Nu = (Re_x)^{1/2}\xi^{-1/2}/g(\xi,0), \ \xi > 0.$$

Equations. (6.7)-(6.8) are nonlinear coupled parabolic partial differential equations under boundary conditions (6.9) for $n = 1$ (steady case) are identical to those of Ramachandran *et al.* (1988). Also, (6.7) under conditions (6.9) for buoyancy parameter $B = 0$ (forced convection flow) is the same as that of Williams *et al.* (1980), if we put $m = 1$ in their equation.

## 6.4 Homotopy series solution

Apply the HAM to solve non-similar boundary layer flows governed by the coupled nonlinear partial differential equations (i.e. eqs. (6.7)-(6.8)) with subject to the boundary conditions (6.9). The set of base functions, initial guesses and auxiliary linear operators as follows

$$f(\eta,\xi) = A_{0,0}^{\ell} + \sum_{\ell=0}^{+\infty}\sum_{i=1}^{+\infty}\sum_{j=0}^{+\infty}[A_{i,j}^{\ell}\eta^j e^{-i\eta}] \tag{6.10}$$

$$g(\eta,\xi) = \sum_{\ell=0}^{+\infty}\sum_{i=1}^{+\infty}\sum_{j=0}^{+\infty}[K_{i,j}^{\ell}\eta^j e^{-i\eta}]. \tag{6.11}$$

In which $A_{i,j}^{\ell}$ and $K_{i,j}^{\ell}$ are the coefficients to be determined.

$$f_0(\eta,\xi) = 1 - e^{-\eta}, \ g_0(\eta,\xi) = e^{-\eta} \tag{6.12}$$

$$\mathscr{L}_f = f_{\eta\eta\eta} - f_\eta; \ \mathscr{L}_g = g_{\eta\eta} - g, \tag{6.13}$$

so as to obtain a simpler form of solution as

$$\mathscr{L}_f\left[C_1+C_2e^{\eta}+C_3e^{-\eta}\right]=0;\ \ \mathscr{L}_g\left[C_4e^{\eta}+C_5e^{-\eta}\right]=0, \tag{6.14}$$

where $C_i$'s are arbitrary constants and can be obtained from (6.9).

### 6.4.1 Zeroth-order deformation problem

To obtain the HAM solution for the governing eqs. (6.7)-(6.8), let $\gamma\in[0,1]$ be an embedding parameter and $c_X$ is the basic convergence control parameter and $H(\eta,\xi)$ be a non-zero auxiliary parameter. Then the zeroth order deformation equation takes the form,

$$(1-\gamma)L_X[X(\eta,\xi;\gamma)-X_0(\eta,\xi)]=\gamma H(\eta,\xi)c_X\mathscr{N}_X[X(\eta,\xi;\gamma)], \tag{6.15}$$

where, $X=f$ and $g$; $X_0=f_0$ and $g_0$.

The non linear operator of each of these flow variables can be explicitly written from the governing equations as

$$\begin{aligned}\mathscr{N}_f[f(\eta,\xi;\gamma),\ g(\eta,\xi;\gamma)] &= f'''+2^{-1}\eta(1-\xi)f''+\xi(1+ff'' \\ &\quad -f'^2+Bg)-\xi(1-\xi)\frac{\partial f'}{\partial\xi}\end{aligned} \tag{6.16}$$

$$\begin{aligned}\mathscr{N}_g[f(\eta,\xi;\gamma),\ g(\eta,\xi;\gamma)] &= g''+2^{-1}(1-\xi)\eta Prg'+Pr\xi(fg' \\ &\quad -nf'g)-Pr\xi(1-\xi)\frac{\partial g'}{\partial\xi}.\end{aligned} \tag{6.17}$$

### 6.4.2 Higher-order deformation problem

For obtaining the $\ell^{th}$-order deformation equations, differentiate eq. (6.15) $\ell$-times with respect to $\gamma$, and divide by $\ell!$. Setting $\gamma=0$, we get

$$\mathscr{L}_{\mathscr{X}}[X_\ell(\eta,\xi;c_X)-\Omega_\ell X_{\ell-1}(\eta,\xi;c_X)]=c_X\mathscr{R}_\ell^X X_{\ell-1}(\eta,\xi;c_X), \tag{6.18}$$

where,

$$\mathscr{R}_\ell^X X_{\ell-1}(\eta,\xi;c_X)=\frac{1}{\ell!}\frac{\partial^\ell}{\partial\gamma^\ell}\bigg|_{\gamma=0}, \tag{6.19}$$

where the function $\Omega_\ell$ denotes the characteristic function defined as

$$\Omega_\ell=\begin{cases}0 & \text{if } \ell=1\\ 1 & \text{if } \ell>1.\end{cases} \tag{6.20}$$

In (6.18), the term $\mathscr{R}_\ell^X X_{\ell-1}(\eta,\xi;c_X)$ denotes $\mathscr{R}_\ell^f f_{\ell-1}(\eta,\xi;c_f)$ and $\mathscr{R}_\ell^g g_{\ell-1}(\eta,\xi;c_g)$. These are the remainder terms from the linear operators which are given by

$$\begin{aligned}
\mathscr{R}_\ell^f f_{\ell-1}(\eta,\xi;c_f) &= \frac{1}{(\ell-1)!}\frac{\partial^{\ell-1}}{\partial\gamma^{\ell-1}}\mathscr{N}_f[f(\eta,\xi;\gamma),g(\eta,\xi;\gamma)]|_{\gamma=0} \\
&= (f_{\eta\eta\eta})_{\ell-1}+2^{-1}\eta(1-\xi)(f_{\eta\eta})_{\ell-1} \\
&+ \xi\left(1+\sum_{k=0}^{\ell-1}[f_{\ell-1-k}(f_{\eta\eta})_k-(f_\eta)_{\ell-1-k}(f_\eta)_k)]\right) \\
&+ \xi(Bg(\eta,\xi)-(1+\xi))(g_{\eta\xi})_{\ell-1},
\end{aligned} \tag{6.21}$$

$$\begin{aligned}
\mathscr{R}_\ell^g g_{\ell-1}(\eta,\xi;c_g) &= \frac{1}{(\ell-1)!}\frac{\partial^{\ell-1}}{\partial\gamma^{\ell-1}}\mathscr{N}_g[f(\eta,\xi;\gamma),g(\eta,\xi;\gamma)]|_{\gamma=0} \\
&= (g_{\eta\eta})_{\ell-1}+2^{-1}\eta Pr(1-\xi)(g_\eta)_{\ell-1} \\
&+ \xi Pr\left(\sum_{k=0}^{\ell-1}[f_{\ell-1-k}(g_\eta)_k-n(f_\eta)_{\ell-1-k}g_k)]\right) \\
&- \xi Pr(1-\xi)(g_{\eta\xi})_{\ell-1}.
\end{aligned} \tag{6.22}$$

The $\ell^{th}$-order deformations in the frame of HAM are $f_\ell(\eta,\xi;c_f)$ and $g_\ell(\eta,\xi;c_g)$ can be obtained using the following recursive formulae,

$$f_\ell(\eta,\xi;c_f)=\Omega_\ell f_{\ell-1}(\eta,\xi;c_f)+f_\ell^*(\eta,\xi;c_X)+C_1^\ell+C_2^\ell e^\eta+C_3^\ell e^{-x} \tag{6.23}$$

$$g_\ell(\eta,\xi;c_g)=\Omega_\ell g_{\ell-1}(\eta,\xi;c_g)+g_\ell^*(\eta,\xi;c_X)+C_4^\ell+C_5^\ell e^{-x}, \tag{6.24}$$

where,

$$\begin{aligned}
C_1^\ell &= (f_\eta)_\ell^*(0,0)-f_\ell^*(0,0);\ C_2^\ell=(f_\eta)_\ell^*(0,\xi); \\
C_3^\ell &= C_4^\ell=0;\ C_5^\ell=-g_\ell^*(0,\xi),
\end{aligned} \tag{6.25}$$

where, $f_\ell^*(\eta,\xi;c_f)$, $g_\ell^*(\eta,\xi;c_g)$ are the particular solutions defined by

$$f_\ell^*(\eta,\xi;c_f)=\mathscr{L}_f^{-1}\left[c_f\mathscr{R}_\ell^f f_{\ell-1}(\eta,\xi;c_f)\right] \tag{6.26}$$

$$g_\ell^*(\eta,\xi;c_g)=\mathscr{L}_g^{-1}\left[c_g\mathscr{R}_\ell^g g_{\ell-1}(\eta,\xi;c_g)\right]. \tag{6.27}$$

By solving (6.26)-(6.27) one after the other in the order $\ell=1,2,3,...$ by means of the symbolic computation software Mathematica, it is shown that the solution for the profiles can be expressed as an infinite series of any desired order. The approximate analytical solutions computed for $f$ and $g$ for $\ell=1,2,3,...$ are given in **Appendix-E**.

The solution series for $f(\eta,\xi)$ and $g(\eta,\xi)$ are expressed as,

$$f(\eta,\xi)=\sum_{\ell=0}^{+\infty} f_\ell(\eta,\xi;c_f); \quad g(\eta,\xi)=\sum_{\ell=0}^{+\infty} g_\ell(\eta,\xi;c_g). \tag{6.28}$$

In all of the figures, we use $Pr=0.7$, $B=n=1.0$, $\xi=0.5$, $c_f=-1.63203$ and $c_g=-0.45538$ unless it is mentioned otherwise.

### 6.4.3 The error estimation at high orders

At the $\ell^{th}$-order of approximation, the exact squared residual errors of the governing eqs. (6.16)-(6.17) are defined as

$$\Delta_\ell^X(c_X)=\int_0^\infty\left(N_X\left[\sum_{i=0}^{\ell}X_i\right]\right)^2 d\eta. \tag{6.29}$$

We define, $\Delta_\ell^{total}(c_X)=\Delta_\ell^f(c_f)+\Delta_\ell^g(c_g)$. Here $\Delta_\ell^{total}$ is the total exact squared residual errors at $\ell^{th}$-order of approximation solution.

Whenever, the (6.28) is known to be convergent series, the (6.23) and (6.24) are represent the exact solution of governing equations. But, (6.29) requires too much CPU time to compute the exact squared residual errors even for the lesser order of approximation. For example (see the Table 6.1), it needs 25.04, 372.44, 835.6 and 1023.25 seconds of CPU time for $\ell=1,5,10$ and 15 respectively and therefore not very useful in practice.

To over come this, we compute average squared residual error suggested by Liao (2012)

$$E_\ell^X(c_X)\simeq\frac{1}{N+1}\sum_{i=0}^{N}\left[\mathcal{N}_X\left(\sum_{J=0}^{\ell}(X_j)\right)\Bigg|_{t=q\delta x;x=i\delta x}\right]^2, \tag{6.30}$$

where, $N$ is an integer. It is reasonable to set $N=80.0$ and $\delta x=0.1$.

We define $E_\ell^{total}(c_X)=E_\ell^f(c_f)+E_\ell^g(c_g)$, where $E_\ell^{total}$ is the total average squared residual error at $\ell^{th}$-order of approximation solution. Obviously, the smaller the values of $E_\ell^{total}$ for given iteration $\ell$, the better the approximation.

The total average squared residual attained its minimum values at $c_f=-1.632037$ and $c_g=-0.455381$ and these values are used for all computation of results. The convergent non-similar HAM solutions for governing equations in the whole domain $0\le\xi\le1$ and $0\le\eta\le+\infty$. These calculations, not only give the efficiency region of the convergence control parameters but also their appropriate values to enable faster convergence of the non-similar HAM solutions. The HAM solutions which depend on optimal convergence control parameters $c_f$ and $c_g$ can be obtained accurately by the proper choice of convergence-control parameters.

## 6.5 Numerical solution

Though several numerical results are available in the literature, to compare the present approximate analytical results for different parametric values and performed numerical computation with the simple and still popular technique KBM. The numerical solution of (6.7)-(6.8) subject to the boundary conditions (6.9) is obtained using the KBM (see, Shafie (2013), Srinivasacharya *et al.* (2014)). The KBM discussed in detail in introductory chapter. Since the focus is on the approximate analytical solutions, the detailed mathematical derivations for numerical solutions are not presented here for sake of brevity. The numerical results and approximate analytical results agree very well in all the calculations, which are shown in the tables.

## 6.6 Result Analysis

The approximate analytical solutions are obtained in the form of general series for the flow variables $f(\eta,\xi)$ and $g(\eta,\xi)$. The computational software **Mathematica** is used for all algebraic and numerical calculations. The expressions for $f(\eta,\xi)$ and $g(\eta,\xi)$ are evaluated up to $8^{th}$-order. It is to be mentioned here that, though computations could be done easily up to $25^{th}$ order of deformations equations, to retain the results up to five decimal places accuracy and stopped at the $8^{th}$ order.

The effect of various parameters such as Buoyancy parameter $B$, unsteady parameter $\xi$ and Prandtl number $Pr$ are analysed. The influence of these parameters on velocity $f'(\eta,\xi)$ and temperature $g(\eta,\xi)$ profiles as well as in shear stress rates and heat transfer rates for both PST and PHF cases are studied. Computations have been carried out for several combinations of parameters $B$, $\xi$ and $Pr$, and all representative results are presented here in the form of Tables 6.1-6.3 and Figures. 6.2-6.35.

The convergence of the non-similar HAM solutions strongly depends on the convergence control parameters which provide a better way to control the convergence rate and guarantee the convergence solution due to the fixed values of the basic optimal convergence control parameters $c_f$ and $c_g$. It is customary in HAM analysis to plot $c_f$ and $c_g$-curves to identify the interval of optimal convergence control parameters within which any value can be chosen to obtain convergent of the non-similar HAM solution.

At every $\ell^{th}$-order of approximation, $\Delta_\ell^X$ takes at most three convergence control parametric values for eq. (6.15) and at most two for (6.18). The convergence control parameters are represented by $c_f$ and $c_g$ for (6.7) and (6.8), respectively. When $\Delta_\ell^X$ decrease to zero rapidly then the non-similar HAM series solutions converges faster. Whenever, the (6.28) is known to be convergent series, the (6.23) and (6.24) are represent the exact solution of governing equations.

It can be seen in Tables 6.1 that as we increase the order of iteration the corresponding average squared residual errors are decreasing. The computation is stopped when a certain convergence criterion is satisfied. This illustrative example validates the reliability of the non-similar HAM series solutions.

Tables 6.2 and Tables 6.3 present the convergence of surface shear stress $f''(0,\xi)$ and heat transfer rate $-g'(0,\xi)$ for the PST and PHF cases when $\xi = 0.5$, $n = B = 1$ at various values of Prandtl number. Numerical calculations obtained from KBM are carried out for various values of the dimensionless parameters of the problem. Numerical results of present HAM and KBM are compared and are found to be in good agreement.

Figures. 6.4-6.15 show the effect of the present study physical parameters on the velocity, temperature profiles and 6.16-6.35 show variation of shear stresses and heat transfer rates on both PST and PHF cases.

The $c_f$ and $c_g$ curves have been drawn for $8^{th}$-order non-similar solution series for different values of unsteady parameter $\xi$ such as $\xi = 0, 0.5$ and $1.0$ which are shown in 6.2-6.3. It is seen that at $\xi = 0.0$ and $1.0$, shear stress rates $f''(0,\xi)$ converges to the values for all $c_g$ in the interval $[-1.9,-0.3]$ and $[-1.5,-0.0]$, respectively. At $\xi = 0.5$, it also converges to the same value (which is different from that at $\xi = 0.0$ and $1.0$) when in the interval $[-2.1,-0.4]$. However, at $\xi = 0.5$, $f''(0,\xi)$ converges in the region $[-2.1,-0.4]$. Similarly, at $\xi = 0.0$ and $1.0$, heat transfer rate $-g'(0,\xi)$ converges to the values for all $c_f$ in the interval $[-1.9,-0.3]$ and $[-1.6,-0.2]$, respectively. At $\xi = 0.5$, it also converges to the values (which is different from that at $\xi = 0.0$ and

1.0) when in the interval $[-1.3, -0.2]$. However, at $\xi = 0.5$, $-g'(0,\xi)$ converges in the region $[-1.3, -0.2]$. Therefore, $c_f$ in the interval $[-1.6, -0.4]$ does not affect the values of shear stress rates and $c_g$ is $[-1.5, -0.3]$ for heat transfer rate. But the computation of average squared residual errors helps to obtain the optimal value of these optimal convergence control parameters within that interval.

The effect of $\xi$ on the velocity and temperature profiles $f'(\eta,\xi)$ and $g(\eta,\xi)$ when $n = 0,1, B_1 = 1, B_2 = -1$ and $Pr = 0.7$ plotted in 6.4-6.7. It is observed from these figures that, the velocity increases and temperature decreases with increasing the unsteady parameter $\xi$. Also, reverse flow occurs for negative values of $B_2$ seen in 6.6-6.7.

For PST and PHF case, the effect of buoyancy parameter in assisting flow and opposing flow respectively, on the velocity and temperature profiles for $Pr = 0.7$ and $\xi = 1$ displayed in 6.8-6.11. It is seen from theses figures that the velocity decreases and temperature increases with increasing the buoyancy assisting flow parameter $B_1$. Also, opposite trend occurs for negative values of buoyancy parameter $B_2$ seen in 6.10-6.11. The reason for this trend is that, the temperature decreases at $B_2 < 0$ when non-isothermal surface case (i.e. $n = 1$). The positive buoyancy force acts like a favorable pressure gradient and hence accelerates the fluid in the boundary layer. This results in higher velocity as buoyancy parameter increases. For $B_2 = -1.5$, the velocity of the fluid near the wall is more than that on the wall. Since thermal boundary layer is also reduced with increasing $B_2$, the temperature is lowered. It is also observed that the temperature at and near the wall is higher than that of the PHF case.

The effect of Prandtl number in the presence of the unsteady parameter $\xi = 1$ on the velocity $f'(\eta,\xi)$ and temperature profiles $g(\eta,\xi)$ for the PST case is displayed in 6.12-6.13. These figures demonstrate the fact that the velocity and temperature profiles decrease with the increase of $Pr$. Physically, $Pr = 0.7$ and 7.0, correspond to air and water respectively. Since the increase in the $Pr$ from 0.7 to 10 reduces both the momentum and thermal boundary layers, hence velocity and temperature profiles decrease with increasing $Pr$. Also for large $Pr$ the thermal boundary layer is much thinner than the momentum boundary layer, because the effect of $Pr$ is more pronounced on the temperature profiles than on the velocity profiles. This is due to the fact that $Pr$ occurs explicitly in the energy equation.

The effect of the Prandtl number on the velocity and temperature profiles $(f'(\eta,\xi)$

and $g(\eta,\xi)$ ) for the PHF case when $\xi = n = 1$ depicted in 6.14 - 6.15. The temperature at and near the wall changes very significantly unlike the PST case where the change is small. The velocity profiles are qualitatively similar to those of the PST case.

Figures. 6.16-6.23 presents the effect of the Prandtl number $Pr$ on shear stress rate and heat transfer rate for $B_1 = B_2 = \pm 1$, $0 \leq \xi \leq 1$ and for the PST and PHF case when $n = 0$ (isothermal surface case) and $n = 1$ (non-isothermal case). Since an increase in the $Pr$ reduces both the momentum and thermal boundary layers, shear stress rates and heat transfer rates increase with $Pr$. For $\xi = 1$, shear stress rates and heat transfer rates increase, respectively, by about 130% and 346% as $Pr$ increases from 0.7 to 10 seen in 6.16 to 6.17. It is observed from these figures that, the $n = 0$ (isothermal surface case), the heat transfer is found has to be less (about 34%) than that of $n = 1$ (non-isothermal case). The surface shear stress and heat transfer for buoyancy assisting flow ($B_1(B_2) > 0$) are more than those of the buoyancy opposing flow ($B_1(B_2) < 0$). Also, surface shear stress and heat transfer rate for PHF case are less than those of the PST case. Therefore, large Prandtl number, the thermal boundary layer is much thinner than the momentum boundary layer.

The influence of the shear stress $f''(0,\xi)$ and heat transfer rate $-g'(0,\xi)$ with $\xi$ for the PST case when the buoyancy assisting case when $B_1 = 0, 0.5, 1.0, 1.5$ at fixed $Pr = 0.7$ plotted in 6.24 to 6.27. It is observed that, the shear stress and the heat transfer rates increase with $B_1$, because positive buoyancy force acts like favourable pressure gradient which accelerates the motion and reduces both momentum and thermal boundary layers. Therefore, both the shear stress and the surface heat transfer rates increased. For $\xi = n = 1$ and $Pr = 0.7$, the shear stress and heat transfer rates increase by about 57% and 41%, respectively, as $B_1$ increases from 0 to 1.5.

The influence of the shear stress $f''(0,\xi)$ and heat transfer rate $-g'(0,\xi)$ with $\xi$ for the PHF case when the buoyancy opposing case when $B_2 < 0$ at fixed $Pr = 0.7$ plotted in 6.28-6.31. It is observed that, both the shear stress and the surface heat transfer rates decreases with effect of $B_2$ values. For $n = 0$ (isothermal surface case), the heat transfer is found has to be less (about 37%) than that of $n = 1$ (non-isothermal case). The reason for this trend is that for $n = 0$ the surface temperature difference $(T_w - T_\infty)$ is less than that of $n = 1$. This results in lower heat transfer for $n = 0$ as compared to $n = 1$. Also, for gases $(\mu \alpha T)$ reduction in surface temperature causes thinner boundary layer which in turn increases the shear stress rates. Therefore, surface shear stress and heat transfer for buoyancy assisting flow are more than those of the buoyancy opposing flow. For buoyancy assisting flow, the surface shear stress and heat transfer for the PHF case are slightly less than those of the PST case, but for the buoyancy opposing flow the reverse trend is observed.

The surface shear stress $f''(0,\xi)$ and heat transfer rate $-g'(0,\xi)$ for $n = 1,0$ and for $n = -0.5,-1$ with $\xi$ for the PST and PHF cases corresponding buoyancy flow $B_1 > 0$ and $B_2 < 0$ at fixed $Pr = 0.7$ plotted in Figures. 6.31 to 6.35. These figures demonstrate the fact that, the shear stress is increase and heat transfer decrease with decreasing $n$ values. For buoyancy assisting flow $B_1 > 0$, the shear stress and heat transfer rates for the prescribed surface heat flux are slightly less than those of the prescribed surface temperature, but for the buoyancy opposing flow $B_2 < 0$ the reverse trend is observed.

## 6.7 Summary

The present study discusses the development of flow and heat transfer near the stagnation region in the presence of buoyancy forces over a heated vertical plate. The solutions has been obtained for flow and heat transfer in the form of series solution using HAM while the numerical results are computed using the KBM. The effects of various parameters such as the buoyancy parameter, unsteadiness in the flow and Prandtl number on the velocity and temperature distributions as well as on skin friction and heat transfer coefficients are studied. The following conclusions are drawn from the present study.

- The velocity increases and temperature decreases with increasing the unsteady parameter. Also, reverse flow occurs for negative values of buoyancy parameter.
- The velocity decreases and temperature increases with increasing the buoyancy assisting flow parameter. Also, opposite trend occurs for negative values of buoyancy parameter.
- The surface shear stress and heat transfer are found to be increasing with time and there is a smooth transition from the small-time solution to the large-time solution.

- The surface shear stress and heat transfer for buoyancy assisting flow are more than those of the buoyancy opposing flow.
- The surface heat transfer increases with increasing Prandtl number, but the surface shear stress decreases for the buoyancy assisting flow and increases for the buoyancy opposing flow. For large Prandtl number, the thermal boundary layer is much thinner than the momentum boundary layer.
- For buoyancy assisting flow, the surface shear stress and heat transfer for the PHF case is slightly less than those of the PST case, but for the buoyancy opposing flow the reverse trend is observed.
- The surface heat transfer can considerably be reduced by using a lower Prandtl number fluid. It can also be reduced by imposing the buoyancy force in the opposite direction to that of the forced flow or by maintaining uniform temperature or heat flux on the surface.

Table 6.1: Average squared residual error at different order of iterations for $Pr = 0.7$, $\xi = 0.5$ and $n = B = 1.0$ by using $c_f = -1.63203$ and $c_g = -0.45538$.

| $\ell$ | $E_\ell^f$ | $E_\ell^g$ | CPU time(S) |
|---|---|---|---|
| 1 | $1.646122 \times 10^{-4}$ | $1.094900 \times 10^{-3}$ | 25.04 |
| 5 | $1.867819 \times 10^{-5}$ | $1.784361 \times 10^{-4}$ | 372.44 |
| 10 | $2.092342 \times 10^{-6}$ | $3.002289 \times 10^{-5}$ | 835.62 |
| 15 | $4.109238 \times 10^{-7}$ | $2.338722 \times 10^{-6}$ | 1023.25 |
| 20 | $3.228370 \times 10^{-8}$ | $5.931709 \times 10^{-7}$ | 1289.88 |
| 25 | $2.356275 \times 10^{-9}$ | $1.777216 \times 10^{-8}$ | 1501.06 |
| 30 | $1.209200 \times 10^{-10}$ | $1.074358 \times 10^{-9}$ | 1723.15 |

Table 6.2: The shear stress rate $f''(0,\xi)$ and heat transfer rate $-g'(0,\xi)$ for the PST case when $n = 1.0$ and $\xi = 0.5$.

| $Pr$ | $B$ | $f''(0,\xi)$ | | $-g'(0,\xi)$ | |
|---|---|---|---|---|---|
| | | HAM | KBM | HAM | KBM |
| 0.7 | 1.0 | 1.78181 | 1.78182 | 1.09499 | 1.09500 |
| 7.0 | 1.0 | 1.59513 | 1.59513 | 1.79373 | 1.79375 |
| 20.0 | 1.0 | 1.49738 | 1.49739 | 2.51995 | 2.51999 |
| 60.0 | 1.0 | 1.41685 | 1.41685 | 3.52916 | 3.52916 |
| 0.7 | -1.0 | 0.72629 | 0.72630 | 0.79108 | 0.79109 |
| 7.0 | -1.0 | 0.95669 | 0.95673 | 1.58257 | 1.58251 |
| 20.0 | -1.0 | 1.11155 | 1.11159 | 2.32438 | 2.32437 |
| 60.0 | -1.0 | 1.22744 | 1.22746 | 3.30649 | 3.30649 |

Table 6.3: The surface shear stress $f''(0,\xi)$ and heat transfer rate $-g'(0,\xi)$ for the PHF case when $n = 1.0$ and $\xi = 0.5$.

| $Pr$ | $B$ | $f''(0,\xi)$ | | $-g'(0,\xi)$ | |
|---|---|---|---|---|---|
| | | HAM | KBM | HAM | KBM |
| 0.7 | 1.0 | 1.42964 | 1.42968 | 1.14646 | 1.14646 |
| 7.0 | 1.0 | 1.39860 | 1.39860 | 1.63280 | 1.63287 |
| 20.0 | 1.0 | 1.32140 | 1.32140 | 2.45475 | 2.45475 |
| 60.0 | 1.0 | 1.28246 | 1.28248 | 3.51652 | 3.51652 |
| 0.7 | -1.0 | 0.78391 | 0.78390 | 1.08767 | 1.08767 |
| 7.0 | -1.0 | 1.08172 | 1.08175 | 1.52549 | 1.52550 |
| 20.0 | -1.0 | 1.19559 | 1.19559 | 2.40008 | 2.40009 |
| 60.0 | -1.0 | 1.23501 | 1.23503 | 3.45576 | 3.45576 |

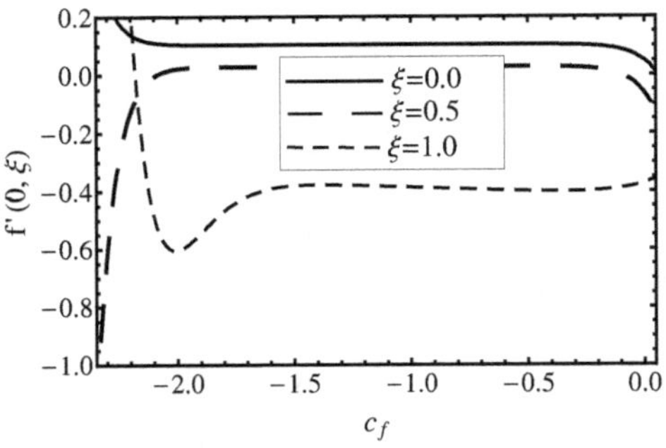


Figure 6.2: $c_f$ curve of $f''(0,\xi)$ for various values of $\xi$.

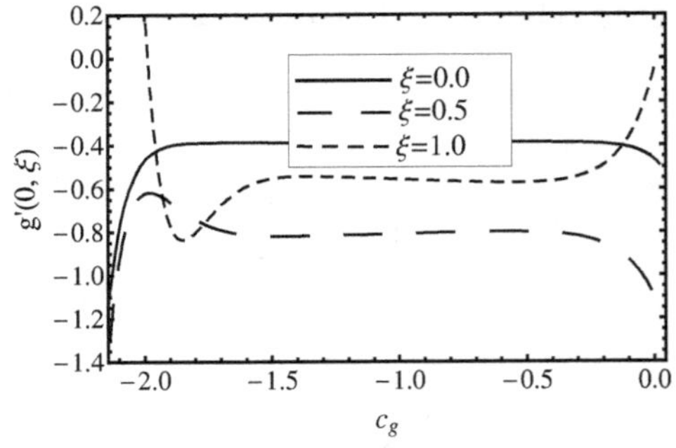


Figure 6.3: $c_g$ curve of $-g'(0,\xi)$ for various values of $\xi$.

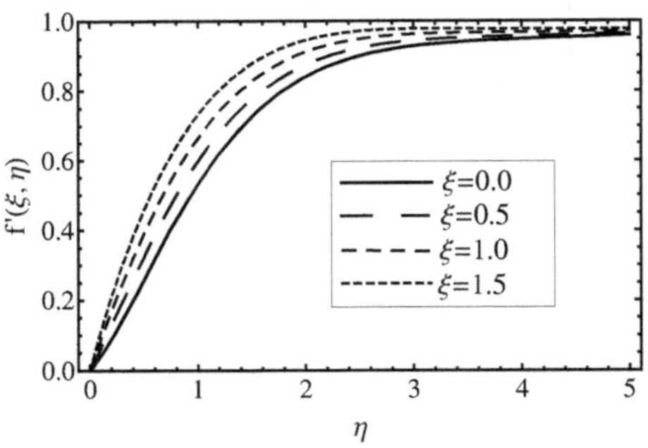


Figure 6.4: Velocity profiles for various values of $\xi$ for the PST case when $n = 0$.

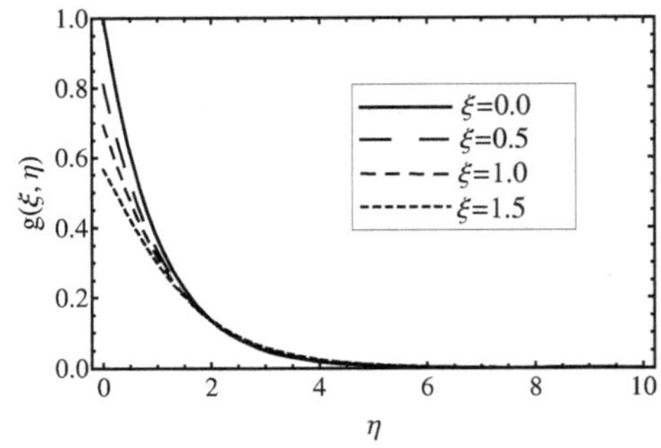


Figure 6.5: Temperature profiles for various values of $\xi$ for the PST case at $n = 0$.

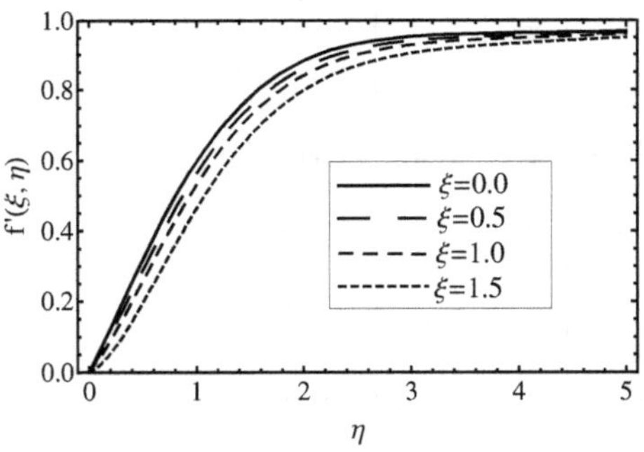


Figure 6.6: Velocity profiles for various values of $\xi$ for the PHF case when $n = 1$.

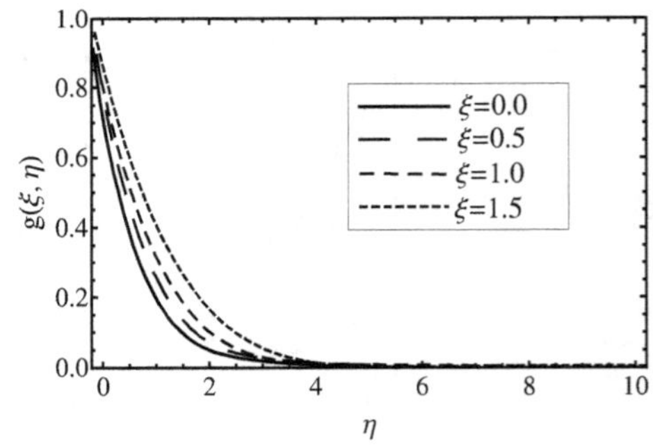


Figure 6.7: Temperature profiles for various values of $\xi$ for the PHF case at $n = 1$.

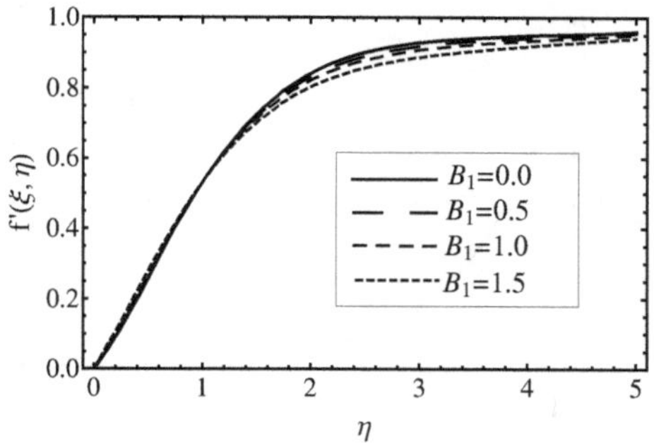


Figure 6.8: Velocity profiles for various values of $B_1$ for the PST case when $n = 0$ and $\xi = 1$.

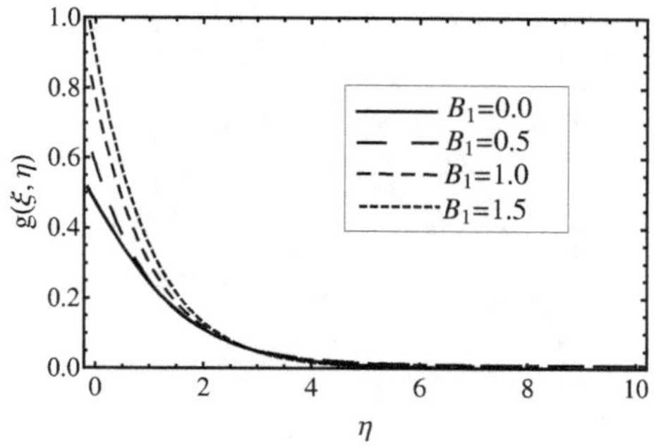


Figure 6.9: Temperature profiles for various values of $B_1$ for the PST case when $n = 0$ and $\xi = 1$.

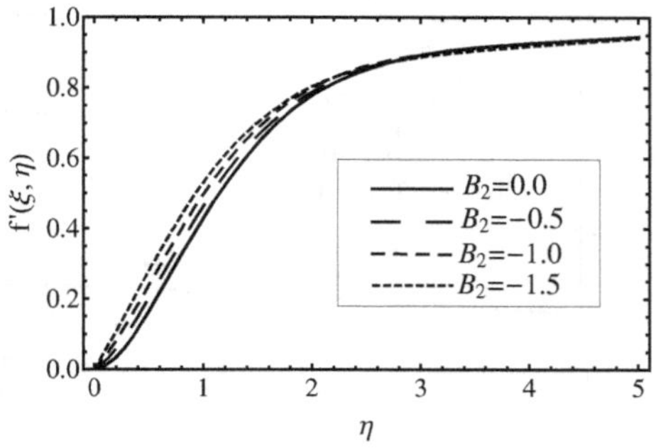


Figure 6.10: Velocity profiles for various values of $B_2$ for the PHF case when $n = 0$ and $\xi = 1$.

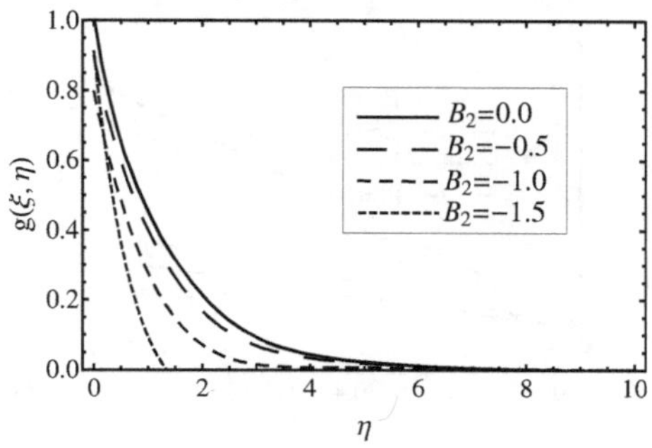


Figure 6.11: Temperature profiles for various values of $B_2$ for the PHF case when $n = 0$ and $\xi = 1$.

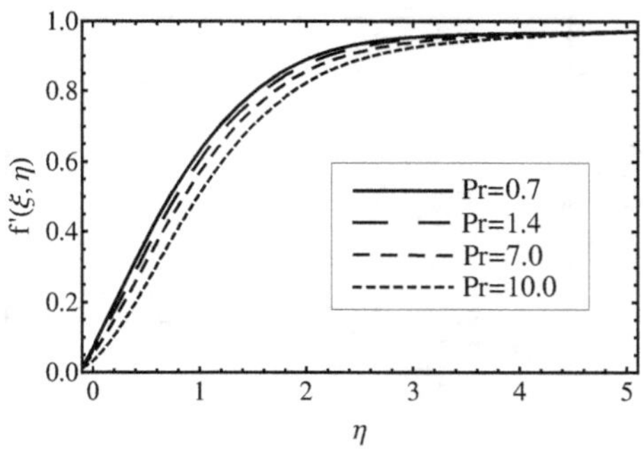


Figure 6.12: Velocity profiles for various values of $Pr$ for the PST case when $n = 0$ and $\xi = 1$.

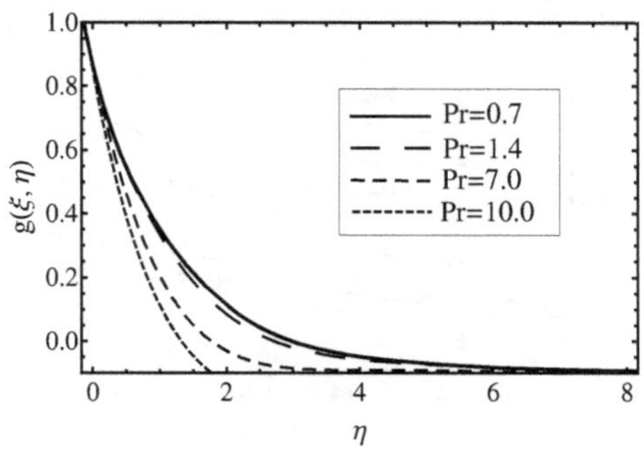


Figure 6.13: Temperature profiles for various values of $Pr$ for the PST case when $n = 0$ and $\xi = 1$.

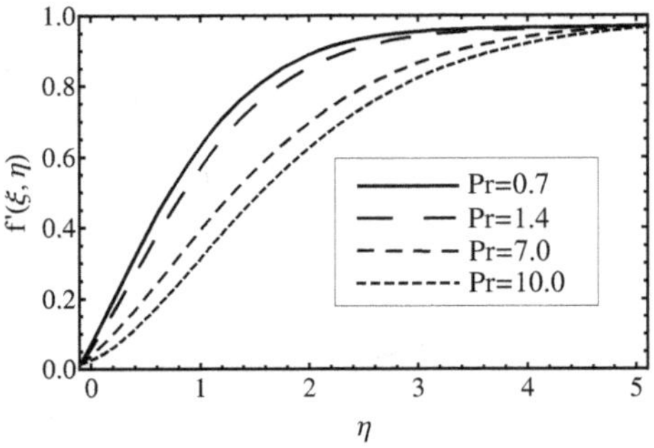


Figure 6.14: Velocity profiles for various values of $Pr$ for the PHF case when $n = 1$ and $\xi = 1$.

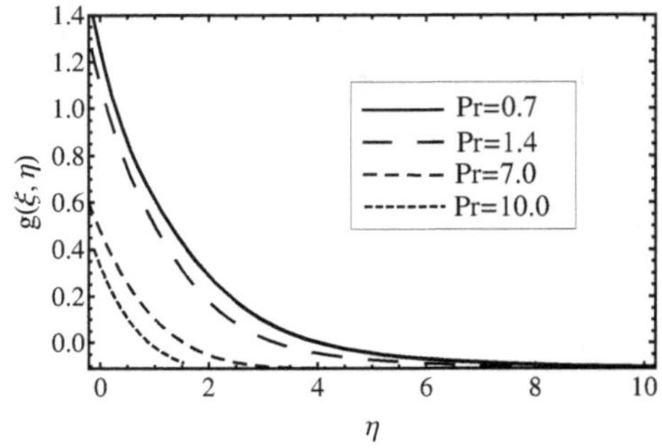


Figure 6.15: Temperature profiles for various values of $Pr$ for the PHF case when $n = 1$ and $\xi = 1$.

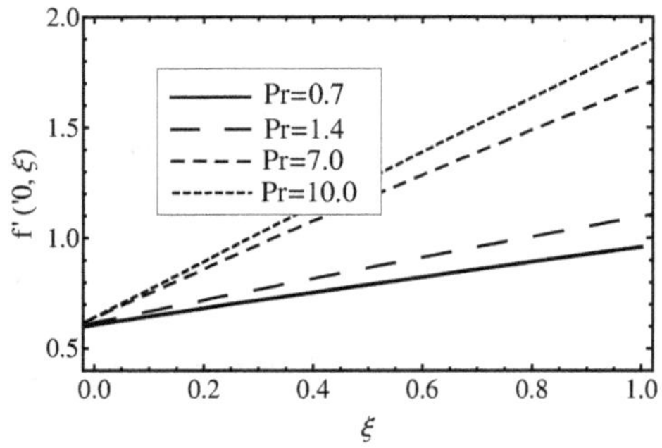


Figure 6.16: Effect of $\xi$ on $f''(0,\xi)$ for different values of $Pr$ for the PST case when $n = B_1 = 1$.

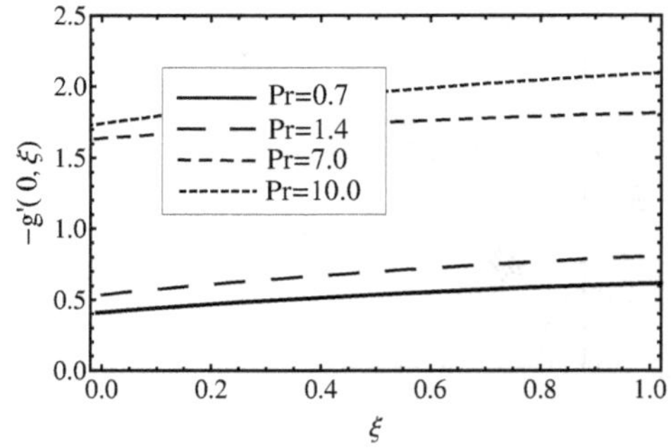


Figure 6.17: Effect of $\xi$ on $-g'(0,\xi)$ for different values of $Pr$ for the PST case when $n = B_1 = 1$.

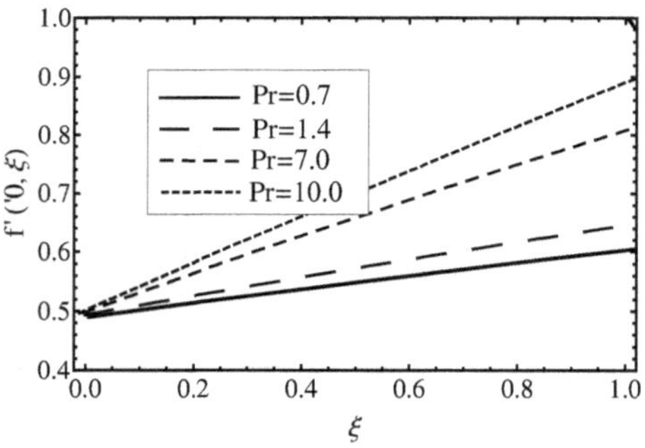


Figure 6.18: Effect of $\xi$ on $f''(0,\xi)$ for different values of $Pr$ for the PST case when $n = 1$ and $B_1 = -1$.

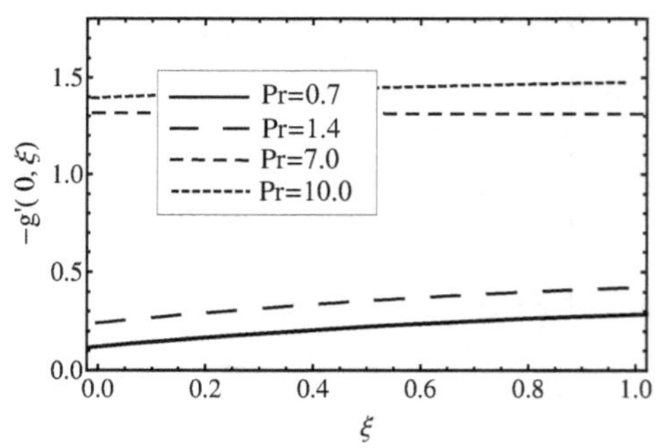


Figure 6.19: Effect of $\xi$ on $-g'(0,\xi)$ for different values of $Pr$ for the PST case when $n = 1$ and $B_1 = -1$.

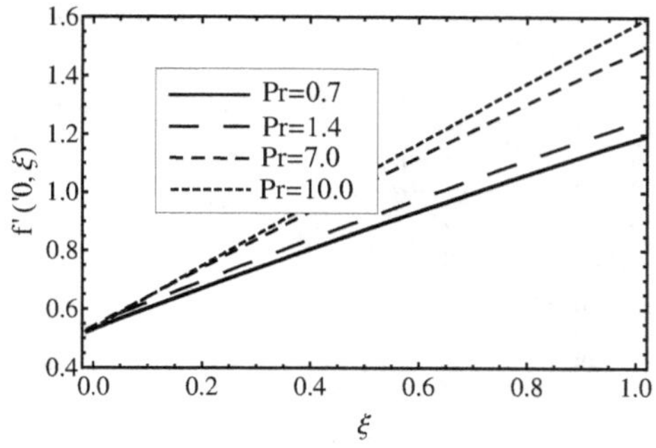


Figure 6.20: Effect of $\xi$ on $f''(0,\xi)$ for different values of $Pr$ for the PHF case when $n = B_2 = 1$.

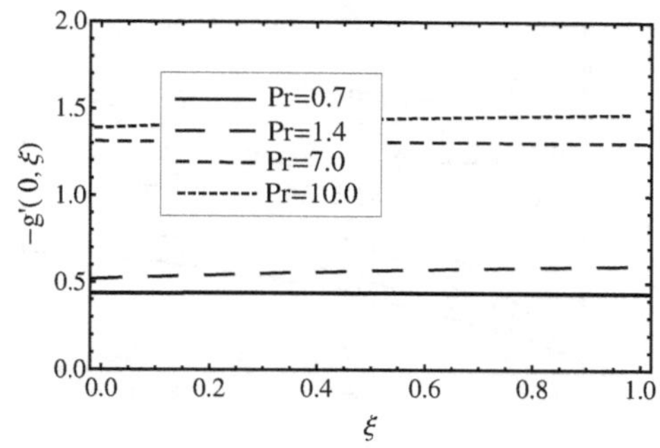


Figure 6.21: Effect of $\xi$ on $-g'(0,\xi)$ for different values of $Pr$ for the PHF case when $n = B_2 = 1$.

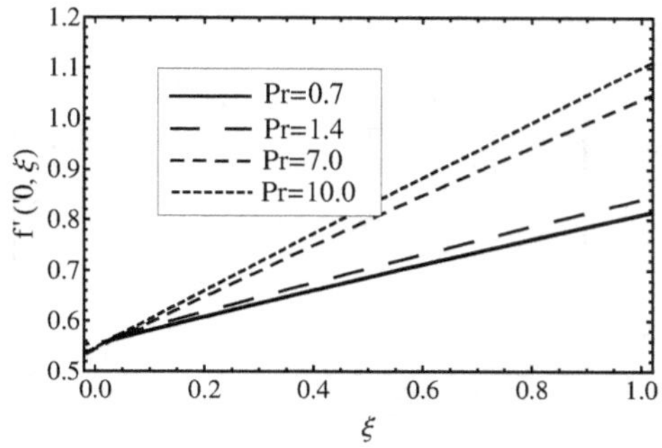


Figure 6.22: Effect of $\xi$ on $f''(0,\xi)$ for different values of $Pr$ for the PHF case when $n = 1$ and $B_2 = -1$.

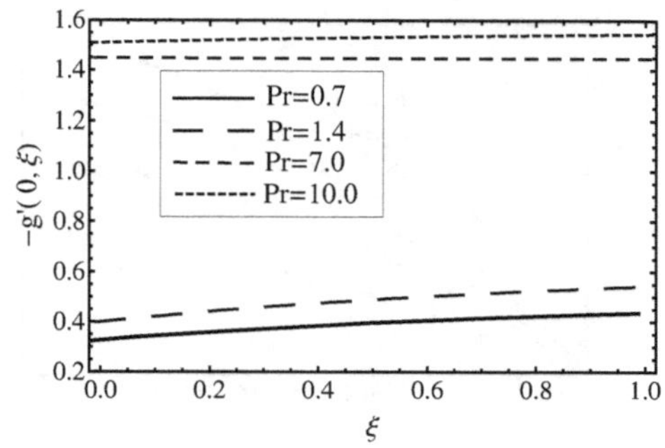


Figure 6.23: Effect of $\xi$ on $-g'(0,\xi)$ for different values of $Pr$ for the PHF case when $n = 1$ and $B_2 = -1$.

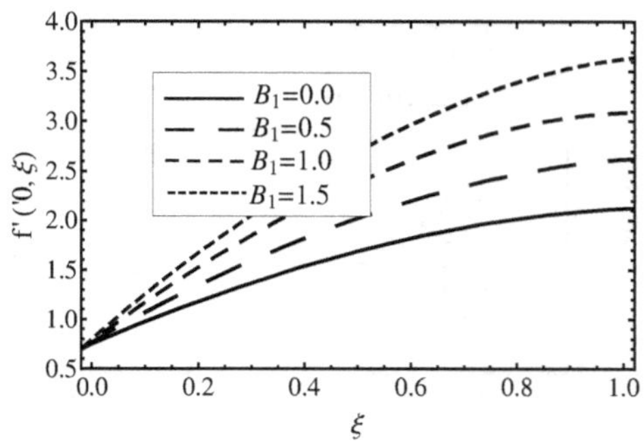


Figure 6.24: Effect of $\xi$ on $f''(0,\xi)$ for different values of $B_1$ for the PST case when $n = 0$.

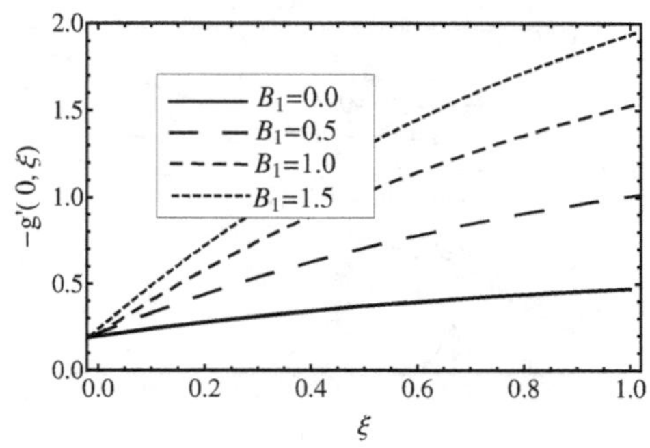


Figure 6.25: Effect of $\xi$ on $-g'(0,\xi)$ for different values of $B_1$ for the PST case when $n = 0$.

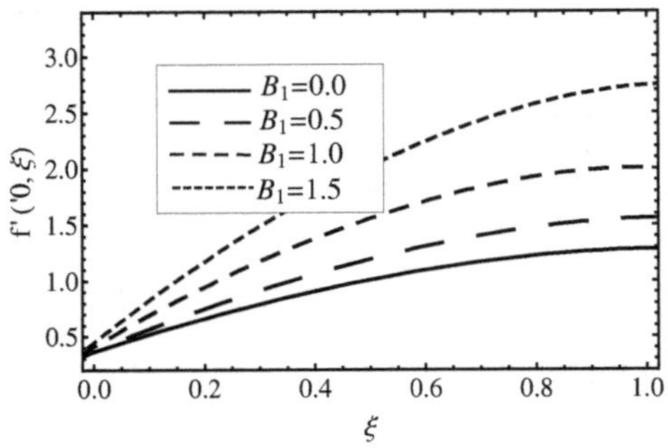


Figure 6.26: Effect of $\xi$ on $f''(0,\xi)$ for different values of $B_1$ for the PST case when $n = 1$.

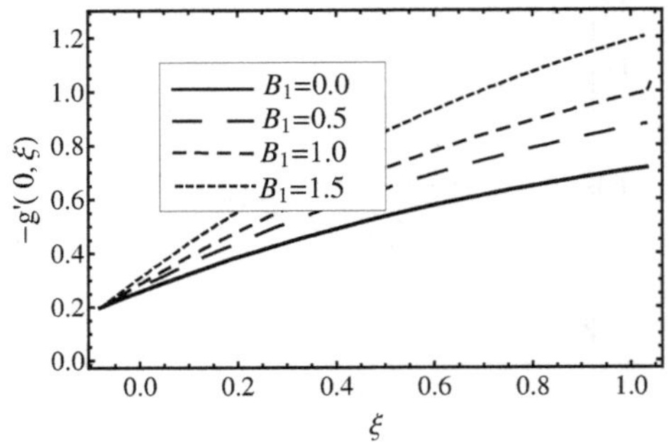


Figure 6.27: Effect of $\xi$ on $-g'(0,\xi)$ for different values of $B_1$ for the PST case when $n = 1$.

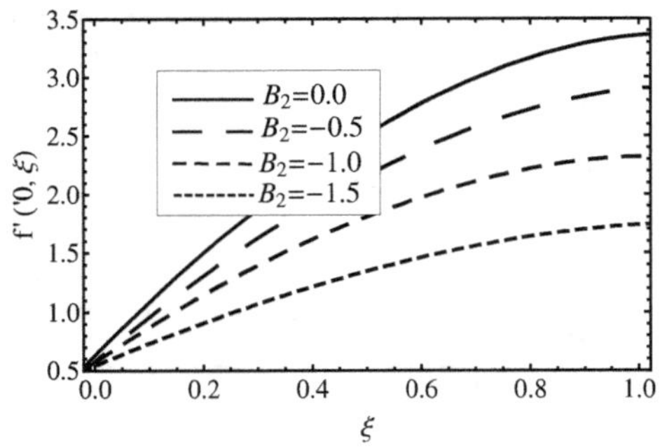


Figure 6.28: Effect of $\xi$ on $f''(0,\xi)$ for different values of $B_2$ for the PHF case when $n = 0$.

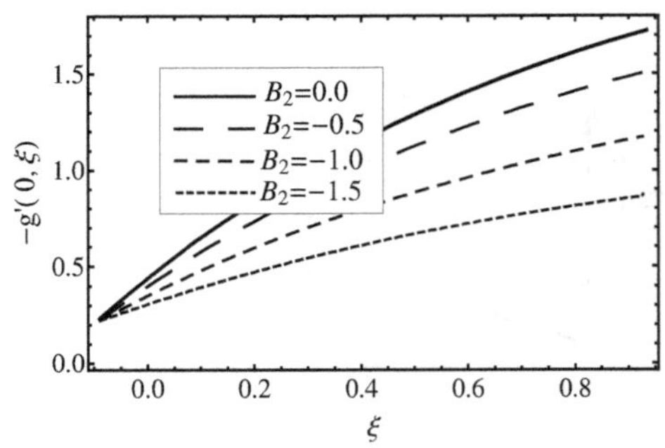


Figure 6.29: Effect of $\xi$ on $-g'(0,\xi)$ for different values of $B_2$ for the PHF case when $n = 0$.

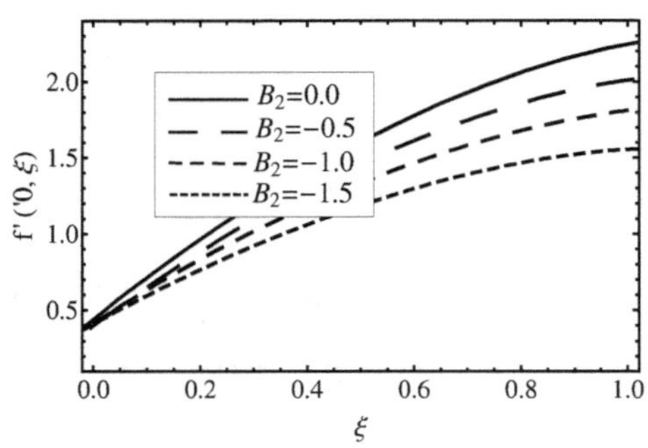


Figure 6.30: Effect of $\xi$ on $f''(0,\xi)$ for different values of $B_2$ for the PHF case when $n = 1$.

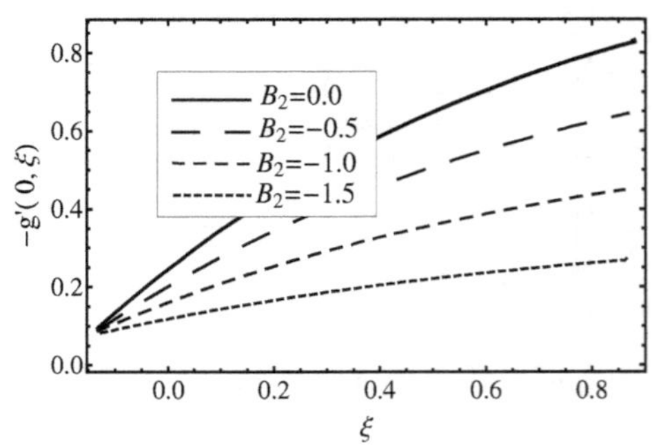


Figure 6.31: Effect of $\xi$ on $-g'(0,\xi)$ for different values of $B_2$ for the PHF case when $n = 1$.

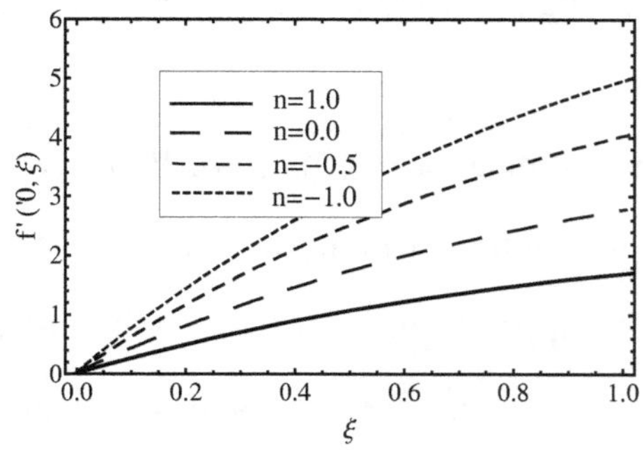


Figure 6.32: Effect of $\xi$ on $f''(0,\xi)$ for different values of $n$ for the PST case when $B_1 = 1$.

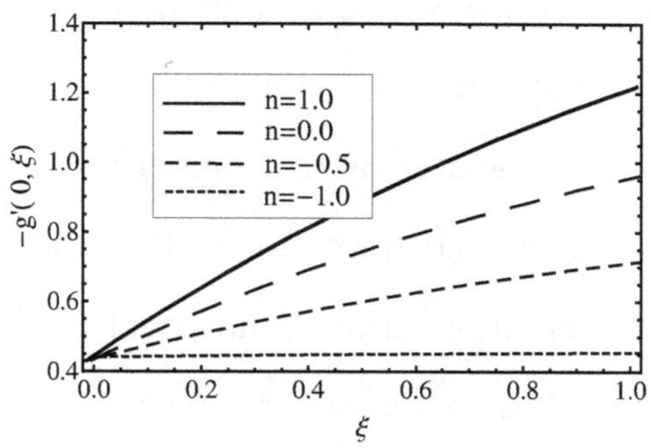


Figure 6.33: Effect of $\xi$ on $-g'(0,\xi)$ for different values of $n$ for the PST case when $B_1 = 1$.

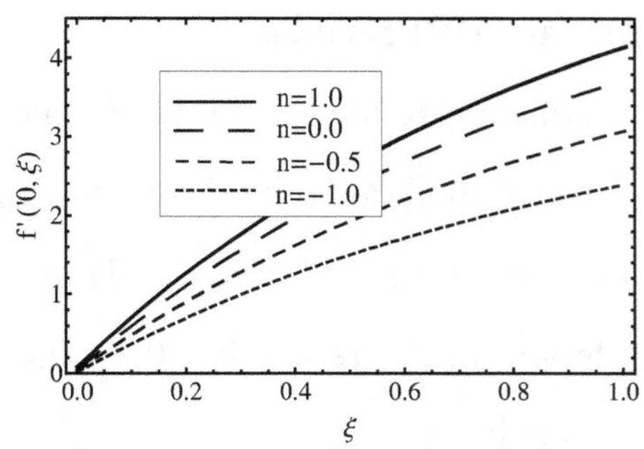


Figure 6.34: Effect of $\xi$ on $f''(0,\xi)$ for different values of $n$ for the PHF case when $B_2 = -1$.

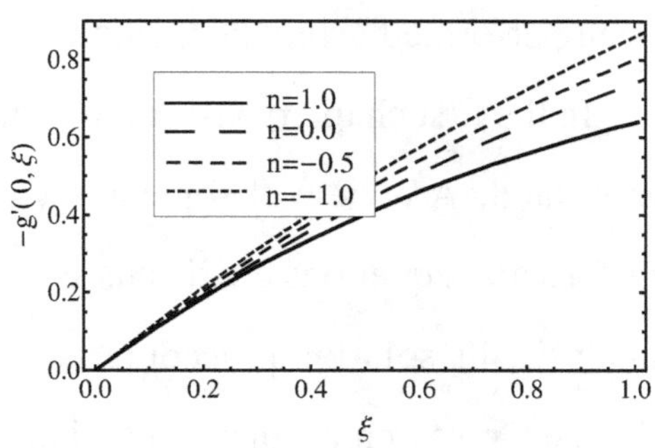


Figure 6.35: Effect of $\xi$ on $-g'(0,\xi)$ for different values of $n$ for the PHF case when $B_2 = -1$.

# CONCLUDING REMARKS AND OPEN PROBLEMS

In general, many physical phenomena in fluid dynamics are controlled by non linear differential equations. Therefore, it becomes important to be familiar with the traditional and recently developed methods for solving non linear differential equations and the implementation of these methods. Hence, in this thesis, some non linear differential equations resulted as a mathematical model of some practical engineering problems in fluid dynamics have been analysed.

The analytical and numerical methods of non-linear problems have their own advantages and limitations. It is more difficult to obtain an analytical solution than a numerical solution. Numerical methods give the approximate functions whereas analytical methods give the exact or actual functions. Since, analytical solution is always has some advantage over numerical solutions, in the present work, analytical solutions are derived for all the study problems using homotopy analysis method. The solution obtained is in the form of a power series hence it is an approximate analytical solution. However, the results can be improved to any desired accuracy by increasing the number of terms in the series solution. The entire algebraic calculations and computations have been performed using the Computer Algebra Software Mathematica.

In the first chapter, basic definitions and some concepts related to fluid dynamics are presented. A review of some analytical and numerical methods for solving non linear differential equations are discussed. Since our focus is on the application of Homotopy analysis, its solution procedure is explained in detail. In the remaining five chapters, five new research problems and their solutions are analysed.

In the second Chapter, the hydromagnetic heat and mass transfer by mixed convection flow due to a vertical flat plate is considered for analysis. The importance of the present study has many applications in various chemical and engineering processes such as petroleum and chemical industry, thermal insulation, cooling of nuclear reactors. The Convective heat transfer condition applied in our study are very useful in understanding processes involving high temperature and concentration, for example, gas turbines and thermal energy storage. Present results show that the thermal boundary layer decreases with increasing chemical reaction parameter. The shear stress rates increases but heat and mass transfer rates are decreases with increasing the magnetic field. The present study is useful in identifying a suitable parameter that can be altered so that, the heat and mass transfer rates in the flow field can be adjusted, there by influencing cooling/heating effect in the system.

In the third Chapter, the unsteady three-dimensional flow of an incompressible viscous fluid in the neighborhood of a stagnation point is studied. The study of laminar boundary layers to variations in the external free stream with time has many practical applications in flow over helicopters, missile aerodynamics, turbo-machines and in flutter phenomena involving wings. The importance of studying the unsteady boundary layer flow near stagnation region is that the heat transfer is maximum near the stagnation point. When the free stream velocity varies arbitrarily with time, the unsteadiness is caused in the flow field which influences the flow and heat transfer to a great extent. The analytical solution using HAM and the numerical solutions using the RKFM with a shooting technique have been presented. An important conclusion drawn from the present study is that, by modifying the magnetic field of suitable strength, one can control the heat transfer rates there by delay the occurrence of flow reversal near stagnation point region. The percentage increase or decrease of a certain flow variable with respect to the change in a given parameter have been analysed. As a result, the study parameter that has the strongest influence on flow variables have be identified.

In several mechanical processes such as extrusion, melt spinning etc., the extruded material issues through a die. The ambient fluid condition is stagnant, but the flow is induced near the material surface being extruded due to entrainment of the fluid caused by stretching of a moving surface. In these processes, the quality of the final product depends largely on the skin friction and heat transfer rates at the surface. Hence it is important to control the flow and heat transfer rate in order to obtain the final product of desired characteristics. Therefore, flow and heat transfer analysis is carried out on stretching surfaces in the next two chapters for the two and three dimensional viscoelastic fluids.

In chapter 4, the two-dimensional flow of non-Newtonian incompressible viscoelastic fluid due to a continuous stretching surface is studied. Calculations are performed to obtain the shear stress, heat and mass transfer rates for various combinations of the parametric values. In the case of increasing values suction ($\alpha < 0$), the profiles tend to approach to the free stream values faster where as in the case of injection ($\alpha > 0$)

there is a slight overshoot in the temperature profiles close to the wall. The present study revealed that the viscoelastic parameter, heat and mass transfer parameters helps in controlling the boundary layer thicknesses of both velocity and temperature. The presence of source/sink in the flow influences the heat transfer rate to a great extent. The prescribed wall temperature always has a higher heat transfer rate compared to prescribed heat flux condition.

In chapter 5, a steady three dimensional viscoelastic fluid flow and heat transfer due to a stretching sheet with an applied magnetic field is considered for analysis. Industrial processes such as the extrusion of polymer sheets, the cooling of a metallic plate in a cooling bath, drawing of plastic films have viscoelastic fluids in the molten form before solidification. Hence the present study of heat transfer effects due to a stretching surface of a viscoelastic fluid is significant. The heat transfer analysis has been carried out for two heating processes, viz., the constant wall temperature (CWT) and the constant heat flux (CHF). The ratio of the velocity gradient, magnetic parameter and the viscoelastic parameters have significant effect on the velocity and temperature as well as on skin friction and heat transfer rates. The solutions shows that the heat transfer rate decrease with the increasing viscoelastic parameter, but they increase with the stretching ratio. The special cases of our results compare very well with the results available in the literature.

In the last Chapter, the mixed convection flow in the stagnation region of a heated vertical plate subjected to impulsive motion is analysed. The results reveal that when there is an impulsive change in the velocity field, the inviscid flow is developed instantaneously, but the flow in the viscous layer near the wall is developed slowly which becomes fully developed steady flow after sometime. For small time the flow is dominated by the viscous forces and the unsteady acceleration, but for large time it is dominated by the viscous forces. For a fixed time, heat transfer rates increases with Prandtl number, because the higher Prandtl number fluid has a lower thermal conductivity which results in thinner thermal buoyancy layer and hence a higher heat transfer rate at the surface. Through this analysis, the validity of the homotopy analysis solution for non-linear partial differential equations related to non-similar boundary layer problems is illustrated. It is believed that, this method can be applied to unsteady boundary layer flows to get accurate analytic solutions valid for all time.

Present results revealed that for the buoyancy assisting flow, the surface shear stress and heat transfer for the prescribed surface heat flux are less than those of the prescribed surface temperature, but for the buoyancy opposing flow the reverse trend is observed. The solution of flow variables presented here in a series form is very handy in computing the effect of one or more parameters on the flow with least computational effort.

Like any other method of solution, homotopy analysis method also has its own limitations. When the number of unknown convergence-control parameters and the the order of approximation increases, it becomes time consuming in practice to solve the nonlinear algebraic equations related to the high-order approximations. To overcome this difficulty, several analytic and semi-analytic techniques based on the HAM to solve more complicated nonlinear problems are available in the literature.

They are homotopy perturbation method, the optimal homotopy asymptotic method, the spectral homotopy analysis method, the generalized boundary element method, and the generalized scaled boundary finite element method.

Since HAM provides a great freedom to choose the auxiliary linear operator and the initial guess, it should be possible to develop a generalized HAM which can use a proper special function such as Chebyshev polynomial, Hermite polynomial, Legendre polynomial, Airy function, Bessel function, hypergeometric functions and so on, for a given nonlinear problem. It is known that, any continuous function in a bounded interval can be best approximated by some kind of special function. Generalized HAM using spectral form has great potential to solve more complicated nonlinear problems in science and engineering, although further modifications in theory and more applications are needed. Thus, the present study is expected show way to explore opportunities in this direction of future studies.

# Appendix-A

## Approximate analytical solutions of flow variables of Chapter 2

When $\ell = 1$ in equations. (2.36)-(2.38), we get solution series

$$
\begin{aligned}
f_1(\eta) &= \left(1-e^{-\eta}\right)\eta + \frac{25c_f}{27(1+Bi)} + \frac{25Bic_f}{27(1+Bi)} \\
&- \frac{5Bi\mathrm{GcGr}c_f}{36(1+Bi)} + \frac{c_f\mathrm{Ha}}{4(1+Bi)} + \frac{Bic_f\mathrm{Ha}}{4(1+Bi)} \\
&+ \left(\frac{181c_f}{216(1+Bi)} - \frac{181Bic_f}{216(1+Bi)} + \frac{4Bi\mathrm{GcGr}c_f}{9(1+Bi)} - \frac{c_f\mathrm{Ha}}{4(1+Bi)}\right)e^{-\eta} \\
&- \left(\frac{Bic_f\mathrm{Ha}}{4(1+Bi)} + \frac{7c_f\eta}{8(1+Bi)} + \frac{7Bic_f\eta}{8(1+Bi)} + \frac{c_f\mathrm{Ha}\eta}{4(1+Bi)} + \frac{Bic_f\mathrm{Ha}\eta}{4(1+Bi)}\right)e^{-\eta}. \\
g_1(\eta) &= \frac{Bie^{-\eta}}{1+Bi} - \left(\frac{2Bic_g\mathrm{Pr}}{9(1+Bi)} + \frac{Bic_g\eta}{2(1+Bi)} - \frac{Bic_g\mathrm{Pr}\,\eta}{8(1+Bi)} + \frac{Bic_g\mathrm{Pr}\,S\eta}{2(1+Bi)}\right)e^{-\eta}. \\
G_1(\eta) &= e^{-\eta} - \left(\frac{2}{9}c_G\mathrm{Sc} - c_G\mathrm{KrNcSc} + \frac{1}{2}c_G\eta - \frac{1}{8}c_G\mathrm{Sc}\eta - \frac{1}{2}c_G\mathrm{KrSc}\eta\right)e^{-\eta} \\
&- c_G\mathrm{KrNcSc}.
\end{aligned}
$$

In the similar way, we can obtain the series solution for $f_2(\eta)$, $g_2(\eta)$, $G_2(\eta)$ and $f_3(\eta)$, $g_3(\eta)$, $G_3(\eta)$ and so on. Since the series solution expressions are too long to be fitted in a page even for $f_2(\eta)$, $g_2(\eta)$ and $G_2(\eta)$ they are not given here.

However, for a fixed set of values of the study parameters such as $Ha = Gr = Gc = Kr = Nc = Bi = 0.1$; $Sc = 0.6$; $Sr = 1.0$ and $Pr = 0.72$, the series solution for $\ell = 2$ in eqs. (2.36)-(2.38), we get solution series,

$$
\begin{aligned}
f_2(\eta) &= 2.001c_f + 0.7736c_f^2 + (1-c_f)\eta - (1.8201c_f + 0.4444c_f^2)e^{-\eta} \\
&- (0.1753c_f + 0.3198c_f^2)e^{-2\eta} - (1 + 1.8931c_f - 0.6197c_f^2)e^{-\eta}\eta \\
&+ (0.2714c_f + 0.4605c_f^2)e^{-2\eta}\eta + (0.2001c_f - 0.0264c_f^2)e^{-\eta}\eta^2 \\
&- (0.1613c_f + 0.2001c_f^2)e^{-2\eta}\eta^2. \\
g_2(\eta) &= (0.0922 - 0.0281c_g + 0.0355c_g^2)e^{-\eta} - (0.0213c_g - 0.0355c_g^2)e^{-2\eta} \\
&- (0.1704c_g + 0.01c_g^2)e^{-\eta}\eta - (0.0222c_g - 0.01c_g^2)e^{-2\eta}\eta \\
&+ (0.01c_g + 0.0321c_g^2)e^{-\eta}\eta^2 + (0.001c_g - 0.006c_g^2)e^{-2\eta}\eta^2. \\
G_2(\eta) &= (1 - 0.0181c_G - 0.0003c_G^2)e^{-\eta} + (0.3111c_G + 0.5302c_G^2)e^{-2\eta} \\
&+ (1 + 1.5457c_G + 0.6101c_G^2)e^{-\eta}\eta - (0.3333c_G + 0.5601c_G^2)e^{-2\eta}\eta \\
&- (0.4587c_G + 0.3104c_G^2)e^{-\eta}\eta^2 + (0.2c_G + 0.2605c_G^2)e^{-2\eta}\eta^2.
\end{aligned}
$$

When $\ell = 3$ in equations. (2.36)-(2.38), we get solution series,

$$
\begin{aligned}
f_3(\eta) &= 3.1528c_f + 2.2c_f^2 + 0.6799c_f^3 + (1 - 0.3333c_f - 0.01c_f^2 - 0.5c_f^3)\eta \\
&- (2.8c_f + 1.2888c_f^2 + 0.0413c_f^3)e^{-\eta} - (0.2c_f + 0.9c_f^2 + 0.5c_f^3)e^{-2\eta} \\
&- (0.0333c_f^2 + 0.07c_f^3)e^{-3\eta} - (1 + 2.7c_f + 1.8c_f^2 + 0.4c_f^3)e^{-\eta}\eta \\
&- (0.4129c_f + 1.42c_f^2 + 0.7793c_f^3)e^{-2\eta}\eta - (0.1c_f^2 + 0.1c_f^3)e^{-3\eta}\eta \\
&- (0.3c_f - 0.08c_f^2 - 0.1c_f^3)e^{-\eta}\eta^2 - (0.2c_f + 0.6c_f^2 + 0.3c_f^3)e^{-2\eta}\eta^2 \\
&- (0.0761c_f^2 + 0.1c_f^3)e^{-3\eta}\eta^2 - (0.25c_f + 0.4c_f^2 + 0.15c_f^3)e^{-\eta}\eta^3 \\
&- (0.0055c_f^2 + 0.0492c_f^3)e^{-2\eta}\eta^3 + (0.0278c_f^2 + 0.0333c_f^3)e^{-3\eta}\eta^3. \\
g_3(\eta) &= (0.09 - 0.04c_g - 0.11c_g^2)e^{-\eta} + (0.04c_g + 0.1c_g^2 + 0.04c_g^3)e^{-2\eta} \\
&+ (0.007c_g^2 + 0.01c_g^3)e^{-3\eta} + (0.31c_g + 0.05c_g^2 - 0.02c_g^3)e^{-\eta}\eta \\
&+ (0.03c_g + 0.02c_g^2 - 0.003c_g^3)e^{-2\eta}\eta + (0.009c_g^2 + 0.01c_g^3)e^{-3\eta}\eta \\
&- (0.02c_g + 0.12c_g^2 + 0.01c_g^3)e^{-\eta}\eta^2 - (0.02c_g + 0.02c_g^2 + 0.006c_g^3)e^{-2\eta}\eta^2 \\
&+ (0.003c_g^2 + 0.002c_g^3)e^{-3\eta}\eta^2 - (0.02c_g^2 + 0.01c_g^3)e^{-\eta}\eta^3 \\
&+ (0.005c_g^2 + 0.006c_g^3)e^{-2\eta}\eta^3 - (0.0001c_g^2 + 0.0002c_g^3)e^{-3\eta}\eta^3. \\
G_3(\eta) &= 0.036c_G - 0.001c_G^2 - 0.0002c_G^3 - (0.43c_G + 1.66c_G^2 + 1.26c_G^3)e^{-\eta} \\
&+ (0.46c_G + 1.6c_G^2 + 1.138c_G^3)e^{-2\eta} + (0.06c_G^2 + 0.12c_G^3)e^{-3\eta} \\
&+ (2.34ec_G + 1.84c_G^2 + 0.33c_G^3)e^{-\eta}\eta + (0.5c_G + 1.69c_G^2 + 1.1c_G^3)e^{-2\eta}\eta \\
&+ (0.12c_G^2 + 0.23c_G^3)e^{-3\eta}\eta - (0.66c_G + 0.91c_G^2 + 0.33c_G^3)e^{-\eta}\eta^2 \\
&+ (0.3c_G + 0.79c_G^2 + 0.48c_G^3)e^{-2\eta}\eta^2 + (0.09c_G^2 + 0.16c_G^3)e^{-3\eta}\eta^2 \\
&+ (0.15c_G + 0.33c_G^2 + 0.16c_G^3)e^{-\eta}\eta^3 - (0.01c_G^2 - 0.01c_G^3)e^{-2\eta}\eta^3 \\
&+ (0.03c_G^2 + 0.05c_G^3)e^{-3\eta}\eta^3.
\end{aligned}
$$

# Appendix-B

## Approximate analytical solutions of flow variables of Chapter 3

When order $\ell = 1$ in equation. (3.40), we obtain the solution series in the form given by:

$$
\begin{aligned}
f_1(\eta) &= (\eta+1-e^{-\eta}) + \frac{7c_f}{4} + \frac{13cc_f}{12} + \frac{c_f M}{2} - \frac{7c_f\lambda}{8} + c_f\lambda \\
&- \left(\frac{7c_f}{4} + \frac{11}{12}cc_f + \frac{1}{2}c_f M + c_f\lambda\right)e^{-\eta} \\
&- \left(\frac{7c_f}{4} + \frac{7}{8}cc_f + \frac{1}{2}c_f M + \frac{1}{8}c_f\lambda\right)\eta e^{-\eta}. \\
g_1(\eta) &= (\eta+1-e^{-\eta}) + \frac{7c_g}{12} + \frac{9cc_g}{4} + \frac{c_g M}{2} - \frac{7c_g\lambda}{8} + c_g\lambda \\
&- \left(\frac{5c_g}{12} + \frac{9}{4}cc_g + \frac{1}{2}c_g M + c_g\lambda\right)e^{-\eta} \\
&- \left(\frac{3}{4}c_g + \frac{9}{4}cc_g + \frac{1}{2}c_g M + \frac{1}{8}c_g\lambda\right)\eta e^{-\eta}. \\
s_1(\eta) &= 1 - e^{-x} + 2c_s \Pr\lambda + \left(\frac{1}{3}c_s \Pr + \frac{1}{3}cc_s \Pr - 2c_s \Pr\lambda\right)e^{-\eta} \\
&- \left(\frac{1}{2}c_s - \frac{5}{8}c_s \Pr - \frac{3}{4}cc_s \Pr - c_s \Pr\lambda\right)\eta e^{-\eta}. \\
\Phi_1(\eta) &= \eta e^{-\eta} - c_\Phi M \Pr\alpha \\
&+ \left(\frac{7}{9}c_\Phi \Pr - \frac{1}{9}cc_\Phi \Pr - \frac{1}{3}c_\Phi \Pr\alpha + \frac{2}{3}c_\Phi M \Pr\alpha\right)e^{-\eta} \\
&+ \left(\frac{3}{4}c_\Phi + \frac{1}{4}c_\Phi \Pr - \frac{1}{4}cc_\Phi \Pr - e^{-x}c_\Phi M \Pr\alpha + \frac{1}{4}c_\Phi \Pr\lambda\right)\eta e^{-\eta}. \\
\theta_1(\eta) &= \eta e^{-\eta} - c_\theta M \Pr\beta \\
&- \left(\frac{1}{9}c_\theta \Pr - \frac{7}{9}cc_\theta \Pr + \frac{1}{3}c_\theta \Pr\beta - \frac{2}{3}c_\theta M \Pr\beta\right)e^{-\eta} \\
&+ \left(\frac{3}{4}c_\theta - \frac{1}{4}c_\theta \Pr + \frac{1}{4}cc_\theta \Pr - c_\theta M \Pr\beta + \frac{1}{2}e^{-x}c_\theta \Pr\lambda\right)\eta e^{-\eta}.
\end{aligned}
$$

In the similar way, we can obtain the series solution for $f_2(\eta)$, $g_2(\eta)$, $s_2(\eta)$, $\Phi_2(\eta)$, $\theta_2(\eta)$ and $f_3(\eta)$, $g_3(\eta)$, $s_3(\eta)$, $\Phi_3(\eta)$, $\theta_3(\eta)$ and so on. Since the series solution expressions are too long to be fitted in a page even for $f_2(\eta)$, $g_2(\eta)$, $s_2(\eta)$, $\Phi_2(\eta)$ and $\theta_2(\eta)$ they are not given here.

However, for a fixed set of values of the study parameters such as $Pr = 0.72$, $\lambda = -1.0$ and $c = -0.5$, $M = 0.5$ and $\alpha = \beta = 0.2$, the series solution for $\ell = 2$ in eq. (3.40), we get solution series,

$$\begin{aligned}
f_2(\eta) &= -3c_f - 1.7222c_f^2 + (1 - 3.5c_f - 1.5c_f^2)\eta + (3c_f)\eta^2 + (3c_f)e^{-\eta} \\
&+ (0.5092c_f - 0.1389c_f^2)e^{-2\eta} - (1 + 2.75c_f + 3.7187c_f^2)e^{-\eta}\eta \\
&- (0.75c_f + 1.3692c_f^2)e^{-\eta}\eta^2 + 0.2777c_f + 0.3411c_f^2)e^{-2\eta}\eta \\
&+ (0.1667c_f + 0.1458c_f^2)e^{-2\eta}\eta^2. \\
g_2(\eta) &= 3.2871c_g - 1.7745c_g^2 + (1 + 2c_g + 1.5c_g^2)\eta \\
&- (2.7685c_g - 3.2368c_g^2)e^{-\eta} - (0.5185c_g + 1.5595c_g^2)e^{-2\eta} \\
&+ (1 - 1.25c_g + 0.5625c_g^2)e^{-\eta}\eta - (0.5555c_g + 1.9251c_g^2)e^{-2\eta}\eta \\
&+ (0.75c_g + 0.5c_g^2)e^{-\eta}\eta^2 - (0.3333c_g + 0.7083c_g^2)e^{-2\eta}\eta^2. \\
s_2(\eta) &= (1 - 0.3111c_s - 1.4748c_s^2)e^{-\eta} + (0.3111c_s + 1.5241c_s^2)e^{-2\eta} \\
&- (3.1c_s - 0.2033c_s^2)e^{-\eta}\eta + (0.2333c_s + 0.7249c_s^2)e^{-2\eta}\eta \\
&+ (0.0691c_s - 0.0875c_s^2)e^{-\eta}\eta^2 + (0.545c_s + 0.175c_s^2)e^{-2\eta}\eta^2. \\
\Phi_2(\eta) &= -0.14c_\Phi + 0.091c_\Phi^2 + (1.5711c_\Phi + 2.2039c_\Phi^2)e^{-\eta} \\
&- (1.4311c_\Phi + 2.3788c_\Phi^2)e^{-2\eta} + (2 + 2.67c_\Phi + 0.1002c_\Phi^2)e^{-\eta}\eta \\
&- (1.8433c_\Phi + 1.9488c_\Phi^2)e^{-2\eta}\eta - (0.91c_\Phi + 0.7707c_\Phi^2)e^{-2\eta}\eta^2 \\
&- (0.47c_\Phi + 0.2268c_\Phi^2)e^{-\eta}\eta^2. \\
\theta_2(\eta) &= -0.14c_\theta + 0.287c_\theta^2 + (1.8355c_\theta + 4.8108c_\theta^2)e^{-2\eta} \\
&- (1.6955c_\theta + 5.1053c_\theta^2)e^{-\eta} + (2 + 0.395c_\theta + 0.5124c_\theta^2)e^{-\eta}\eta \\
&+ (1.6566c_\theta + 4.5826c_\theta^2)e^{-2\eta}\eta - (2.745c_\theta + 0.3718c_\theta^2)e^{-\eta}\eta^2 \\
&+ (1.19c_\theta + 2.1214c_\theta^2)\eta^2 e^{-2\eta}\eta^2.
\end{aligned}$$

When $\ell = 3$ in equation. (3.40), we obtain the solution series in the form given by:

$$
\begin{aligned}
f_3(\eta) &= 11.9722c_f + 19.1278c_f^2 + 8.4921c_f^3 - (12.7361c_f + 21.5049c_f^2 \\
&+ 9.6316c_f^3)e^{-\eta} + (0.7638c_f + 2.4313c_f^2 + 1.1166c_f^3)e^{-2\eta} \\
&- (0.7272c_f + 0.0542c_f^2 - 0.0306c_f^3)e^{-3\eta} + (1 + 7.5c_f + 6.75c_f^2 \\
&+ 1.25c_f^3)\eta - (1 - 4.125c_f + 11.1563c_f^2 - 5.4068c_f^3)e^{-\eta}\eta \\
&+ (0.4166c_f + 1.1481c_f^2 - 0.7817c_f^3)e^{-2\eta}\eta + (0.1078c_f \\
&+ 1.2222c_f^2 - 0.5c_f^3)e^{-3\eta}\eta - (0.1078c_f - 4.1076c_f^2 \\
&+ 3.9792c_f^3)e^{-\eta}\eta^2 + (0.2552c_f + 0.4375c_f^2 - 0.2226c_f^3)e^{-2\eta}\eta^2 \\
&- (0.0468c_f - 0.0001c_f^2 - 0.1134c_f^3)e^{-3\eta}\eta^2 - (0.5c_f + 0.9375c_f^2 \\
&+ 0.6249c_f^3)e^{-\eta}\eta^3 + (0.1111c_f^2 + 0.0189c_f^3)e^{-2\eta}\eta^3 + (0.0321c_f^3)e^{-3\eta}\eta^3. \\
g_3(\eta) &= 4.93056c_g - 5.7821c_g^2 + 3.086c_g^3 + (1 - 3c_g + 4.5c_g^2 - 2.75c_g^3)\eta \\
&- (0.7778c_g + 4.6369c_g^2 + 6.6096c_g^3)e^{-2\eta} - (4.1528c_g - 10.6827c_g^2 \\
&- 4.4152c_g^3)e^{-\eta} - (0.2636c_g + 0.2636c_g^2 + 0.8863c_g^3)e^{-3\eta} \\
&- (1 + 1.875c_g + 2.4375c_g^2 + 0.2449c_g^3)e^{-\eta}\eta - (0.8333c_g + 6.0621c_g^2 \\
&+ 7.8063c_g^3)e^{-2\eta}\eta - (0.294271c_g^2 + 1.1577c_g^3)e^{-3\eta}\eta + (1.1256c_g \\
&- 0.9305c_g^2 - 0.3208c_g^3)e^{-\eta}\eta^2 - (0.5c_g - 2.125c_g^2 + 3.0211c_g^3)e^{-2\eta}\eta^2 \\
&- (0.1822c_g^2 + 0.7787c_g^3)e^{-3\eta}\eta^2 - (0.0625c_g^2 + 0.2458c_g^3)e^{-3\eta}\eta^3 \\
&- (0.2222c_g^2 + 0.9412c_g^3)e^{-2\eta}\eta^3 - (0.375c_g^2 - 0.6496c_g^3)e^{-\eta}\eta^3. \\
s_3(\eta) &= (1 - 0.4666c_s - 4.7926c_s^2 - 7.1035c_s^3)e^{-\eta} + (0.4666c_s + 4.9405c_s^2 \\
&+ 7.1888c_s^3)e^{-2\eta} + (0.1479c_s + 0.2532c_s^2 + 0.0702c_s^3)e^{-3\eta} - (5.7c_s \\
&- 1.1213c_s^2 - 1.1213c_s^3)e^{-\eta}\eta + (0.35c_s + 2.0931c_s^2 + 2.5332c_s^3)e^{-2\eta}\eta \\
&- (0.0671c_s - 0.1835c_s^2 - 3.6185c_s^3)e^{-3\eta}\eta + (0.0001c_s + 2.475c_s^2 \\
&- 0.5c_s^3)e^{-\eta}\eta^2 + (0.1c_s + 1.5c_s^2 + 0.4607c_s^3)e^{-2\eta}\eta^2 \\
&- (0.0131c_s + 0.589c_s^2 - 0.1071c_s^3)e^{-3\eta}\eta^2 - (0.3211c_s^2 \\
&+ 0.85c_s^2)e^{-\eta}\eta^3 + (0.05c_s^2 + 0.1c_s^3)e^{-2\eta}\eta^3 + (0.02e^{-3\eta}c_s^3)\eta^3.
\end{aligned}
$$

$$
\begin{aligned}
\Phi_3(\eta) &= -0.28c_\Phi + 0.483c_\Phi^2 + 0.3017c_\Phi^3 + (4.2311c_\Phi + 10.4187c_\Phi^2 \\
&+ 3.5378c_\Phi^3)e^{-\eta} - (3.9511c_\Phi + 11.1526c_\Phi^2 + 4.0583c_\Phi^3)e^{-2\eta} \\
&+ (0.2508c_\Phi^2 + 0.2248c_\Phi^3)e^{-3\eta} - (4.8533c_\Phi + 9.0007c_\Phi^2 \\
&+ 1.4449c_\Phi^3)e^{-2\eta}\eta + (4 + 6.84c_\Phi - 0.0417c_\Phi^2 - 2.5c_\Phi^3)e^{-\eta}\eta \\
&+ (0.6899c_\Phi^2 + 0.4338c_\Phi^3)e^{-3\eta}\eta - (1.44c_\Phi + 1.3791c_\Phi^2 \\
&+ 0.6852c_\Phi^3)e^{-\eta}\eta^2 - (2.52c_\Phi + 3.6131c_\Phi^2 - 0.5061c_\Phi^3)e^{-2\eta}\eta^2 \\
&+ (0.5886c_\Phi^2 + 0.2419c_\Phi^3)e^{-3\eta}\eta^2 + (0.6231c_\Phi^2\eta^3 + 0.9333c_\Phi^3)e^{-\eta}\eta^3 \\
&- (0.5931c_\Phi^2\eta^3 - 0.9333c_\Phi^3)e^{-2\eta}\eta^3 + (0.1432c_\Phi^2 + 0.0744c_\Phi^3)e^{-3\eta}\eta^3. \\
\theta_3(\eta) &= 0.28c_\theta + 1.106c_\theta^2 - 0.7c_\theta^3 - 4.48e^{-\eta}c_\theta + 4.76e^{-2\eta}c_\theta - 4.9e^{-3\eta}c_\theta \\
&- (22.3623c_\theta^2 - 23.1694c_\theta^3)e^{-\eta} + (21.1476c_\theta^2 + 23.1799c_\theta^3)e^{-2\eta} \\
&+ (0.1087c_\theta^2 + 0.8135c_\theta^3)e^{-3\eta} + (4 + 0.54c_\theta + 3.5354c_\theta^2 \\
&+ 4.4342c_\theta^3)e^{-\eta}\eta + (4.48c_\theta + 19.677c_\theta^2 + 20.2c_\theta^3)e^{-2\eta}\eta \\
&- (0.31c_\theta^2 + 0.6905c_\theta^3)e^{-3\eta}\eta - (7.74c_\theta + 1.3251c_\theta^2 \\
&- 0.3822c_\theta^3)e^{-\eta}\eta^2 + (3.08c_\theta + 8.3851c_\theta^2 + 7.3605c_\theta^3)e^{-2\eta}\eta^2 \\
&- (0.2c_\theta^2 - 0.7259c_\theta^3)e^{-3\eta}\eta^2 + (0.9c_\theta + 2c_\theta^2 - 0.01c_\theta^3)e^{-\eta}\eta^3 \\
&+ (0.4552c_\theta^2 + 1.5471c_\theta^3)e^{-2\eta}\eta^3 + (0.0198c_\theta^2 + 0.3426c_\theta^3)e^{-3\eta}\eta^3.
\end{aligned}
$$

# Appendix-C

## Approximate analytical solutions of flow variables of Chapter 4

When $\ell = 1$ in eqs. (4.32)-(4.34), we obtain the solution series in the form given by:

$$
\begin{aligned}
f_1(\eta) &= 1 - e^{-\eta} + \alpha + \frac{c_f\alpha}{2} + \frac{c_f\lambda}{2} - \left(\frac{1}{2}c_f\alpha + \frac{1}{2}c_f\alpha\lambda\right)e^{-\eta} \\
&- \left(\frac{1}{2}c_f\alpha + \frac{1}{2}c_f\alpha\lambda\right)\eta e^{-\eta}. \\
g_1(\eta) &= e^{-\eta} - \left(\frac{1}{3}c_g\,\mathrm{Pr} - \frac{1}{3}c_g\,\mathrm{Pr}\,\beta\right)e^{-\eta} \\
&- \left(\frac{1}{2}c_g - \frac{1}{2}c_g\,\mathrm{Pr} + \frac{1}{2}c_g s - \frac{1}{2}c_g\,\mathrm{Pr}\,\alpha\right)\eta e^{-\eta}. \\
G_1(\eta) &= e^{-\eta} - \left(\frac{1}{3}c_G\,\mathrm{Pr} - \frac{1}{3}c_G\,\mathrm{Pr}\,\beta\right)e^{-\eta} \\
&- \left(\frac{1}{2}c_G - \frac{1}{2}c_G\,\mathrm{Pr} + \frac{1}{2}c_G s - \frac{1}{2}c_G\,\mathrm{Pr}\,\alpha\right)\eta e^{-\eta}.
\end{aligned}
$$

In the similar way, we can obtain the series solution for $f_2(\eta)$, $g_2(\eta)$, $G_2(\eta)$ and $f_3(\eta)$, $g_3(\eta)$, $G_3(\eta)$ and so on. Since the series solution expressions are too long to be fitted in a page even for $f_2(\eta)$, $g_2(\eta)$ and $G_2(\eta)$ they are not given here.

However, for a fixed set of values of the study parameters such as $Pr = 0.7$, $\lambda = 0.2$ and $\beta = 0.5$, $s = 0.1$ and $\alpha = 0.1$, the series solution for $\ell = 2$ in eqs. (4.32)-(4.34), we get solution series,

$$
\begin{aligned}
f_2(\eta) &= 1+0.3221c_f+0.15c_f^2-(1+0.3333c_f+0.3221c_f^2)e^{-\eta} \\
&- (0.3221c_f+0.01c_f^2)e^{-\eta}\eta-(0.15c_f+0.1536c_f^2)e^{-2\eta}\eta \\
&- (0.1c_f+0.15c_f^2)e^{-2\eta}\eta^2. \\
g_2(\eta) &= (1-0.23c_g-0.18c_g^2)e^{-\eta}+(0.23e^{-2\eta}c_g+0.16c_g^2)e^{-2\eta} \\
&- (0.38e^{-\eta}c_g\eta+0.01c_g^2)e^{-\eta}\eta-(0.0005e^{-2\eta}c_g^2\eta-0.013c_g^2)e^{-\eta}\eta^2 \\
G_2(\eta) &= (1-0.23c_G-0.18c_G^2)e^{-\eta}+(0.23e^{-2\eta}c_G+0.16c_G^2)e^{-2\eta} \\
&- (0.38e^{-\eta}c_G\eta+0.01c_G^2)e^{-\eta}\eta-(0.0005e^{-2\eta}c_G^2\eta-0.013c_G^2)e^{-\eta}\eta^2.
\end{aligned}
$$

When $\ell = 3$ in eqs. (4.32)-(4.34), we get solution series,

$$
\begin{aligned}
f_3(\eta) &= 1+0.975c_f+0.8409c_f^2+0.2516c_f^3-(1+0.975c_f+0.8409c_f^2 \\
&+ 0.2516c_f^3)e^{-\eta}-(0.975c_f+0.8409c_f^2+0.1585c_f^3)e^{-\eta}\eta \\
&- (0.48c_f+0.46c_f^2+0.15c_f^3)e^{-2\eta}\eta-(0.1584c_f^2+0.0739c_f^3)e^{-\eta}\eta^2 \\
&- (0.001c_f^2+0.0007c_f^3)e^{-2\eta}\eta^2-(0.0057c_f^3)e^{-\eta}\eta^3.
\end{aligned}
$$

$$
\begin{aligned}
g_3(\eta) &= (1+0.35c_g-0.7292c_g^2-0.3179c_g^3)e^{-\eta}+(0.35c_g+0.0459c_g^2 \\
&+ 0.2631c_g^3)e^{-2\eta}+(0.0459c_g^2+0.0531c_g^3)e^{-3\eta}-(0.645c_g-0.1187c_g^2 \\
&- 0.1515c_g^3)e^{-\eta}\eta-(0.0501c_g^2-0.0594c_g^3)e^{-2\eta}\eta+(0.0491c_g^2 \\
&- 0.0058c_g^3)e^{-\eta}\eta^2-0.0007e^{-\eta}c_g^3\eta^3+0.0014e^{-2\eta}c_g^3\eta^2+0.0023e^{-3\eta}c_g^3\eta.
\end{aligned}
$$

$$
\begin{aligned}
G_3(\eta) &= (1+0.35c_G-0.7292c_G^2-0.3179c_G^3)e^{-\eta}+(0.35c_G+0.0459c_G^2 \\
&+ 0.2631c_G^3)e^{-2\eta}+(0.0459c_G^2+0.0531c_G^3)e^{-3\eta}-(0.645c_G-0.1187c_G^2 \\
&- 0.1515c_G^3)e^{-\eta}\eta-(0.0501c_G^2-0.0594c_G^3)e^{-2\eta}\eta+(0.0491c_G^2 \\
&- 0.0058c_G^3)e^{-\eta}\eta^2-0.0007e^{-\eta}c_G^3\eta^3+0.0014e^{-2\eta}c_G^3\eta^2+0.0023e^{-3\eta}c_G^3\eta.
\end{aligned}
$$

# Appendix-D

## Approximate analytical solutions of flow variables of Chapter 5

When $\ell=1$ in eqs. (5.35)-(5.38), we obtain the solution series in the form given by:

$$
\begin{aligned}
f_1(\eta) &= 1-e^{-\eta}+\frac{c_fM}{2}+\frac{cc_f}{3}+\frac{5}{6}cc_f\lambda+\frac{cc_fM}{2} \\
&- \left(\frac{1}{6}cc_f+\frac{1}{2}c_fM+\frac{1}{2}c_f\lambda+\frac{7}{6}cc_f\lambda+\frac{1}{2}cc_fM\right)e^{-\eta} \\
&- \left(\frac{1}{2}cc_f+\frac{1}{2}c_fM+\frac{1}{2}c_f\lambda+\frac{1}{2}cc_fM+\frac{1}{2}cc_f\lambda\right)\eta e^{-\eta}. \\
s_1(\eta) &= c\left(1-e^{-\eta}\right)+\frac{c_sM}{2}-\frac{cc_s}{6}+\frac{cc_s}{6}\lambda+\frac{cc_sM}{2} \\
&+ \left(\frac{1}{3}cc_s-\frac{1}{3}c_sM-\frac{1}{6}c_s\lambda-\frac{1}{2}cc_s\lambda-\frac{1}{2}cc_sM\right)e^{-\eta} \\
&- \left(\frac{1}{2}cc_s+\frac{1}{2}c_sM+\frac{1}{2}c_s\lambda+\frac{1}{2}cc_sM+\frac{1}{2}cc_s\lambda\right)\eta e^{-\eta}. \\
g_1(\eta) &= e^{-x}-\left(\frac{1}{3}c_g\,\mathrm{Pr}+\frac{1}{3}cc_g\,\mathrm{Pr}\right)e^{-\eta} \\
&- \left(\frac{1}{2}c_g-\frac{1}{2}c_g\,\mathrm{Pr}-\frac{1}{2}cc_g\,\mathrm{Pr}\right)\eta e^{-\eta}. \\
G_1(\eta) &= e^{-\eta}-\left(\frac{1}{3}c_G\,\mathrm{Pr}+\frac{1}{3}cc_G\,\mathrm{Pr}\right)e^{-\eta} \\
&- \left(\frac{1}{2}c_G-\frac{1}{2}c_G\,\mathrm{Pr}-\frac{1}{2}cc_G\,\mathrm{Pr}\right)\eta e^{-\eta}.
\end{aligned}
$$

In the similar way, we can obtain the series solution for $f_2(\eta)$, $s_2(\eta)$, $g_2(\eta)$, $G_2(\eta)$ and $f_3(\eta)$, $s_3(\eta)$, $g_3(\eta)$, $G_3(\eta)$ and so on. Since the series solution expressions are too long to be fitted in a page even for $f_2(\eta)$, $s_2(\eta)$, $g_2(\eta)$ and $G_2(\eta)$ they are not given here.

However, for a fixed set of values of the study parameters such as $Pr=0.7$, $\lambda=0.1$, $c=0.5$ and $M=0.5$, the series solution for $\ell=2$ in eqs. (5.35)-(5.38), we get solution series,

$$
\begin{aligned}
f_2(\eta) &= 1+1.0083c_f+0.7974c_f^2-(1+0.9416c_f+0.7391c_f^2)e^{-\eta} \\
& \quad (0.0667c_f+0.0543c_f^2)e^{-2\eta}-(1.075c_f+0.826c_f^2)e^{-\eta}\eta \\
&+ (0.0325e^{-2\eta})c_f^2\eta-(0.1444e^{-\eta}c_f^2-0.0387e^{-2\eta}c_f^2)\eta^2. \\
s_2(\eta) &= 0.5+0.3666c_s+0.2794c_s^2-(0.5+0.2958c_s+0.1772c_s^2)e^{-\eta} \\
&- (0.0708c_s+0.1005c_s^2)e^{-2\eta}-(0.0016c_s^2)e^{-3\eta} \\
&- (0.4375c_s+0.3469c_s^2)e^{-\eta}\eta-(0.0364c_s^2)e^{-2\eta}\eta \\
&- 0.0478c_s^2e^{-\eta}\eta^2. \\
g_2(\eta) &= (1-1.1668c_g-0.7507c_g^2)e^{-\eta}+(1.1666c_g+0.4865c_g^2)e^{-2\eta} \\
&+ (0.7501c_g+0.3155c_g^2)e^{-\eta}\eta+(0.07e^{-\eta}\eta^2+0.5206e^{-2\eta}\eta)c_g^2. \\
G_2(\eta) &= (1-1.1668c_G-0.7507c_G^2)e^{-\eta}+(1.1666c_G+0.4865c_G^2)e^{-2\eta} \\
&+ (0.7501c_G+0.3155c_G^2)e^{-\eta}\eta+(0.07e^{-\eta}\eta^2+0.5206e^{-2\eta}\eta)c_G^2.
\end{aligned}
$$

When $\ell = 3$ in eqs. (5.35)-(5.38), we get solution series,

$$
\begin{aligned}
f_3(\eta) &= (1+1.5125c_f+2.3911c_f^2+1.2816c_f^3)-(1-1.4125c_f \\
&- 2.2173c_f^2-1.1795c_f^3)e^{-\eta}-(0.1c_f+0.1631c_f^2+0.091c_f^3)e^{-2\eta} \\
&- (0.01c_f^2+0.0104c_f^3)e^{-3\eta}-(1.6c_f+2.4786c_f^2+1.2c_f^3)e^{-\eta}\eta \\
&- (0.0975c_f^2+0.0909c_f^3)e^{-2\eta}\eta-(0.0052c_f^3)e^{-3\eta}\eta \\
&- (0.4333e^{-\eta}c_f^2+0.3759e^{-\eta}c_f^3)\eta^2 \\
&- (0.0158c_f^3)e^{-2\eta}\eta^2-(0.0258c_f^3)e^{-\eta}\eta^3.
\end{aligned}
$$

$$
\begin{aligned}
s_3(\eta) &= 0.5+0.55c_s+0.8384c_s^2+0.4283c_s^3-(0.5+0.4437c_s \\
&+ 0.5318c_s^2+0.2c_s^3)e^{-\eta}-(0.1062c_s+0.3016c_s^2+0.2c_s^3)e^{-2\eta} \\
&- (0.0049c_s^2+0.01c_s^3)e^{-3\eta}-(0.6c_s+1.0407c_s^2+0.5c_s^3)e^{-\eta}\eta \\
&- (0.1092c_s^2+0.1418c_s^3)e^{-2\eta}\eta-(0.0026c_s^3)e^{-3\eta}\eta \\
&- (0.1435c_s^2+0.1376c_s^3)e^{-\eta}\eta^2-(0.0185c_s^3)e^{-2\eta}\eta^2 \\
&- (0.0069c_s^3)e^{-\eta}\eta^3. \\
g_3(\eta) &= (1-1.75c_g-2.2522c_g^2-0.8c_g^3)e^{-\eta}+(1.75c_g+1.4598c_g^2 \\
&+ 0.1c_g^3)e^{-2\eta}+(0.7924c_g^2+0.6c_g^3)e^{-3\eta}+(1.1c_g+0.9465c_g^2 \\
&+ 0.1c_g^3)e^{-\eta}\eta+(1.5c_g^2+1.0825c_g^3)e^{-2\eta}\eta+(0.3333c_g^3)e^{-3\eta}\eta \\
&+ (0.2109c_g^2+0.1593c_g^3)e^{-\eta}\eta^2+(0.2328c_g^3)e^{-2\eta}\eta^2 \\
&+ (0.0087c_g^3)e^{-\eta}\eta^3+(0.0007c_g^3)e^{-3\eta}\eta^3. \\
G_3(\eta) &= (1-1.75c_G-2.2522c_G^2-0.8c_G^3)e^{-\eta}+(1.75c_G+1.4598c_G^2 \\
&+ 0.1c_G^3)e^{-2\eta}+(0.7924c_G^2+0.6c_G^3)e^{-3\eta}+(1.1c_G+0.9465c_G^2 \\
&+ 0.1c_G^3)e^{-\eta}\eta+(1.5c_G^2+1.0825c_G^3)e^{-2\eta}\eta+(0.3333c_G^3)e^{-3\eta}\eta \\
&+ (0.2109c_G^2+0.1593c_G^3)e^{-\eta}\eta^2+(0.2328c_G^3)e^{-2\eta}\eta^2 \\
&+ (0.0087c_G^3)e^{-\eta}\eta^3+(0.0007c_G^3)e^{-3\eta}\eta^3.
\end{aligned}
$$

# Appendix-E

## Approximate analytical solutions of flow variables of Chapter 6

When $\ell = 1$ in eqs. (6.26)-(6.27), the solution series for $f(\eta,\xi)$ and $g(\eta,\xi)$ are expressed as,

$$
\begin{aligned}
f_1(\eta,\xi) &= 1-e^{-\eta}+\eta+\frac{c_f}{2}-\frac{7c_f\xi}{2}+Bc_f\xi \\
&+ \left(\frac{c_f}{2}-\frac{1}{2}c_f\eta\right)e^{-\eta}+\left(\frac{7}{2}c_f-Bc_f+\frac{1}{2}c_f\eta\right)\xi e^{-\eta}. \\
g_1(\eta,\xi) &= e^{-\eta}+c_g-\frac{c_g\,\mathrm{Pr}}{2}-c_g\,\mathrm{Pr}\,\xi-\frac{3}{2}c_g n\,\mathrm{Pr}\,\xi \\
&+ \left(c_g-\frac{1}{2}c_g\,\mathrm{Pr}+\frac{1}{2}c_g\,\mathrm{Pr}\,\eta\right)e^{-\eta} \\
&+ \left(\frac{3}{2}c_g\,\mathrm{Pr}+\frac{1}{2}c_g n\,\mathrm{Pr}+c_g n\,\mathrm{Pr}+\frac{1}{2}c_g\,\mathrm{Pr}\,\eta\right)\xi e^{-\eta}.
\end{aligned}
$$

In the similar way, we can obtain the series solution for $f_2(\eta,\xi)$, $g_2(\eta,\xi)$ and $f_3(\eta,\xi)$, $g_3(\eta,\xi)$ and so on. Since the series solution expressions are too long to be fitted in a page even for $f_2(\eta,\xi)$ and $g_2(\eta,\xi)$ they are not given here.

However, for a fixed set of values of the study parameters such as $Pr = 0.7$, $B = 1.0$ and $n = 1.0$ the series solution for $\ell = 2$ in eqs. (6.26)-(6.27), we get solution series,

$$
\begin{aligned}
f_2(\eta,\xi) &= 1+\eta+c_f+1.2542c_f^2-(1+1.001c_f+1.2542c_f^2)e^{-\eta} \\
&- (6.5177c_f-0.9502c_f^2)\xi+(c_f+0.7511c_f^2)e^{-\eta}\eta \\
&+ (6c_f-0.2983c_f^2)e^{-\eta}\xi+(c_f+0.6541c_f^2)\eta\xi \\
&+ (0.5c_f-0.7531c_f^2)e^{-2\eta}\xi+(c_f-1.85c_f^2)e^{-\eta}\eta\xi \\
&- (0.25c_f^2+0.5\xi c_f^2)\eta^2-(1.6209e^{-\eta}c_f^2\xi^2+0.5e^{-2\eta\xi}c_f^2)\eta \\
&+ (3.1c_f^2-5.3e^{-\eta}c_f^2-1.75c_f^2\eta-0.25e^{-\eta}c_f^2\eta^2+0.5e^{-2\eta}c_f^2\eta)\xi^2. \\
g_2(\eta,\xi) &= 1.3c_g-0.895c_g^2+(1-1.3c_g+0.895c_g^2)e^{-\eta}-(3.5c_g-1.5c_g^2)\xi \\
&+ (0.7c_g-0.455c_g^2)e^{-\eta}\eta+(3.5c_g-1.855c_g^2)e^{-\eta}\xi \\
&+ (0.7932c_g+0.525c_g^2)e^{-\eta}\eta\xi+(0.2975\xi+0.2975\xi^2)e^{-2\eta}c_g^2 \\
&- (0.455c_g^2-2.7755\,10^{-17}e^{-2\eta})c_g^2\eta\xi-(1.9775-1.4702\eta e^{-\eta})c_g^2\xi^2 \\
&+ (0.1225\eta^2+1.68\xi^2+0.245\eta^2\xi)e^{-\eta}c_g^2+(0.1225c_g^2)e^{-\eta}\eta^2\xi^2 \\
&+ (1.225+2.7755\,10^{-17}e^{-2\eta})c_g^2\eta\xi^2.
\end{aligned}
$$

When $\ell = 3$ in eqs. (6.26)-(6.27), we get solution series,

$$
\begin{aligned}
f_3(\eta,\xi) &= 1+\eta+1.5c_f+3.75c_f^2+2.625c_f^3-(12.c_f-1.8c_f^2+1.9275c_f^3)\xi \\
&- (1+1.5c_f+3.75c_f^2+2.625c_f^3)e^{-\eta}+(1.5c_f+2.25c_f^2 \\
&- 2.375c_f^3)e^{-\eta}\eta-(0.75c_f^2-0.75c_f^3)e^{-\eta}\eta^2+(10.5c_f-0.8c_f^2)e^{-\eta}\xi \\
&+ (1.5c_f-1.004c_f^2)e^{-2\eta}\xi+(6.49e^{-\eta}-4.5625e^{-2\eta})c_f^3\xi \\
&+ (4c_f+1.6c_f^2+1.5e^{-\eta}c_f+e^{-2\eta}c_f^2-6.4e^{-\eta}c_f^2-1.545c_f^3)\eta\xi \\
&+ (2.125e^{-2\eta}c_f^3+1.435e^{-\eta}c_f^3)\eta\xi-(1.5c_f^2+0.3025c_f^3)e^{-\eta}\eta^2\xi \\
&- (19.15e^{-\eta}-7e^{-2\eta}+0.8333e^{-3\eta})c_f^2\xi^2+(0.375e^{-\eta}\eta^3 \\
&- 0.375e^{-2\eta})c_f^3\eta^2\xi+(11.3167c_f^2-4.67181c_f^3+5.7075c_f^3\eta \\
&- 0.2275c_f^3\eta^2)\xi^2-(6c_f^2\eta+2.04875e^{-2\eta}c_f^3+2.19444e^{-3\eta}c_f^3)\xi^2 \\
&- (4.65e^{-\eta}c_f^2-e^{-2\eta}c_f^2)\eta\xi^2+(4.01e^{-\eta}c_f^3+0.4e^{-2\eta}c_f^3 \\
&+ 1.16667e^{-3\eta}c_f^3)\eta\xi^2-(0.75e^{-\eta}c_f^2+0.75e^{-2\eta}c_f^3+1.355e^{-\eta}c_f^3)\eta^2\xi^2 \\
&- (8.32e^{-\eta}-4.11375e^{-2\eta}-5.47222e^{-3\eta})c_f^3\xi^3 \\
&- (2.64e^{-\eta}-0.275e^{-2\eta}+1.16667e^{-3\eta})c_f^3\eta\xi^3 \\
&+ 0.125e^{-\eta}c_f^3\eta^3-6.4775c_f^3\eta\xi^3.
\end{aligned}
$$

$$
\begin{aligned}
g_3(\eta,\xi) &= 1.95c_g - 2.685c_g^2 + 1.11025c_g^3 + (1 - 1.95c_g + 2.685c_g^2 \\
&- 1.1c_g^3)e^{-\eta} - (5.25c_g - 4.6c_g^2 + 4.2337c_g^3)\xi + (1.05c_g - 1.3c_g^2 \\
&+ 0.9397c_g^3)e^{-\eta}\eta + (0.3675c_g^2 + 0.8085c_g^3)e^{-\eta}\eta^3 + (0.1286e^{-\eta}\eta^3\xi \\
&+ 0.0428c_g^3)e^{-\eta} + (5.2586c_g - 5.5651c_g^2 + 4.9787c_g^3)e^{-\eta}\xi + (1.05c_g \\
&- 1.575c_g^2)e^{-\eta}\eta\xi - (0.7451e^{-2\eta}c_g^3 + 0.0796c_g^3\eta^2)\xi \\
&- (1.365c_g^2 - 0.945c_g^3)\eta\xi - (1.0272e^{-\eta} - 0.0148e^{-2\eta})c_g^3\eta\xi \\
&+ (0.735c_g^2 - 0.0918c_g^3)e^{-\eta}\eta^2\xi + (2.7755\,10^{-17}e^{-2\eta}c_g^3)\eta^2\xi \\
&- (6.1658c_g^2 - 3.6333c_g^3)\xi^2 + (5.39e^{-\eta}0.8925e^{-2\eta} - 0.1e^{-3\eta})c_g^2\xi^2 \\
&- (2.8245e^{-\eta} + 0.9922e^{-2\eta} - 0.1833e^{-3\eta})c_g^3\xi^2 \\
&+ (3.675 + 5.11e^{-\eta}c_g^2 - 3.41c_g^3)\eta\xi^2 - (0.9118e^{-\eta} - 0.02e^{-2\eta} \\
&+ 0.1166e^{-3\eta})c_g^3\eta\xi^2 + (0.3675c_g^2\eta^2 + 0.1286c_g^3\eta^3)e^{-\eta}\xi^2 \\
&+ (0.294 + 5.5511\,10^{-17}e^{-2\eta})c_g^3\eta^2\xi^2 + (7.1435e^{-\eta} + 0.6908e^{-2\eta} \\
&- 0.5e^{-3\eta})c_g^3\xi^3 + (3.9 + 5.1082e^{-\eta} + 0.01e^{-2\eta} - 0.1e^{-3\eta})c_g^3\eta\xi^3 \\
&- (0.2143 + 0.9004e^{-\eta} + 0.0429e^{-\eta})c_g^3\eta^2\xi^3 \\
&+ (2.7755\,10^{-17}e^{-2\eta}c_g^3)\eta^2\xi^3.
\end{aligned}
$$

www.ingramcontent.com/pod-product-compliance
Lightning Source LLC
LaVergne TN
LVHW082339200926
848481LV00012B/3387
* 9 7 9 8 2 3 1 1 3 5 8 2 0 *